General Knowledge

Compiled & Edited
Research & Editorial Deptt.

Published by:

F-2/16, Ansari road, Daryaganj, New Delhi-110002
☎ 23240026, 23240027 • *Fax:* 011-23240028
Email: info@vspublishers.com • *Website:* www.vspublishers.com

Regional Office : Hyderabad
5-1-707/1, Brij Bhawan (Beside Central Bank of India Lane)
Bank Street, Koti, Hyderabad - 500 095
☎ 040-24737290
E-mail: vspublishershyd@gmail.com

Branch Office : Mumbai
Jaywant Industrial Estate, 1st Floor–108, Tardeo Road
Opposite Sobo Central Mall, Mumbai – 400 034
☎ 022-23510736
E-mail: vspublishersmum@gmail.com

Follow us on:

© **Copyright:** V&S PUBLISHERS
ISBN 978-93-579415-6-3
New Edition

DISCLAIMER

While every attempt has been made to provide accurate and timely information in this book, neither the author nor the publisher assumes any responsibility for errors, unintended omissions or commissions detected therein. The author and publisher make no representation or warranty with respect to the comprehensiveness or completeness of the contents provided.
All matters included have been simplified under professional guidance for general information only without any warranty for applicability on an individual. Any mention of an organization or a website in the book by way of citation or as a source of additional information doesn't imply the endorsement of the content either by the author or the publisher. It is possible that websites cited may have changed or removed between the time of editing and publishing the book.
Results from using the expert opinion in this book will be totally dependent on individual circumstances and factors beyond the control of the author and the publisher.
It makes sense to elicit advice from well informed sources before implementing the ideas given in the book. The reader assumes full responsibility for the consequences arising out from reading this book. For proper guidance, it is advisable to read the book under the watchful eyes of parents/guardian. The purchaser of this book assumes all responsibility for the use of given materials and information. The copyright of the entire content of this book rests with the author/publisher. Any infringement/ transmission of the cover design, text or illustrations, in any form, by any means, by any entity will invite legal action and be responsible for consequences thereon.

Printed at Repro Knowledgecast Limited, Thane

PUBLISHER'S NOTE

V&S Publishers is constant in its effort to identify the problems faced by the aspirants of various competitive examinations held at state and national levels, and to sort out those problems effectively. After a thorough search in the market, we realised that there are a few books available on comprehensive General Knowledge, which are too costly and too large to go through in short span of time during preparation. The present book, **'General Knowledge'** with all genres of general awareness has been designed to meet the specific needs of the contestants of various entrance exams and competitive exams as well. Not only does the book spreads awareness, but also can be a facilitator of change in life.

The book has been strategically planned in order to be user friendly. It covers up-to-date knowledge on *Indian Polity and Indian Economy*. The primary goal is to fulfil the quest for knowledge on various topics of study at national and international levels.

The book is recommended for various competitive examinations such as:

- Civil Services
- Staff Selection Commission (SSC)
- Institute of Banking Personnel Selection (IBPS)
- Defence Services – CDSE, NDA and other defence services
- Management Aptitude Test (MAT), Common Admission Test (CAT), and Graduate Management Admission Test (GMAT)
- Indian Engineering Services
- Railway Recruitment Services
- Test of English as a Foreign Language (TOEFL)
- International English Language Testing System (IELTS)

We hope that the book will be of immense help to the readers to upgrade their knowledge on various topics of general knowledge. A regular revision of all the topics covered in the book is advised to get up-to-date with the required information. We wish all aspirants good luck for their future endeavours.

CONTENTS

INDIAN POLITY AND GOVERNANCE   1-96

1. Evolution of Indian Constitution 2. Constituent Assembly and Making of the Constitution 3. The Constitution of India 4. Different Sources of the Indian Constitution 5. Important Articles of the Constitution 6. Important Amendments to the Constitution of India 7. Special Features of the Indian Constitution 8. Federal and Unitary Features of the Indian Union 9. The Preamble 10. Lapse of Paramountcy 11. Integration and Merger of Indian States 12. The Union and its Territories 13. Reorganization of States 14. Citizenship 15. Fundamental Rights 16. Directive Principles of State Policy 17. Fundamental Duties 18. Procedure for Amending the Constitution 19. Executives of Union Government 20. The Parliament 21. Executive of the States – The Governor 22. Inter-State Relations 23. Special Position of Jammu & Kashmir 24. Panchayats 25. Municipalities 26. Union-State Relations 27. The Supreme Court and the High Courts 28. The Political Processes in India 29. Order of Precedence 30. Offices under the Government of India 31. Inter-State Council 32. Finance Commission 33. NITI Aayog 34. National Development Council (NDC) 35. National Integration Council 36. Public Service Commissions 37. Election 38. Delimitation Commission of India 39. The Official Languages 40. National Symbols 41. Glossary of Constitutional Terms

INDIAN ECONOMY   97-176

1. Indian Economy 2. Characteristics of Indian Economy 3. Types of Economies in the World 4. Agriculture and Land Development 5. National Income 6. Planning in India 7. Unemployment 8. Trade and Commerce 9. New Economic Policy 10. The Policy of Liberalisation 11. Indian Financial System 12. Indian Fiscal System 13. Banking in India 14. Adoption of Banking Technology 15. Tax System 16. Industry 17. Foreign Trade

1. Evolution of Indian Constitution

Although the systems of ancient India do have their reflections in the Constitution of India, the direct sources of the Constitution lie in the administrative and legislative developments of the British period. A concise and chronological description of the Acts, documents and events that culminated in the framing of the world's largest written Constitution is given here.

Administrative and Legislative Reforms Before 1857

Regulating Act of 1773

- This Act was based on the report of a committee headed by the British Prime Minister Lord North.
- Governance of the East India Company was put under British parliamentary control.
- The Governor of Bengal was nominated as Governor General for all the three Presidencies of Calcutta, Bombay and Madras. Warren Hastings was the first such Governor General.
- A Supreme Court was established in Calcutta (now Kolkata).
- Governor General was empowered to make rules, regulations and ordinances with the consent of the Supreme Court.

Pitts India Act of 1784

- It was enacted to improve upon the provisions of Regulating Act of 1773 to bring about better discipline in the Company's system of administration.
- A 6-member Board of Controllers was set up which was headed by a minister of the British Government. All political responsibilities were given to this board.
- Trade and commerce related issues were under the purview of the Court of Directors of the company.
- Provinces had to follow the instructions of the Central Government, and Governor General was empowered to dismiss the failing provincial government.

Charter Act of 1793

- Main provisions of the previous Acts were consolidated in this Act.
- Provided for the payment of salaries of the members of the Board of Controllers from Indian revenue.
- Courts were given the power to interpret rules and regulations.

Charter Act of 1813
- Trade monopoly of the East India Company came to an end.
- Powers of the three Councils of Madras, Bombay and Calcutta were enlarged, they were also subjected to greater control of the British Parliament.
- The Christian Missionaries were allowed to spread their religion in India.
- Local autonomous bodies were empowered to levy taxes.

Charter Act of 1833
- The Governor General and his Council were given vast powers. This Council could legislate for the whole of India subject to the approval of the Board of Controllers.
- The Council got full powers regarding revenue, and a single budget for the country was prepared by the Governor General.
- The East India Company was reduced to an administrative and political entity and several Lords and Ministers were nominated as ex-officio members of the Board of Controllers.
- For the first time the Governor-General's Government was known as the 'Government of India' and his Council as the 'Indian Council'.

Charter Act of 1853
- This was the last of the Charter Acts and it made important changes in the system of Indian legislation.
- This Act followed a report of the then Governor General Dalhousie for improving the administration of the company.
- A separate Governor for Bengal was to be appointed.
- Legislative and administrative functions of the Council were separately identified.
- Recruitment of the Company's employees was to be done through competitive exams.
- British Parliament was empowered to put Company's governance of India to an end at any suitable time.

Administrative and Legislative Reforms After 1857

Government of India Act, 1858
- British Crown decided to assume sovereignty over India from the East India Company in an apparent consequence of the Revolt of 1857, described as an armed sepoy mutiny by the British historians and remembered as the First War of Independence by the Indians.
- The first statute for the governance of India, under the direct rule of the British Government, was the Government of India Act, 1858.
- It provided for absolute (British) imperial control over India without any popular participation in the administration of the country.
- The powers of the crown were to be exercised by the Secretary of State for India, assisted by a council of fifteen members, known as the Council of India.

- The country was divided into provinces headed by a Governor or Lieutenant-Governor aided by his Executive Council.
- The Provincial Governments had to function under the superintendence, direction and control of the Governor-General in all matters.
- All the authority for the governance of India was vested in the Governor-General in Council who was responsible to the Secretary of State.
- The Secretary of State was ultimately responsible to the British Parliament.

Indian Councils Act, 1861
- This is an important landmark in the constitutional history of India. By this Act, the powers of the crown were to be exercised by the Secretary of State for India, assisted by a council of fifteen members (known as the Council of India). The Secretary of State, who was responsible to the British Parliament, governed India through the Governor General, assisted by an Executive council.
- This Act enabled the Governor General to associate representatives of the Indian people with the work of legislation by nominating them to his expanded council.
- This Act provided that the Governor General's Executive Council should include certain additional non-official members also while transacting legislative business as a Legislative Council. But this Legislative Council was neither representative nor deliberative in any sense.
- It decentralised the legislative powers of the Governor General's Council and vested them in the Governments of Bombay and Madras.

Indian Councils Act, 1892
- The non-official members of the Indian Legislative Council were to be nominated by the Bengal Chamber of Commerce and the Provincial Legislative Councils while the non-official members of the Provincial Councils were to be nominated by certain local bodies such as universities, district boards, municipalities, *zamindars* etc.
- The Councils were to have the power of discussing the Budget and addressing questions to the Executive.

Morley-Minto Reforms and the Indian Councils Act, 1909
- Reforms recommended by the then Secretary of States for India (Lord Morley) and the Viceroy (Lord Minto) were implemented by the Indian Councils Act, 1909.
- The maximum number of additional members of the Indian Legislative Council (Governor-General's Council) was raised from 16 (under the Act of 1892) to 60 (excluding the Executive Councillors).
- The size of Provincial Legislative Councils was enlarged by including elected non-official members so that the official majority was gone.
- An element of election was also introduced in the Legislative Council at the centre also but the official majority was maintained there.
- The Legislative Councils were empowered to move resolutions on the Budget, and on any matter of public interest, except certain specified subjects, such as the Armed forces, Foreign Affairs and the Indian States.

- It provided, for the first time, for separate representation of the Muslim community and thus sowed the seeds of separatism.

The Government of India Act, 1915
- This act was passed to consolidate the provisions of the preceding Government of India Acts.

Montague-Chelmsford Report and the Government of India Act, 1919
- The then Secretary of State for India Mr. E.S. Montagu and the Governor General Lord Chelmsford formulated proposals for the Government of India Act, 1919.
- Responsible Government in the Provinces was to be introduced, without impairing the responsibility of the Governor (through the Governor General), for the administration of the Province, by resorting to device known as 'Dyarchy' or dual government.
- The subjects of administration were to be divided into two categories *Central* and *Provincial*.
- *Central subjects* were those which were exclusively kept under the control of the Central Government.
- The *provincial subjects* were sub-divided into 'transferred' and 'reserved' subjects.
- The *'transferred subjects'* were to be administered by the Governor with the aid of Ministers responsible to the Legislative Council in which the proportion of elected members was raised to 70 percent.
- The *'reserved subjects'* were to be administered by the Governor and his Executive Council with no responsibility to the Legislature.
- The previous Central control over the provinces in administrative, legislative and financial matters was relaxed. Sources of revenue were divided into two categories so that the provinces could run the administration with the revenue raised by the provinces themselves.
- The provincial budget was separated from the central budget.
- The provincial legislature was empowered to present its own budget and levy its own taxes relating to the provincial sources of revenue.
- The Central Legislature, retained power to legislate for the whole country on any subject.
- The control of the Governor General over provincial legislation was retained by providing that a Provincial Bill, even though assented to by the Governor, would become law only when assented to also by the Governor-General.
- The Governor was empowered to reserve a Bill for the consideration of the Governor General if it was related to some specified matters.
- The Governor General in Council continued to remain responsible only to the British Parliament through the Secretary of State for India.
- The Indian Legislature was made more representative and, for the first time *'bi-cameral'*.

- The Upper House was named the *Council of State*. This was composed of 60 members of whom 34 were elected.
- The Lower House was named the *Legislative Assembly*. This was composed of about 144 members of whom 104 were elected.
- The electorates were arranged on a communal and sectional basis, developing the Morley-Minto device further.
- The Governor General's overriding powers in respect of Central legislation were retained as follows :
 (a) His prior sanction was required to introduce Bills relating to certain matters; (b) he had the power to veto or reserve for consideration of the Crown any Bill passed by the Indian Legislature; (c) he had the converse power of certifying Bill or any grant refused by the Legislature; (d) he could make Ordinances, in case of emergency.

Simon Commission
- This commission, headed by Sir John Simon, constituted in 1927 to inquire into the working of the Act of 1919, placed its report in 1930.
- The report was examined by the British Parliament and the Government of India Bill was drafted accordingly.

The Government of India Act, 1935
- The Act of 1935 prescribed a federation, taking the Provinces and the Indian States (native states) as units.
- It was optional for the Indian States to join the Federation, and since they never joined, the *Federation never came into being*.
- The Act divided legislative powers between the Centre and Provinces.
- The executive authority of a Province was also exercised by a Governor on behalf of the Crown and not as a subordinate of the Governor General.
- The Governor was required to act with the advice of Ministers responsible to the Legislature.
- In certain matters, the Governor was required to act 'in his discretion' without ministerial advice and under the control and directions of the Governor General, and, through him, of the Secretary of State.
- The executive authority of the Centre was vested in the Governor General (on behalf of the Crown).
- Counsellors or Council of Ministers responsible to the Legislature was not appointed although such provisions existed in the Act of 1935.
- The Central Legislature was bi-cameral, consisting of the Federal Assembly and the Council of State.
- In six provinces, the legislature was bi-cameral, comprising a Legislative Assembly and a Legislative Council. In other provinces, the Legislature was uni-cameral.
- Apart from the Governor General's power of veto, a Bill passed by the Central Legislature was also subject to *veto by the Crown*.
- The Governor General could prevent discussion in the Legislature and suspend the proceedings on any Bill if he was satisfied that it would affect the discharge of his special responsibilities.

- The Governor General had independent powers of legislation, concurrently with those of the Legislature.
- On some subjects no bill or amendment could be introduced in the Legislature without the Governor-General's previous sanction.
- A three-fold division in the Act of 1935 — There was a Federal List over which the Federal Legislature had exclusive powers of legislation. There was a Provincial List of matters over which the Provincial Legislature had exclusive jurisdiction. There was a Concurrent List also over which both the Federal and Provincial Legislature had competence.
- The Governor-General was empowered to authorise either the Federal or the Provincial Legislature to enact a law with respect to any matter which was not enumerated in the above noted Legislative Lists.
- *Dominion Status*, which was promised by the Simon Commission in 1929, was *not conferred* by the Government of India Act, 1935.

Cripps Mission
- In March 1942, Sir Stafford Cripps, a member of the British cabinet came with a draft declaration on the proposals of the British Government.
- These proposals were to be adopted at the end of the Second World War provided the Congress and the Muslim League could accept them.
- According to the proposals:
  - The Constitution of India was to be framed by an *elected Constituent Assembly* by the Indian people.
  - The Constitution should give India Dominion Status.
  - There should be one Indian Union comprising all the Provinces and Indian States;
  - Any Province (or Indian State) not accepting the Constitution would be free to retain its constitutional position existing at that time and with such non-acceding Provinces, the British Government could enter into separate Constitutional arrangements.

Cabinet Mission Plan
- In March 1946, Lord Attlee sent a Cabinet Mission to India consisting of three Cabinet Ministers, namely Lord Pethick Lawrence, Sir Stafford Cripps and Mr. A.V. Alexander.
- The *object of the Mission* was to help India achieve its independence as early as possible, and to set up a Constituent Assembly.
- The Cabinet Mission rejected the claim for a separate Constituent Assembly and a separate State for the Muslim.
- According to Cabinet Mission Plan there was to be a Union of India, comprising both British India and the States, and having jurisdiction over the subjects of Foreign Affairs, Defence and Communication. All residuary powers were to be vested in the Provinces and the States.
- The Union was to have an Executive and a Legislature consisting of representatives of the Provinces and the States.
- Any decision involving a major communal issue in the legislature was to require a majority support of representatives of each of the two major

communities present and voting as well as a majority of all the members present and voting.
- The provinces could form groups with executives and legislatures, and each group could be competent to determine the provincial subjects.

The Mountbatten Plan
- The plan for transfer of power to the Indians and partition of the country was laid down in the Mountbatten Plan.
- It was given a formal shape by a statement made by the British Government on 3rd June, 1947.

The Indian Independence Act, 1947 of the British Parliament
- In pursuance of this Act, the Government of India Act, 1935, was amended by the Adaptation Orders, both in India and Pakistan, for setting up an interim Constituent Assembly to draw up the future Constitution of the country.
- From the 15th August, 1947 India ceased to be a Dependency, and the suzerainty of the British Crown over the Indian States and the treaty relations with Tribal Areas lapsed from that date.
- The office of the Secretary of State for India was abolished.
- The Governor-General and the Governors lost extraordinary powers of legislations to compete with the Legislature.
- The Central Legislature of India, composed of the Legislative Assembly and the Council of States, ceased to exist on August 14,1947.
- The Constituent Assembly itself was to function also as the Central Legislature with complete sovereignty.

2. Constituent Assembly and Making of the Constitution

- The Cabinet Mission envisaged the establishment of a Constituent Assembly to frame a Constitution for the country. Members of the Constituent Assembly were elected by the Provincial Legislative Assemblies.
- Each Province and each Indian State were allotted seats in proportion of its population, roughly in the ratio of one to a million. The seats so ascertained were distributed among the main communities in each Province. The main communities recognised were Sikh, Muslim and General.

Committees of the Constituent Assembly and their Chairman

S.No.	Committee	Chairman
1.	Committee on the Rules of Procedure	
2.	Steering Committee	
3.	Finance and Staff Committee	Dr. Rajendra Prasad
4.	Ad hoc Committee on the National Flag	

5.	Union Constitution Committee	
6.	Union Powers Committee	Pt. Jawaharlal Nehru
7.	State Committee	
8.	Advisory Committee on Fundamental Rights, Minorities and Tribal and Excluded Areas	Sardar Vallabhbhai Patel
9.	Drafting Committee	Dr. B.R. Ambedkar
10.	Credential Committee	Alladi Krishnaswami Ayyar
11.	House Committee	B.Pattabhi Sitaramayya
12.	Order of Business Committee	K.M. Munshi
13.	Committee on the Functions of the Constituent Assembly	G.V. Mavalankar
14.	Minorities Sub-Committee	H.C. Mookherjee
15.	Fundamental Rights Sub-committee	J. B. Kripalani
16.	North-East Frontier Tribal Areas and Assam Excluded & Partially Excluded Areas Sub-Committee	Gpinath Bardoloi
17.	Excluded and Partially Excluded Areas (other than those in Assam) Sub-Committee	A. V. Thakkar

⇨ The total number of members of the Constituent Assembly was 385, of whom 93 were representatives from the Indian States and 292 from the Provinces (British India).

⇨ After the partition of India the number of members of the Constituent Assembly came to 299, of whom 284 were actually present on the 26th November, 1949 and signed on the finally approved the Constitution of India. The Assembly, which had been elected for undivided India held its first meeting on December 9, 1946, and reassembled on Augus 14, 1947, as the sovereign Constituent Assembly for the dominion of India.

⇨ It took two years, eleven months and eighteen days for the Constituent Assembly to finalise the Constitution.

⇨ *Objective Resolution* was moved in the first session of the Constituent Assembly (on 13th December, 1946) by Pandit Jawaharlal Nehru which was adopted after considerable deliberation and debate in the Assembly on 22nd January, 1947. The following objectives were embodied in the resolution :
- To foster unity of the Nation and to ensure its economic and political security, to have a written Constitution, and to proclaim India as a Sovereign Democratic Republic.

- To have a federal form of Government with the distribution of powers between the centre and states.
- To guarantee and secure justice, equality, freedom of thought, expression, belief, faith, worship, vocation, association and action to all the people of India.
- To provide adequate safeguards for minorities, backward and tribal areas and depressed and other backward classes.
- To maintain the integrity of the territory of the republic and its sovereign rights on land, sea and air according to justice and the law of civilised nations.
- To attain rightful and honoured place in the world and make its full and willing contribution to the promotion of the world peace and the welfare of mankind.
- The principles of the Constitution were outlined by various committees of the Assembly, and there was a general discussion on the reports of these Committees. The Assembly appointed the Drafting Committee with Dr. B.R. Ambedkar as the Chairman on August 29, 1947.
- The Drafting Committee, headed by Dr. B.R.Ambedkar, submitted a Draft constitution of India to the President of the assembly on 21st February 1948.
- The members of Drafting Committee were N. Gopalaswamy Ayyangar, Alladi Krishnaswamy Ayyar, K.M. Munshi, Mohd. Saadullah, B.L. Mitter (later replaced by N. Madhava Rao), Dr. D.P. Khaitan (replaced on death by T.T. Krishnamachari).
- The third and final reading of the draft was completed on November 26, 1949. On this date, the signature of the President of the Assembly was appended to it and the Constitution was declared as passed.
- The provisions relating to citizenship, elections and provisional Parliament etc. were implemented with immediate effect, that is, from the 26th November, 1949. The rest of the provisions of the constitution came into force on January 26, 1950 and this date is referred to in the Constitution as the date of its commencement.

3. The Constitution of India

The Constitution of India is the supreme law of the land. The Constitution is a set of laws and rules setting up the machinery of the government of the country. This set of laws defines and determines the relation between different institutions and organs of the government, such as, the *executive*, the *legislature* and the judiciary. The Constitution of India also lays down the laws that define relationship between the central, regional and local governments.

The Constitution of India was enacted by the **Constituent Assembly** on November 26, 1949 and came into effect on January 26, 1950. The date,

January 26 for this purpose was fixed to commemorate the **Purna Swaraj declaration of 1930**. With the adoption of Constitution, India officially became a **Republic** and replaced the **Government of India Act of 1935**, the fundamental governing principle.

The framers of the Constitution of India drew much from American Constitution, the British Constitution – by enacting the Government of India Act of 1935 and some parts from the constitutions of other countries.

The Constitution of India originally, when drafted, contained *395 articles* and *9 schedules,* many of which contain a number of exceptions and limitations. However, presently, our Constitution contains *448 articles in 22 parts, 12 schedules* and has undergone *97 amendments* up to January, 2012. This is considered the longest and the bulkiest Constitution of the World.

Unlike United Kingdom, the Indian Constitution is a written one. The Indian Constitution is federal in form characterised by the supremacy of the Constitution, division of power between the Union and the State governments, existence of judiciary and a rigid system to amend it. The Constitution duly establishes a political system with clearly defined areas of authority of the Union and State governments. Also, the Constitution provides for an independent judiciary to determine issues between the Union and the States or between two States.

However, the Constitution exhibits centralising tendencies in several of its provisions like adoption of a lengthy Concurrent List, supremacy of Parliament over State Legislatures, residuary legislative power being vested with Parliament and the power of governors to resolve Bills for the consideration of the Parliament.

The Constitution operates as supreme and fundamental law of the land. Various organs of the government owe their origin to the Constitution, derive authority and discharge their responsibilities within the framework laid down by the Constitution. The Indian Constitution provides that neither the parliament nor the state legislatures are sovereign. The validity of any law enacted by Parliament or State Legislatures is judged with reference to the respective jurisdictions as defined in the Constitution.

4. Different Sources of the Indian Constitution

Although the skeleton of the constitution was derived from the Government of India Act 1935, many provisions were imported from other constitutions of the world. Some of them are listed below along with the Government of India Act, 1935:

Government of India Act, 1935 : This Act formed the basis or 'blueprint' of the consititution of India with the features of Federal system, office of Governor, emergency powers etc. Besides, the Constitution of India has borrowed from the:

Constitution of Britain: Law making procedures, Rule of law, Single citizenship, Bi-cameral Parliamentary system, office of CAG.

Constitution of USA: Independence of judiciary, judicial review, fundamental rights, removal of Supreme Court and High Court judges, Preamble and functions of President and Vice-president.

Constitution of Canada: Federation with strong Centre, to provide residuary powers to the Centre, Supreme Court's advisory jurisdiction.

Constitution of Ireland: Directive Principles of State policy, method of presidential elections, and the nomination of members to Rajya Sabha by the President.

Weimar Constitution of Germany: Provisions concerning the suspension of fundamental rights during emergency.

Constitution of Australia: Idea of the Concurrent List, Trade and Commerce provisions.

Constitution of South Africa: Amendment with 2/3rd majority in Parliament and election of the Members of Rajya Sabha on the basis of proportional representation.

Constitution of France: Republican System, Principles of Liberty, Equality and Fraternity.

Constitution of former USSR: Fundamental Duties, Ideals of justice in Preamble.

5. Important Articles of the Constitution

	Articles	Subject
Part I	Art. 1-4	The Union and its territory
Part II	Art. 5-1	Citizenship
Part III	**Fundamental Rights**	
Art. 12		Definition
Art. 13		Laws inconsistent with or in derogation of the fundamental rights

Right to Equality

Art. 14	Equality before law
Art. 15	Prohibition of discrimination on grounds of religion, race, caste, sex or place of birth
Art. 16	Equality of opportunity in matters of public employment
Art. 17	Abolition of untouchability
Art. 18	Abolition of titles

Right to Freedom

Art. 19	Protection of certain rights regarding freedom of speech, etc.
Art. 20	Protection in respect of conviction for offences
Art. 21	Protection of life and personal liberty

21A.	Right to education
Art. 22	Protection against arrest and detention in certain cases

Right against Exploitation

Art. 23	Prohibition of traffic in human beings and forced labour
Art. 24	Prohibition of employment of children in factories, etc.

Right to Freedom of Religion

Art. 25	Freedom of conscience and free profession, practice and propagation of religion
Art. 26	Freedom to manage religious affairs
Art. 27	Freedom as to payment of taxes for promotion of any particular religion
Art. 28	Freedom as to attendance at religious instruction or religious worship in certain educational institutions

Cultural and Educational Rights

Art. 29	Protection of interests of minorities
Art. 30	Right of minorities to establish and administer educational institutions

Saving of certain Laws

Art. 31A	Saving of laws providing for acquisition of estates, etc.
Art. 31B	Validation of certain Acts and Regulations
Art. 31C	Saving of laws giving effect to certain directive principles

Right to Constitutional Remedies

Art. 32	Remedies for enforcement of rights conferred by this Part
Art. 33	Power of Parliament to modify the rights conferred by this Part in their application to Forces, etc.
Art. 34	Restriction on rights conferred by this Part while martial law is in force in any area
Art. 35	Legislation to give effect to the provisions of this Part
Part IV	**Directive Principles of State Policy**
Art. 36	Definition
Art. 37	Application of the principles contained in this Part
Art. 38	State to secure a social order for the promotion of welfare of the people
Art. 39	Certain principles of policy to be followed by the State
Art. 39A	Equal justice and free legal aid
Art. 40	Organisation of village panchayats
Art. 41	Right to work, to education and to public assistance in certain cases
Art. 42	Provision for just and humane conditions of work and maternity relief

Art. 43	Living wage, etc. for workers
Art. 43A	Participation of workers in management of industries
Art. 43B	The State shall endeavour to promote voluntary formation, autonomous functioning, democratic control and professional management of co-operative societies.
Art. 44	Uniform civil code for the citizens
Art. 45	Provision for early childhood care and education to children below the age of six years
Art. 46	Promotion of educational and economic interest of Scheduled Castes, Scheduled Tribes and other weaker sections
Art. 47	Duty of the State to raise the level of nutrition and the standard of living and to improve public health
Art. 48	Organisation of agriculture and animal husbandry
Art. 48A	Protection and improvement of environment and safeguarding of forests and wild life
Art. 49	Protection of monuments and places and objects of national importance
Art. 50	Separation of judiciary from executive
Art. 51	Promotion of international peace and security
Part IVA	**Art. 51A Fundamental Duties**
Part V	**The Union**
Chapter–I:	**The Executive**
Art. 52	The President of India
Art. 53	Executive power of the Union
Art. 54	Election of President
Art. 61	Procedure for impeachment of the President
Art. 63	The Vice-President of India
Art. 64	The Vice-President to be ex-officio Chairman of the Council of States
Art. 65	The Vice-President to act as President or to discharge his functions during casual vacancies in the office, or during the absence of President
Art. 66	Election of Vice-President
Art. 72	Power of President to grant pardons, etc. and to suspend, remit or commute sentences in certain cases
Art. 74	Council of Ministers to aid and advise President
Art. 76	Attorney-General for India
Chapter–II:	**Parliament**
Art. 79	Constitution of Parliament

Art. 80	Composition of the Council of States (Rajya Sabha)
Art. 81	Composition of the House of the People (Lok Sabha)
Art. 83	Duration of Houses of Parliament
Art. 84	Qualification for membership of Parliament
Art. 85	Sessions of Parliament, prorogation and dissolution
Art. 86	Right of President to address and send messages to Houses
Art. 87	Special address by the President
Art. 88	Rights of Ministers and Attorney General as respects Houses
Art. 89	The Chairman and Deputy Chairman of the Council of States
Art. 90	Vacation and resignation of, and removal from, the office of Deputy Chairman
Art. 93	The Speaker and Deputy Speaker of the House of the People
Art. 94	Vacation and resignation of, and removal from, the offices of Speaker and Deputy Speaker
Art. 95	Power of the Deputy Speaker or other person to perform the duties of the office of, or to act as, Speaker
Art. 98	Secretariat of Parliament
Art. 99	Oath or affirmation by members
Art. 100	Voting in Houses, power of Houses to act notwithstanding vacancies and quorum
Art. 105	Powers, privileges, etc. of the Houses of Parliament and of the members and committees thereof
Art. 106	Salaries and allowances of members
Art. 107	Provisions as to introduction and passing of Bills
Art. 108	Joint sitting of both Houses in certain cases
Art. 109	Special procedure in respect of Money Bills
Art. 110	Definition of "Money Bills"
Art. 111	Assent to Bills
Art. 112	Annual financial statement (Budget)
Art. 113	Procedure in Parliament with respect to estimates
Art. 114	Appropriation Bills
Art. 115	Supplementary, additional or excess grants
Art. 116	Votes on account, votes of credit and exceptional grants
Art. 117	Special provisions as to financial Bills
Art. 118	Rules of procedure
Art. 119	Regulation by law of procedure in Parliament in relation to financial business
Art. 120	Language to be used in Parliament

Art. 121	Restriction on discussion in Parliament
Art. 122	Courts not to inquire into proceedings of Parliament
Chapter–III:	**Legislative Powers of the President**
Art. 123	Power of President to promulgate Ordinances during recess of Parliament
Chapter–IV:	**The Union Judiciary**
Art. 124	Establishment and Constitution of Supreme Court
Art. 125	Salaries, etc. of Judges
Art. 126	Appointment of acting Chief Justice
Art. 127	Appointment of ad hoc Judges
Art. 128	Attendence of retired Judge at sittings of the Supreme Court
Art. 129	Supreme Court to be a Court of record
Art. 130	Seat of Supreme Court
Art. 131	Original jurisdiction of Supreme Court
Art. 132	Appellate jurisdiction of Supreme Court in appeals from High Court in certain cases
Art. 133	Appellate jurisdiction of Supreme Court in appeals from High Court in regard to civil matters
Art. 134	Appellate jurisdicition of Supreme Court in regard to criminal matters
Art. 134A	Certificate for appeal to the Supreme Court
Art. 135	Jurisdiction and powers of the Federal Court under existing law to be exercisable by the Supreme Court
Art. 136	Special leave to appeal by the Supreme Court
Art. 137	Review of judgements or orders by the Supreme Court
Art. 138	Enlargement of the jurisdiction of the Supreme Court
Art. 141	Law declared by Supreme Court to be binding on all Courts
Art. 143	Power of President to consult Supreme Court
Art. 144	Civil and judicial authorities to act in aid of the Supreme Court
Chapter–V :	**Comptroller and Auditor-General of India**
Art. 148	Comptroller and Auditor-General of India
Art. 149	Duties and powers of the Comptroller and Auditor-General
Part VI	**The States**
Art. 152-237	The Government at the State level: The Executive, The State Legislature, The High Courts and Subordinate Courts
Part VIII	Art. 239-241 The Union Territories
Part IX	Art. 243 to 243-O The Panchayats

Part IXA	Art. 243-P to 243-ZG The Municipalities
Part IXB	Art. 243-ZH to 243-ZT The Co-operative Societies
Part X	Art. 244-244A The Scheduled and Tribal Areas
Part XI	Art. 245-263 Relations between The Union and the States
Part XII	Art. 264-300 Finance, property, contracts and suits; Distribution of revenue between Union and States; Finance Commission; Borrowing, Property, Contracts, Rights, Liabilities, Obligations and Suits
Art. 300A	Right to Property
Part XIII	Art. 301-307: Trade, commerce and intercourse within India
Part XIV	**Services Under The Union and The States**
Art. 309	Recruitment and conditions of service of persons serving the Union or a State
Art. 310	Tenure of office of persons serving the Union or a State
Art. 311	Dismissal, removal or reduction in rank of persons employed in civil capacities under the Union or a State
Art. 312	All-India Services
Art. 315	Public Service Commissions for the Union and for the States
Art. 316	Appointment and term of office of members
Art. 317	Removal and suspension of a member of a Public Service Commission
Art. 318	Power to make regulations as to conditions of service of members and staff of the Commission
Art. 320	Functions of Public Service Commissions
Art. 321	Power to extend functions of Public Service Commissions
Art. 323	Reports of Public Service Commissions
Part XIVA	**Art. 323A-323B Tribunals**
Part XV	**Elections**
Art. 324	Superintendence, direction and control of elections to be vested in an Election Commission
Art. 325	No person to be ineligible for inclusion in, or to claim to be included in a special, electoral roll on grounds of religion, race, caste or sex
Art. 326	Elections to the House of the People and to the Legislative Assemblies of States to be on the basis of adult suffrage
Art. 327	Power of Parliament to make provision with respect to elections to legislatures
Art. 328	Power of Legislature of a State to make provision with respect to elections to such Legislature
Art. 329	Bar to interference by Courts in electoral matters

Part XVI	Art. 330-342 Special provisions for certain classes
Part XVII	Art. 343-351 Official languages
Part XVIII	Art. 352-360 Emergency Provisions
Part XIX	**Miscellaneous**
Art. 361A	Protection of publication of proceedings of Parliament and State Legislatures
Art. 363	Bar to interference by courts in disputes arising out of certain treaties, agreements, etc.
Art. 363A	Recognition granted to Rulers of Indian States to cease and privy purses to be abolished
Art. 364	Special provisions as to major ports and aerodromes
Art. 365	Effect of failure to comply with, or to give effect to, directions given by the Union
Part XX	Art. 368 Amendment of the Constitution
Part XXI	Art. 369-392 Temporary, Transitional and Special Provisions — Special status of States
Part XXII	Art. 393-395 Short Title, Commencement, Authoritative text in Hindi and Repeals

Schedules of the Indian Constitution

The Constitution of India at the time of its adoption had only eight Schedules to which four more were added during the succeeding sixty-five years.

1st Schedule	28 States and 7 Union Territories with Territorial demarcations
2nd Schedule	
Part 'A'	Salary and emoluments of the President and Governors of the States
Part 'B'	Omitted
Part 'C'	Salary and emoluments of the Speaker / Deputy Speaker or Chairman/Vice Chairman of the Lok Sabha, Rajya Sabha and State Legislative Assemblies or Councils.
Part 'D'	Salary and emoluments of the judge of the Supreme Court and High Courts
Part 'E'	Salary and emoluments of the Comptroller and Auditor General of India
3rd Schedule	Forms of oath and affirmations of members of legislatures, ministers and judges.
4th Schedule	Allocation of seats to States and Union Territories in the Rajya Sabha.
5th Schedule	Administration and control of Scheduled Areas and STs.
6th Schedule	Administration of Tribal Areas of North-Eastern States

7th Schedule	Distribution of power between the Union and the State Government. (Union List, State List and Concurrent List)
8th Schedule	Description of 22 languages recognised by the Constitution.
9th Schedule	Validation of certain Acts and Regulations
10th Schedule	Provisions as to disqualification on ground of defection (Anti-defection Law introduced by the 52nd Constitutional Amendment Act.). This Schedule followed latest developments by 91st amendment to the constitution in 2003.
11th Schedule	Powers, authority and responsibilities of Panchayats, 29 subjects over which the Panchayats have jurisdiction (refer to the 73rd Constitutional Amendment Act).
12th Schedule	Powers, authority and responsiblities of Municipalities, 18 subjects over which the Municipalities have jurisdiction (refer to the 74th Constitutional Amendment Act).

6. Important Amendments to the Constitution of India

- **1st Constitutional Amendment Act, 1951:** This amendment added Article, 15(4) and Article, 19(6) and brought changes in the right to private property in pursuance with the decision of Supreme Court concerning fundamental rights. Ninth schedule to the Constitution was also added by it.
- **7th Constitutional Amendment Act, 1956:** Through this amendment the implementation of State Reorganisation Act was made possible. The categorisation of States into Part A, Part B and Part C ceased henceforth. Part C states were redesignated as Union Territories. The seats in the Rajya Sabha and in the Union and State Legislatures were reallocated. It also effected changes regarding appointment of additional and acting judges, High Courts and their jurisdictions etc.
- **10th Constitutional Amendment Act, 1961:** Incorporated Dadra and Nagar Haveli as Union Territory.
- **12th Constitutional Amendment Act, 1962:** Inclusion of territories of Goa, Daman and Diu into the Indian Union.
- **13th Constitutional Amendment Act, 1962:** Insertion of Art. 371. A to make special provisions for the administration of the State of Nagaland.
- **14th Constitutional Amendment Act, 1962:** Pondicherry, Karaikal, Mahe and Yenam, the former French territories, were specified in the Constitution as the Union Territory of Pondicherry (now Puducherry). Enabled the UTs of Himachal Pradesh, Manipur, Tripura, Goa, Daman and Diu and Pondicherry to have Legislatures and Council of Ministers.
- **15th Constitutional Amendment Act,1963:** It raised the age of retirement of a High Court Judge from 60 to 62. Extended the jurisdiction of a High Court to issue writs under Art. 226 to a Government or authority situated outside its territorial jurisdiction where the cause of action arises within such jurisdictions.

- **16th Constitutional Amendment Act, 1963:** Changes were effected in Art. 19 to enable the Parliament to make laws providing reasonable restrictions on the freedom of expression in the larger interests of sovereignty and integrity of India. Amendments were made in the form of oath contained in the third Schedule with emphasis on upholding the sovereignty and integrity of India.
- **19th Constitutional Amendment Act, 1966:** Art. 324 was amended to clarify the duties of the Election Commission. It deprived the Election Commission of the power to appoint election tribunals for deciding election disputes of members of Parliament and State Legislatures.
- **21st Constitutional Amendment Act, 1967:** Sindhi language was included as 15th regional language in the Eighth Schedule.
- **24th Constitutional Amendment Act, 1971:** It was a retaliatory act of the Parliament to neutralise the effect of the judgement in Golak Nath Case. It affirmed the parliament's power to amend any part of the Constitution, including Fundamental Rights by amending Arts. 368 and 13. It made obligatory for the President to give assent to Amendment Bills, when they are presented to him/her.
- **25th Constitutional Amendment Act, 1971 (came into force on April 20, 1972):** It restricted the jurisdiction of the Courts over acquisition laws with regard to adequacy of Compensation. This amendment came primarily in the wake of Bank Nationalisation case and the word 'amount' was substituted in place of 'compensation' in Article 31.

  It also provided that no law passed by the State to give effect to Directive Principles specified under clauses (b) and (c) of Art. 39 can be declared void on the ground that it was inconsistent with Fundamental Rights conferred by Arts. 14, 19 and 31.
- **26th Constitutional Amendment Act, 1971:** This amendment withdrew the recognition to the rulers of Princely States and their privy purses were abolished.
- **30th Constitutional Amendment Act. 1972 (w.e.f. February 27, 1973):** It provided that only such appeals can be brought to the Supreme Court which involve a substantial question of law. The valuation aspect of Rs. 20,000 for appeals in civil cases to the Supreme Court was abolished.
- **31st Constitutional Amendment Act, 1973:** By this amendment, the seats of the Lok Sabha were increased from 525 to 545 but reduced the representation of UTs in Lok Sabha from 25 to 20.
- **35th Constitutional Amendment Act, 1974 (w.e.f. March 1, 1975):** Accorded status of Associate State to Sikkim by ending its protectorate kingdom status which was a novel concept introduced in the Constitution.
- **36th Constitutional Amendment Act, 1975:** Made Sikkim a full fledged State of the Union of India.
- **38th Constitutional Amendment Act, 1975:** Clarified that declaration of emergency by the President and promulgation of Ordinance by the President or Governor cannot be challenged in any Court on any ground.

- **39th Constitutional Amendment Act, 1975:** The disputes or questions regarding elections of President, Vice-President, Prime Minister and Speaker of Lok Sabha were taken out of the purview judicial review of the Supreme Court or High Courts.
- **42nd Constitutional Amendment Act, 1976 (Mini Constitution):** The 42nd Amendment made fundamental changes in the constitutional structure and it incorporated the words (SOCIALIST', 'SECULAR and 'INTEGRITY in the Preamble. Fundamental Duties were added in Part IVA. Directive Principles were given precedence over Fundamental Rights and any law made to this effect by the Parliament was kept beyond the scope of judicial review by the Court. It made the power of Parliament supreme so far as amendment to the Constitution was concerned. It authorised the Supreme Court to transfer certain cases from one High Court to another and redefined the writ jurisdiction of the High Courts. It provided for Administrative Tribunals for speedy justice. It empowered the Centre to deploy armed forces in any State to deal with the grave law and order situation. It authorised the President to make Proclamation of Emergency for any part of the country or to whole of India. It made it obligatory for the President to act on the advice of the Council of Ministers. Tenure of the Lok Sabha and the State Assemblies was increased by one year.
- **43rd Constitutional Amendment Act, 1977 (w.e.f. April 13, 1978):** The 43rd Amendment omitted many articles inserted by 42nd Amendment. It restored the jurisdiction of the Supreme Court and the High Courts, which had been curtailed under the 42nd Amendment.
- **44th Constitutional Amendment Act, 1978 (w.e.f June–September, 1979):** The amendment was brought by the Janata Party Government which repealed some of the changes effected by 42nd Amendment, omitted a few and provided alterations. Right to property was taken away from the list of Fundamental Rights and placed in a new Art. 300A as an ordinary legal right. Constitutionality of the Proclamation of Emergency by the President could be questioned in a court on the ground of malafide (42nd Amendment had made it immune from judicial review). It brought the revocation of a Proclamation under Parliamentary control. In Article 352 regarding National Emergency, the words 'internal disturbance' were substituted by the words 'armed rebellion'. It authorised the President to refer back the advice to the Council of Ministers for reconsideration, but made it binding for the President to act on the reconsidered advice. The power of the Courts to decide disputes regarding election of Prime Minister and Speaker was restored. Constitutional protection on publication of proceedings of Parliament and State Legislatures was provided.
- **52nd Constitutional Amendment Act, 1985:** This amendment was brought about during Rajiv Gandhi regime with a view to put an end to political defections. It added Tenth Schedule to the Constitution

containing the modes for disqualification in case of defection from the Parliament or State Legislature.

- **55th Constitutional Amendment Act, 1986 (w.e.f. February 20, 1987):** The formation of Arunachal Pradesh took place with special powers given to the Governor. It also provided for a 30-member State Assembly.
- **56th Constitutional Amendment Act, 1987:** Goa was made a full fledged State with a State Assembly but Daman and Diu stayed as UT.
- **57th Constitutional Amendment Act, 1987:** It provided for reservation of seats for Scheduled Tribes of Nagaland, Meghalaya, Mizoram and Arunachal Pradesh in Lok Sabha. Seats were also reserved for the Scheduled Tribes of Nagaland and Meghalaya in the State Assemblies of Nagaland and Meghalaya.
- **58th Constitutional Amendment Act, 1987:** An authoritative text of the Constitution in Hindi was provided to the people of India by the President.
- **59th Constitutional Amendment Act, 1988:** It amended Art. 356 to provide that the declaration of Emergency may remain in operation upto 3 years and also authorised the Government to proclaim emergency in Punjab on ground of 'internal disturbance'. The amendment made in Art. 352 thus provided that the emergency with respect to Punjab shall operate only in that State.
- **61st Constitutional Amendment Act, 1988 (w.e.f. March 28, 1989):** It brought about an amendment to Article 326 for the reduction of voting age from 21 to 18 years.
- **62nd Constitutional Amendment Act, 1989:** It increased the period of reservation of seats provided to the Scheduled Castes and Scheduled Tribes for another 10 years i.e. upto 2000 A.D. The reservation for Anglo-Indians through nomination in case of their inadequate representation, was also extended upto 2000 A.D.
- **65th Constitutional Amendment Act, 1990 (w.e.f. March 12, 1992):** A National Commission for Scheduled Castes and Scheduled Tribes with wide powers was provided to take care of the cause of SCs/STs.
- **66th Constitutional Amendment Act, 1990:** This amendment provided for the inclusion of 55 new land reform Acts passed by the States into the Ninth Schedule.
- **69th Constitutional Amendment Act, 1991 (w.e.f. February 01, 1992):** Arts. 239AA and 239-AB were inserted in the Constitution to provide a National Capital Territory designation to Union Territory of Delhi with a legislative Assembly and Council of Ministers.
- **70th Constitutional Amendment Act, 1992 :** Altered Art. 54 and 368 to include members of legislative assemblies of Union Territories of Delhi and Pondicherry in the electoral college for the election of the President.
- **71st Constitutional Amendment Act, 1992:** It included Manipuri, Konkani and Nepalese languages in the 8th Schedule.
- **73rd Constitutional Amendment Act, 1992 (w.e.f. April 24, 1993):** The institution of Panchayati Raj received Constitutional guarantee, status and legitimacy. XIth Schedule was added to deal with it. It also inserted part IX, containing Arts, 243, 243A to 243 O.

- **74th Constitutional Amendment Act, 1992 (w.e.f. June 01, 1993):** Provided for constitutional sanctity to Municipalities by inserting PartIX-A, containing Arts. 243P to 243ZG and the XIIth Schedule which deals with the items concerning Municipalities.
- **77th Constitutional Amendment Act, 1995:** By this amendment a new clause 4A was added to Art. 16 which authorised the State to make provisions for Scheduled Castes and Scheduled Tribes with regard to promotions in Government jobs.
- **78th Constitutional Amendment Act, 1995:** This amended the Ninth Schedule of the Constitution to insert 27 Land Reform Acts of various States. After this the total number of Acts included in the Ninth Schedule went upto 284.
- **79th Constitutional Amendment Act, 1999:** Amended Art. 334 to extend the reservation of seats for SCs/STs and Anglo-Indians in the Lok Sabha and in the State Legislative Assemblies upto 60 years from the commencement of the Constitution (i.e., till 2010).
- **80th Constitutional Amendment Act, 2000:** Amended Art. 269 and substituted a new Article for Art. 270 and abolished Art. 272 of the Constitution. This was based on the recommendation of the Tenth Finance Commission. This amendment was deemed to have come into operation from 1st April 1996. The Amendment widened the scope of the Central taxes and duties on the consignment of goods levied by the Government of India and distributed among States.
- **81st Constitutional Amendment Act, 2000:** Amended Art. 16(1) of the Constitution and added a new clause (4-B) after clause (4-A) to Art. 16(1) of the Constitution. The new clause (4-B) ends the 50% ceiling on reservation for Scheduled Caste and Scheduled Tribes and other Backward Classes in backlog vacancies.
- **82nd Constitutional Amendment Act, 2000:** This amendment restored the relaxation in qualifying marks and standards of evaluation in both job reservation and promotions to Scheduled Castes and Scheduled. Tribes which was set aside by a Supreme Court's judgement in 1996.
- **84th Constitutional Amendment Act, 2001 (w.e.f. February 21, 2002):** This amendment provided that till the publication of the relevent figures of the first census after 2026 the ascertainment of the population of a State for following purposes shall be made on the basis of the census shown against each of them :
    - Election of the President under Art. 55 — 1971 census.
    - Allotment of seats to each State in Lok Sabha — 1971 census.
    - Division of State into territorial Lok Sabha constituencies — 1991 Census.
    - Composition of Legislative Assemblies under Art. 170 – 1991 census.
    - Reservation of seats for SC/ST in the Lok Sabha under Art. 330 — 1991 Census.

- **85th Constitutional Amendment Act, 2001:** It amended clause (4A) of Art. 16 and substituted the words "in matters of promotion, with consequential seniority, to any class" for the words "in matter of promotion to any class".
  The amendment provided for 'consequential seniority' to the SCs/STs for promotion in government service.
- **86th Constitutional Amendment Act, 2002:** Added a new Art. 21A after. Art. 21 which makes the right of education for children of the age of 6 to 14 years a Fundamental Right. Substitutes Article 45 to direct the State to endeavour to provide early childhood care and education for all children until they complete the age of six years. Added a new Fundamental Duty to Part IV (Art. 51A) of the Constitution.
- **87th Constitutional Amendment Act, 2003 (w.e.f. February 19, 2004):** Provided that the allocation of seats in the Lok Sabha and division of each State into territorial Constituencies will be done on the basis of population as ascertained by the 2001 census' and not by 1991 census.
- **88th Constitutional Amendment Act, 2003 (w.e.f. January 15, 2004):** This amendment inserted a new Article 268A after Article 268 which empowered the Union of India to levy 'service tax'.
  This tax shall be collected and appropriated by the Union and States in the manner as formulated by Parliament.
- **89th Constitutional Amendment Act, 2003:** Provided for the establishment of a separate National Commission for Scheduled Tribes by bifurcating the existing National Commission for Scheduled Castes and Scheduled Tribes. The commission shall consist of a Chairman, Vice-Chairman and three other members. They shall be appointed by the President of India.
- **90th Constitutional Amendment Act, 2003:** This amendment was necessitated due to creation of Bodoland Territorial Areas District within the State of Assam by agreement reached between the Centre and Bodo representatives for solving Bodoland problem. It stated that the representation of Scheduled Tribes and non-Scheduled Tribes in the Constitution of the Bodoland Territorial Areas District shall be maintained. It meant that the representation of the above categories shall remain the same as existed prior to the creation of Bodoland Territorial Areas District.
- **91st Constitutional Amendment Act, 2003 (w.e.f. January 01, 2004):** This amendment limits the size of ministries at the Centre and in States. According to new Clause (1-A) the total number of ministers, including the Prime Minister in the central Council of Ministers or Chief Minister in the State Legislative Assemblies shall not exceed 15 per cent of the total members of the Lok Sabha in the Centre or Vidhan Sabha in the states. The new Clause (1-B) of Article 75 provides that a member of either House of Parliament belonging to any political party who is disqualified for being member of that house on the ground of defection

shall also be disqualified to be appointed as a minister under Clause (1) of Art. 75 and 164 until he is again elected. However, the number of ministers including the Chief Minister in a State shall not be less than 12 (in smaller States like Sikkim, Mizoram and Goa).

- **92nd Constitutional Amendment Act, 2003(w.e.f. January 07, 2004):** It amended the Eighth Schedule of the Constitution and has inserted 4 new languages in it, namely — Bodo, Dogri, Maithili and Santhali. After this amendment the total number of constitutionally recognised official languages has become 22.
- **93rd Constitutional Amendment Act, 2005 (w.e.f. January 20, 2006):** Provided reservation in admissions in private unaided educational institutions for students belonging to scheduled castes/tribes and other backward classes.
- **94th Constitutional Amendment Act, 2006 :** Excluded Bihar from the provision to Clause (1) of Art 164 of the constitution which provides that there shall be a minister in charge of tribal welfare who may in addition be in charge of the welfare of the Scheduled Castes and backward classes in Bihar, Madhya Pradesh and Orissa (now Odisha). It extends the provisions of clause(1) of Art. 164 to the newly formed States of Chhattisgarh and Jharkhand.
- **95th Constitutional Amendment Act, 2009:** Extended the reservation of seats for SCs and STs in the Lok Sabha and State assemblies by another 10 years (beyond January 25, 2010). The time period of 60 years under Art.334 of the constitution was to lapse on January 25, 2010. Through this amendment in Art. 334 the words 'sixty years' has been substituted by 'seventy years'.
- **Ninety-seventh Amendment (2012):** It amended Article 19 and added Part-IXB. The amendment objective was to encourage economic activities of the cooperatives which in turn help the progress of rural India. It is expected to not only ensure autonomous and democratic functioning of cooperatives, but also the accountability of the management to the members and other stakeholders. This amendment came into force on January 12, 2012.
- **Ninety-eighth Amendment (2012):** To insert Article 371 J to empower the Governor of Karnataka to take steps to develop the Hyderabad-Karnataka Region.
- **Ninety-nine Amendment* (2014):** Insertion of Articles 124A, 124B, 124C. Amendments to Articles 127, 128, 217, 222, 224A, 231. Formation of National Judicial Appointments Commission.
- **Hundred Amendment (2015):** India-Bangladesh enclaves transfer.

*The Constitution Bench of the Supreme Court has rejected the 99th Constitution Amendment a 'unconstitutional and void' on October 16,2015.

7. Special Features of the Indian Constitution

- The Constitution of India is the lengthiest and the most comprehensive of all the written Constitutions of the world.
- Originally the Constitution consisted of 395 Articles divided into 22 parts and 8 Schedules.
- Now it consists of about 442 Articles divided into 22 parts and 12 Schedules.
- Unlike the federal Constitutions of the USA and Australia the Indian Constitution lays down provisions relating to the Governmental machinery not only in the Centre but also in the States.
- The Indian Constitution provides for matters of administrative detail.
- The Constitution contains detailed provisions relating to *Centre-State relations* including the emergency provisions.
- Special status has been given to Jammu & Kashmir and some other states such as Nagaland, Mizoram, Assam, Gujarat etc.
- Under the Constitution *the people of India* are *the ultimate sovereign*.
- The Constitution of India establishes a *parliamentary form of Government* both at the Centre and in the States.
- The Indian Constitution, though written, is *sufficiently flexible*.
- The Constitution declares certain *Fundamental Rights* of the individual.
- It is a unique feature of the Indian Constitution that it makes the citizens' duties a part of the basic law of the land.
- One of the most important and unique features of the Indian Constitution is the provisions of *Directive Principles of State Policy* to secure a truly welfare State.
- The Indian Constitution, distributes the legislative subjects on which the Parliament and State Legislature can enact laws under three lists viz. Union List, State List and Concurrent List.
- The Indian Constitution unlike other federal Constitutions provides for a *single unified judiciary* with the Supreme Court at the apex, the High Courts in the middle and the Subordinate Courts at the bottom.
- There are provisions in the Constitution to ensure *independence of judiciary*.
- The Constitution of India has adopted a balance between the American system of Judicial Supremacy and the British principle of Parliamentary Supremacy.
- The most remarkable feature of the Indian Constitution is that being a federal Constitution it *acquires a unitary character during the time of emergency*.
- Under the Indian Constitution every adult above 18 years of age has been given the right to elect representatives for the legislature without prescribing any qualification based either on sex, property, education or the like.
- A distinctive feature of the Indian Constitution is that it provides for the establishment of a *Secular State*. Regardless of their religious beliefs, all Indian citizens enjoy equal rights.

- The State cannot discriminate against anyone on the ground of religion or caste, nor can it compel anybody to pay taxes for the support of any particular religion.
- The Indian Constitution has special *reservation of seats* for the Scheduled Castes and Tribes in public appointments and in educational institutions and in the Union and State Legislatures.
- An outstanding feature of the Constitution is *Panchayati Raj*. The idea for organising village Panchayats was provided in the Constitution under Article 40 of Part IV which received Constitutional legitimacy through the 73rd Amendment to the Indian Constitution.

8. Federal and Unitary Features of the Indian Union

- India is different from the United States of America because in United States the federation is based on an agreement between different States, and the States have the right to secede from the Union.
- The Indian Constitution has the features both of a federal and unitary forms of Government.

Federal features
- Distribution of powers between Union and the States has been made as per the three lists.
- The Union Government as well as the State Governments have to function strictly in accordance with the Constitution. They can neither alter the distribution of powers nor override the dictates of the Constitution.
- Indian Constitution is entirely written. An amendment to it must be passed by the Parliament and if an amendment affects the federal structure it must be ratified by at least half the State Legislatures.
- Like other federal states our country also has an independent Judiciary as an essential feature.

Unitary features of the Indian Constitution
- In a federation, people enjoy dual citizenship, that of the Centre and of the State to which they belong. But the Indian Constitution provides every Indian with single citizenship.
- The most important subjects are included in the Union List which has been allocated to the centre.
- The centre can legislate on the subjects in the concurrent list.
- Residuary powers belong to the Centre.
- Single Constitutional Framework has been provided for the Centre as well as for the State.
- The proclamation of National emergency can immediately turn the federal system of India into a Unitary one.
- In a federation, each State should get equal representation irrespective of its size or population. But in the Rajya Sabha in India, States are represented on the basis of population. Besides, the President has the power to nominate twelve members to the Rajya Sabha.
- The Governors of the States are appointed by the President and they continue to hold office only during his pleasure.

- The Indian Constitution provides for single judiciary, a single system of civil and criminal law and command All India Services.
- The authority of the Comptroller and Auditor General and the Chief Election Commissioner uniformly prevails over the Union as well as States.

9. The Preamble

- The Preamble to the Constitution states the object which the Constitution seeks to establish and promote, and also aids the legal interpretation of the Constitution where the language is found ambiguous.
- The ideals embodied in the Objectives Resolution are faithfully reflected in the Preamble to the Constitution, which, as amended in 1976, summaries the aims and objects of the Constitution.
- *Text of the Preamble*: "We, the People of India having solemnly resolved to constitute India into a Sovereign Socialist Secular Democratic Republic and to secure to all citizens Justice, social, economic and political; Liberty of thought, expression, belief, faith and worship, Equality of status and of opportunity; and to promote among them all Fraternity assuring the dignity of the individual and the unity and integrity of the Nation in our Constituent Assembly on this twenty sixth day of November, 1949, do hereby adopt, enact and give to ourselves this constitution."
- The Preamble specifies the source of authority, i.e. people of India, the system of Government, the objectives to be attained by the political system and the date of adoption and enactment of the Constitution. Though, the Preamble is not enforceable in a court of law, it provides a key to the understanding and interpretation of the Constitution. In case of doubt, the Supreme Court has referred to the Preamble to elucidate vague aspects of the Constitution.
- In the Berubari case, the Supreme Court held that the Preamble was not part of the Constitution, but later, in the Keshavananda Bharti case, it declared that it was part of the Constitution.

10. Lapse of Paramountcy

- When the Indian Independence Act 1947, was passed, it declared the lapse of suzerainty (paramountcy) of the crown, in sec. 7(i)(b) of the Act.
- As from the appointed day – the suzerainty of His Majesty over the Indian States lapses, and with it, all treaties and agreements in force at the date of the passing of this Act between His Majesty and the rulers of Indian States, all functions exercisable by His Majesty at the date with respect to Indian States, all obligations of His Majesty existing at that date towards Indian States or the rulers thereof, and all powers, rights, authority, or jurisdiction exercisable by His Majesty at that date in or in relation to Indian States by treaty, grant, usage, sufferance or otherwise........
- Of the states situated within the geographical boundaries of the Dominion of India, all (numbering 552) indcluding Hyderabad, Kashmir, Bahawalpur, Junagarh and the N.W.F. (North West Frontier)

states (Chitral, Phulra, Dir, Swat and Amb) had acceded to the Dominion of India by the 15th August, 1947, i.e. before the 'appointed day' itself.

11. Integration and Merger of Indian States

▷ The main objective of shaping the Indian States into sizeable or viable administrative units was sought to be achieved by a three-fold process of integration (known as the 'Patel Scheme' after Sardar Vallabhbhai Patel, Minister-in-charge of Home Affairs):
 1. 216 states were merged into respective Provinces, geographically contiguous (connected) to them.
    - These merged states were included in the territories of the states in Part B in the First Schedule of the constitution.
    - The process of merger started with the merger of Orissa and Chhattisgarh States with the then Province of Orissa on January 1,1948.
 2. 61 states were converted into Centrally administered areas and included in Part C of the First Schedule of the Constitution.
 3. The third form of integration was the consolidation of groups of states into new viable units, known as Union of States.
    - As many as 275 states were integrated into 5 Unions — Madhya
    - Bharat, Patiala and East Punjab States Union, Rajasthan, Saurashtra and Travancore — Cochin. These were included in the States in Part B of the First Schedule.
    - The other three States included in Part B were — Hyderabad, Jammu and Kashmir and Mysore.
    - Jammu and Kashmir acceded to India on October 26,1947, and so it was included as a state in Part B, but the Government of India agreed to take the accession subject to confirmation by the people of the state, and a constituent. Assembly subsequently confirmed it, in November, 1956.
    - Hyderabad did not formally accede to India, but the Nizam issued a Proclamation recognising the necessity of entering into a constitutional relationship with the Union of India and accepting the Constitution of India subject to ratification by the Constituent Assembly of the State, and the Constituent Assembly of that state ratified this.

▷ It is noteworthy here that the *Rajpramukhs* of the five Unions as well as the Rulers of Hyderabad, Mysore, Jammu and Kashmir all adopted the Constitution of India, by Proclamations.

▷ The process of integration culminated in the Constitution (7th Amendment) Act, 1956, which abolished Part B states as a class and included all the states in Part A and B in one list.

▷ The special provisions in the constitution relating to Part B states were, consequently omitted. The Indian States thus lost their identity and became a uniform political organisation embodied in the Constitution of India.

12. The Union and its Territories

- *Article 1* lays down that India, i.e. Bharat, shall be a Union of States.
- The Territory of India shall consist of (i) the Territories of the States, (ii) the Union Territories and (iii) any Territories that may be acquired.
- Article 1 of the Constitution describes India as a Union of States not as a federation of states. Union of India is not the result of an agreement, nor has any State the right to secede from it.
- The Federation is called a Union of States, because it is indestructible.
- The Union Territories are not included in the "Union of States". Whereas the expression "Territory of India" includes the States, the Union Territories and such other territories as may be acquired by India.
- The States and their territories are specified in the First Schedule to the Constitution. The Constitution empowers the Parliament for the admission or establishment of new States.
- *Article 2* provides that Parliament may by law admit new States into the Union of India or establishes has new States on such terms and conditions as it deems fit.
- The Parliament has admitted the French settlements of Pondicherry, Karaikal, Mahe and Yenam, the Portuguese settlements of Goa, Diu and Daman and Sikkim, etc. into India after independence.
- *Article 3* of the Constitution empowers the Parliament to form a new State by altering boundaries of existing States.

13. Reorganization of States

- A Bill seeking to create a new State or alter boundaries of existing States can be introduced in either House of the Parliament, only on the recommendation of the President.
- President refers the State Reorganization Bill to the State Legislature concerned for its opinion, fixing a time limit.
- Parliament is not bound to accept or act upon the views of the State Legislature on a state Reorganization Bill. The State Reorganization Bill requires simple majority in both Houses of the Parliament.
- It is not necessary to obtain the views of legislatures of Union territories before a bill affecting their boundaries or names is introduced.
- The States Reorganization Act, 1956 reorganised the boundaries of different States to establish a new State of Kerala and merge the former States of Madhya Bharat, Pepsu, Saurashtra, Travancore, Cochin, Ajmer, Bhopal, Coorg, Kutch and Vindhya Pradesh in other adjoining States and thus 14 states and 6 Union Territories were established in India.
- The Bombay Reorganization Act, 1960, divided the State of Bombay to establish two States of Gujarat and Maharashtra.
- In 1962 Nagaland was created as a separate State.
- In 1966, Punjab was divided into Punjab and Haryana.
- Union Territory of Himachal Pradesh was made the State of Himachal Pradesh by an Act of 1970.

- States of Manipur, Tripura, Meghalaya and Union Territories of Mizoram and Arunachal Pradesh were established in 1971. Later Mizoram and Arunachal Pradesh achieved statehood in 1986.
- Sikkim was made part of India by 36th Amendment of the Constitution.
- In 1987 Goa was made a separate State of the Union.
- Chhattisgarh came into existence on 1st November, 2000.
- Uttaranchal (now Uttarakhand) came into existence on 8th November, 2000.
- The State of Jharkhand, which was established on 15th November 2000 is the newest (28th) State of India.
- The Union Government (on 30th July, 2013) gave a go ahead to create 'Telangana,' (the proposed 29th State) bifurcating Andhra Pradesh.

14. Citizenship

- The Constitution of India provides for a single and uniform citizenship for whole of India.
- Citizenship of India was granted to every person who domiciled in the territory of India at the commencement of the constitution and who was born in the territory of India or:
  - Either of whose parents was born in the territory of India or
  - Who had been ordinarily residing in the territory of India for not less than five years immediately preceding commencement of the Constitution.
- Indian citizens have the following rights under the Constitution, which aliens do not possess:
  - Some of the Fundamental Rights enumerated in part III of the Constitution, e. g. Articles 15, 16,19, 29, 30.
  - Only citizens are eligible for offices of the President, Vice-President, Judge of the Supreme Court or a High Court, Attorney General, Governor of a State, Member of a legislature etc.
  - Only citizens have the right to vote.
- Enemy aliens are not entitled to the benefit of the procedural provisions in clauses (l)-(2) of Article 22 relating to arrest and detention.
- The Citizenship Act, 1955, provides for the acquisition of Indian citizenship in the following ways :
  - Generally, every person born in India on or after January 1950, shall be a citizen of India if either of his parents was a citizen of India at the time of his birth.
  - A person who was outside India on or after 26 January; 1950, shall be a citizen of India by descent, if his father was a citizen of India at the time of that person's birth.
  - A person can apply for and get registered as a citizen of India by the competent authority if he satisfies the conditions laid down.
  - A person residing in India for more than 7 years and having ade-

quate knowledge of a constitutionally recognised Indian language can seek citizenship by naturalisation, provided he is not a citizen of a country where Indian citizens are prevented from becoming citizens by naturalisation.
- If any new territory becomes a part of India, the persons of the territory become citizens of India.

⇨ Citizenship of India may be lost by :
- Renunciation of citizenship.
- Termination of citizenship, if a citizen of India voluntarily aquires the citizenship of another country.
- Deprivation of citizenship by the Government of India.

15. Fundamental Rights

⇨ Six Fundamental Rights have been provided by the Constitution :
1. Right to equality
2. Right to liberty
3. Right against exploitation
4. Right to freedom of religion
5. Cultural and educational rights
6. Right to constitutional remedy

⇨ *Article 14* of the constitution provides that the State shall not deny any person equality before the law or equal protection of the laws within the territory of India.

⇨ Exceptions to the provision of equality before law, allowed by the Indian Constitution are:
- The President or the Governor of a State is not answerable to any Court for the exercise and performance of the powers and duties of his office.
- No criminal proceeding can be instituted or continued against the President or a Governor in any Court during his term of office.
- No civil proceeding in which relief is claimed against the President or the Governor of a State can be instituted during his term of office in any Court in respect of any act done by him in his personal capacity, without a prior notice of two months.
- The above immunities do not bar Impeachment proceeding against the President and Suits or other appropriate proceeding against the Government of India or the Government of a State.
- Exceptions acknowledged by the comity of nations in every civilized country, in favour of foreign Sovereigns and ambassadors.
- The guarantee of 'equal protection' is a guarantee of equal treatment of persons in 'equal circumstances', permitting differentiation in different circumstances.

⇨ **Article 15 of the Constitution** states that the State shall not discriminate against any citizen on grounds only of religion, race, caste, sex, place of birth or any of them.

- No citizen shall, on grounds only of religion, race, caste, sex, place of birth or any of them be subjected to any disability, liability restriction or condition with regard to access to shops, public restaurants, hotels and places of public entertainment or the use of wells, tanks, bathing ghats, roads and places of public resort maintained wholly or partly out of State funds or dedicated to the use of general public.
- Nothing in this article shall prevent the State from making any special provisions for women, children or any socially and educationally backward classes.

➪ **Article 16 guarantees Equality of opportunity** in matters of public employment. It says that:
- There shall be equality of opportunity for all citizens in matters relating to employment or appointment to any office under the State.
- No citizen shall, on grounds only of religion, race, caste, sex, descent, place of birth or any of them, be ineligible for any employment under the State.

The Mandal Commission Case

A nine-Judge Bench of the Supreme Court has laid down in Indra Sawhney's case (popularly known as the Mandal Commission Case) regarding reservation in Government employment, that:
- Under Article 16(4) provisions can be made in favour of the backward Classes in the matter of employment by Executive orders also.
- Backward class of citizens is not defined in the Constitution. A caste may also constitute a class.
- The backwardness contemplated by Art. 16(4) is mainly social. It need not be both social and educational.
- Income or the extent of property can be taken as a measure of social advancement and on that basis the 'creamy layer' of a given caste can be excluded.
- The reservations contemplated in Art. 16(4) should not exceed 50%.
- Reservation of posts under Art. 16(4) is confined to initial appointment only and cannot extend to providing reservation in promotion.

➪ **Note :** *Mandal Commission was set up in 1979 under the Chairmanship of B.N. Madal, M.P. (Former Chief Minister of Bihar).*

➪ The 77th Amendment has provided to continue reservation in promotion for the S.C. and S.T.
➪ Identification of backward classes is subject to judicial review.
➪ *Article 17* ensures *Abolition of Untouchability.* The word 'untouchability' has not been defined either in the Constitution or in the relevant Act of Parliament. It has been assumed that the word has a well known connotation.

- *Article 18 ensures Abolition of titles.* It prevents the State from conferring any title.
- This ban is only against the State and not against other public institutions, such as Universities.
- The State is not debarred from awarding military or academic distinctions, even though they may be used as titles.
- The State is not prevented from conferring any distinction or award which cannot be used as a title. *Bharat Ratna* or *Padma Vibhushan* cannot be used by the recipient as a title and therefore does not come within the Constitutional prohibition.
- Article 19 provides the six freedoms of :
  - Speech and expression;
  - Assemble peacefully and without arms;
  - Form associations or unions;
  - Move freely throughout the territory of India;
  - Reside and settle in any part of the territory of India; and
  - Practise any profession, or to carry on any occupation, trade or business.
- State can impose restrictions on the freedom of speech in the interest of the sovereignty and integrity of India, the security of the State, friendly relations with foreign States, public order, decency or morality, or in relation to contempt of Court, defamation or incitement to an offence.
- Restrictions can be imposed on the right to form associations in the interests of the sovereignty and integrity of India or public order or morality. Restrictions can also be imposed on freedom of movement and reside and settle in the interests of the general public or for the protection of the interests of any Scheduled Tribe. State can prescribe the professional or technical qualifications necessary for practising any profession or carrying on any occupation, trade or business. State can exclude any citizen from a business or industry run by the Government or a body of Government.
- There is no specific provision in the Constitution guaranteeing the freedom of the press because freedom of the press is included in the wider freedom of 'expression' which is guaranteed by freedom of expression under Art. 19.
- *Article 20* guarantees certain *protection in respect of conviction for offences.* It prohibits :
  - Restrospective criminal legislation is commonly known as expost facto legislation.
  - Double jeopardy or punishment for the same offence more than once.
  - Compulsion to give self-incriminating evidence.
- *Article 21 (A)* makes the right of education for children of the age of 6 to 14 years a fundamental right. {Ref.: 86th Amendment Act, 2002}
- *Article 21* of Constitution provides that *no person shall be deprived of his life or personal liberty* except according to the procedure established by law.

- Under the *'Due Process' Clause of the American Constitution*, the Court has assumed the power of declaring unconstitutional any law which deprives a person of his liberty without reasonableness and fairness.
- In England courts have no power to invalidate a law made by Parliament.
- In the case of Gopalan the Supreme Court held that our Constitution had embodied the English concept.
- In Maneka's case the Supreme Court held that a law made by the State which seeks to deprive a person of his personal liberty must prescribe a procedure for such deprivation which must not be arbitrary, unfair or unreasonable, it follows that such law shall be invalid if it violates the principle of natural justice.
- *Article 22* provides that no person who is arrested shall be detained in custody without being informed of the grounds for such arrest.
- No arrested person can be denied the right to consult, and to be defended by a legal practitioner of his choice.
- Every person who is arrested and detained in custody is to be produced before the nearest magistrate within a period of twenty-four hours of arrest excluding the time necessary for the journey from the place of arrest to the court of the magistrate and no such person can be detained in custody beyond that period without the authority of a magistrate.
- The above safeguard is not available to an enemy alien and a person arrested or detained under a law providing for preventive detention.
- The Constitution authorises the Legislature to make laws for preventive *detention* for the security of State, the maintenance of public order, or the maintenance of supplies and services essential to the community, or for reasons connected with Defence and Foreign Affairs {Ref.: Art. 22}
- *Article 23* provides *Right against Exploitation* in following respects :
  - Trafficking in human beings and begary and other similar forms of forced labour are prohibited.
  - The State can impose compulsory service for public purposes, and in imposing such service the State can not make any discrimination on grounds only of religion, race, caste or class or any of them.
  - Special provision for the protection of children is made in Art. 24 which provides that no child below the age of fourteen years can be employed to work in any factory or mine or engaged in any other hazardous employment.
- *Article 25-28 provides Right to Freedom of Religion.*
- *Article 25* provides freedom of conscience and free profession, practice and propagation of religion subject to public order, morality and health.
- Under Art. 25 State can regulate religious activities and provide for social reforms and throw open Hindu religious institutions of public character to all sections of Hindus.
- *Article 26* guarantees following rights to all religious groups subject to public order, morality and health :
  - Establish and maintain institution for religious and charitable purposes;
  - Manage its own affairs in matters of religion;

- Own and acquire movable and immovable property;
- Administer such property in accordance with law.

⇨ The State can not compel any citizen to pay any taxes for the promotion or maintenance of any particular religion or religious institution {Ref.: Art. 27}

⇨ No religious instruction can be provided in any educational institution wholly maintained out of State funds {Ref.: Art. 28}

⇨ Where a religious community is in the minority, the Constitution enables it to preserve its culture and religious interests by providing that the State shall not impose upon it any culture other than the community's own culture {Ref.: Art. 29(1)}

⇨ Such community shall have the right to establish and administer educational institutions of its choice and the State shall not, in granting aid to educational institutions, discriminate against such an educational institution maintained by a minority community on the ground that it is under the management of a religious community {Ref.: Art. 30}.

⇨ Full compensation has to be paid if the State seeks to acquire the property of a minority educational institution {Ref.: Art. 30 (1A)].

⇨ The Fundamental Rights are guaranteed by the Constitution not only against the action of the Executive but also against that of the Legislature.

⇨ Right to constitutional remedy, which was termed *"soul of the constitution"* by Dr. B.R. Ambedkar, has been guaranteed by Art. 32 of the Constitution.

The Writs

⇨ For enforcement of fundamental rights, the judiciary has been armed with the power to issue the writs.

⇨ The power to issue these writs for the enforcement of the Fundamental Rights is given by the Constitution to the Supreme Court {Ref.: Art. 32} and High Courts {Ref. : Art. 226}.

⇨ Supreme Court has the power to issue writs only for the purpose of enforcement of the Fundamental Rights whereas under Art. 226 a High Court can issue writs for the purpose of enforcement of Fundamental Rights and/or for the redress of any other injury or illegality.

⇨ Supreme Court can issue a writ against any person or Government within the territory of India, while High Court can issue a writ against a person, Government or other authority only if they are located within the territorial jurisdiction of the High Court.

⇨ A writ of *Habeas Corpus* calls upon the person who has detained another to produce the latter before the court, in order to let the court know on what ground he has been confined and to set him free if there is no legal justification for the imprisonment. The words 'habeas corpus' literally mean 'to have a body'. This writ may be addressed to an official or a private person, who has another person in his custody.

⇨ *Mandamus* literally means a command. It commands the person to whom it is addressed to perform some public or quasipublic legal duty

- which he has refused to perform and the performance of which cannot be enforced by any other adequate legal remedy. *Mandamus* can not be granted against the President, or the Governor of a state, for the exercise and performance of the powers and duties of his office.
- The writ of prohibition is a writ issued by the Supreme Court or a High Court to an inferior court forbidding the latter to continue proceeding therein in excess if its jurisdiction or to usurp a jurisdiction with which it is not legally vested.
- While *mandamus* is available not only against judicial authorities but also against administrative authorities, prohibition and certiorari are issued only against judicial or quasi-judicial authorities.
- Though prohibition and certiorari are both issued against Courts or Tribunals exercising judicial or quasi-judicial powers, *certiorari* is issued to quash order or decision of the Court or Tribunal while *prohibition* is issued to prohibit the Court or Tribunal from making the ultra vires order or decision. Prohibition is available during the pendency of the proceedings and before the order is made, certiorari can be issued only after the order has been made.
- *Quo warranto* is a proceeding whereby the court enquires into the legality of the claim which a party asserts to a public office, and to oust him from its enjoyment if the claim is not well founded.
- The conditions necessary for the issue of a writ of *quo warranto* are as follows :
  - The office must be public and it must be created by a statute or by the constitution itself.
  - The office must be a substantive one and not merely the function or employment of a servant at the will and during the pleasure of another.
  - There has been a contravention of the Constitution or a statute or statutory instrument, in appointing such person to that office.
- The limitations on the enforcement of the fundamental rights are as follows:
- Parliament has the power to modify the application of the Fundamental Rights to the members of the Armed Forces, Police Forces or intelligence orgnisations so as to ensure proper discharge of their duties and maintenance of discipline amongst them {Ref.: Art. 33}.
  - When martial law is in force, Parliament may indemnify any person in the service of the Union or a State for any act done by him {Ref.: Art. 34).
  - Certain fundamental rights guaranteed by the Constitution may remain suspended, while a Proclamation of Emergency is made by the President under Art. 352.

Right to Information
▷ Right to information has been granted to every citizen of India under Right to information Act, 2005 which came into force on 12th October, 2005.
▷ It is not a Fundamental Right but it entails a clause for penalty in case of delay in giving information to the applicant.
▷ Information Commission has been setup at central and state levels to oversee implementation of the Act.

16. Directive Principles of State Policy

The Directive Principles are contained in Part IV of the Constitution. They aim at providing the social and economic base of a genuine democracy.

Important Directive Principles

Broadly speaking, there are three types of Directive Principles aimed at providing social and economic justice and ushering in a welfare state.

1. **Socio-Economic Principles :** They require the State : (i) to provide adequate means of livelihood to all citizens; (ii) to prevent concentration of wealth and means of production and ensure equitable distribution of wealth and material resources; (iii) to secure equal pay for equal work of men as well as women; (iv) to ensure a decent standard of living and leisure for all workers; (v) to provide necessary opportunities and facilities to children and youth to prevent their exploitation; and (vi) to make efforts to secure the right to work, education and public assistance in case of unemployment, sickness, old age etc.

2. **Gandhian Principles :** These are the embodiment of the Gandhian programme for reconstruction. These include :
(i) the establishment of village panchayats to function as units of self government; (ii) the promotion of educational and economic interests of weaker sections of society; (iii) the promotion of cottage industries; (iv) the prohibition of intoxicating drugs and drinks; and (v) prevention of the slaughter of cows, calves and other milch cattle etc.

3. **Liberal Principles :** The principles are based on liberal thinking and emphasise the need for;
(i) a uniform civil code for the country; (ii) free and compulsory education for all children up to the age of 14 years; (iii) separation of the judiciary and executive; (iv) organisation of agriculture and animal husbandry along scientific lines; (v) securing the participation of workers in the management of industries; (vi) safeguarding the forests and wildlife of the country; and (vii) protecting monuments and places of artistic or historical importance.

The real significance of the directive principles lies in the fact that they intend to provide social and economic democracy in the country without which political democracy is a farce.

Difference Between Fundamental Rights and Directive Principles
- Fundamental rights constitute limitations upon State action, while the Directive Principles are instruments of instruction to the Government.
- The directives require to be implemented by legislation while fundamental rights are already provided in the Constitution.
- The Directives are not enforceable in the Courts and do not create any Justiciable rights in favour of the individuals, while the Fundamental Rights are enforceable by the Courts {Ref.: Arts. 32, 37, 226(1)}
- In case of any conflict between fundamental rights and directive principles, the former should prevail in the Courts.
- *42nd Amendment Act* ensured that though the directives themselves are not directly enforceable, it would be totally immune from unconstitutionality on the ground of contravention of the fundamental rights conferred by Arts. 14 and 19.
- This attempt to confer a primacy upon the directives against the fundamental rights was foiled by the decision of the Supreme Court in *Minerva Mills Case* to the effect that a law would be protected by Art. 31C only if it has been made to implement the directive in Art. 39(b)-(c) and not any of the other Directives included in Part IV.

Directives Provided outside Part IV of the Constitution
- State and every local authority within the state to provide adequate facilities for instruction in the mother-tongue at the primary stage of education to children belonging to linguistic minority groups. (Ref. :Art 350 A}
- Union to promote spread of Hindi language and to develop it as a medium of expression of all the elements of the composite culture of India. {Ref.: Art. 351.}
- The claims of the members of the Scheduled Castes and the Scheduled Tribess shall be taken into consideration, consistently with the maintenance of efficiency of administration, in the making of appointments to services and posts in connection with the affairs of the union or a state. {Ref.: Art. 335}
- Though the Directives contained in Arts. 335, 350A and 351 are not included in Part IV, Courts have given similar attention to them meaning that all parts of the Constitution should be read together.

17. Fundamental Duties
- The Fundamental Duties are eleven in number, incorporated in Art. 51A [Part IVA], which has been incorporated by the 42nd Amendment Act, 1976.
- Under this Article, it is the duty of every citizen of India:
    1. to abide by the Constitution and respect its ideals and institutions, the National Flag and the National Anthem;

2. to cherish and follow the noble ideals which inspired our National Struggle for freedom;
3. to uphold and protect the sovereignty, unity and integrity of India;
4. to defend the country;
5. to promote harmony and the spirit of common brotherhood amongst all the people of India;
6. to value and preserve the rich heritage of our composite culture;
7. to protect and improve the natural environment;
8. to develop the scientific temper and spirit of inquiry;
9. to safeguard public property;
10. to strive towards excellence in all spheres of individual and collective activity.
11. to provide opportunities for education to his child or ward as the case may be between the age of six and fourteen years.

Note : The 11th Fundamental Duty was added by the 86th Constitutional Amendment Act, 2002.

▻ There is no provision in the Constitution for direct enforcement of any of the Fundamental Duties nor for any sanction to prevent their violation.

18. Procedure for Amending the Constitution

▻ The alteration of certain provisions of the Constitution are not considered amendment of the constitution. Such provisions can be altered by the Parliament by a simple majority.

▻ Other provisions of the Constitution can be changed only by the process of 'amendment' prescribed in Art. 368.

▻ In the case of provisions which affect the federal structure, a ratification by the Legislatures of at least half of the states, is required before the Bill is presented to the President for his assent. Such provisions are :
- The manner of election of the President {Ref: Arts. 54,55)
- Extent of the executive power of the Union and the States {Ref: Arts. 73, 162);
- The Supreme Court and the High Courts {Art. 241, Chap. IV of part V, Chap. V of part VI);
- Distribution of legislative power between the Union and the States [Chap.I of Part XI];
- Any of the Lists in the 7th Schedule;
- Representation of the States in Parliament {Arts. 80-81, 4th Schedule};
- Provisions of Art. 368 itself,

▻ There is no separate Constituent body provided for by our Constitution for the amending process.

▻ An amendment of the Constitution can be initiated only by the introduction of a Bill for the purpose in either House of Parliament.

- The Amendment Bill should be passed by each House by a *special majority* i.e., more than 50% of the total membership of that House and by a majority of not less than two-thirds of the members of that House present and voting,
- Constitution stands amended in accordance with the terms of the Amendment Bill after President's assent is accorded to it.

The blend of rigidity and flexibility in the procedure for amendment
- The procedure for amendment is 'rigid' in so far as it requires a *special majority* and a special procedure.
- There is no separate body for amending the Constitution, as exists in some other countries (e.g., a Constitutional convention)
- The State Legislatures cannot initiate any Bill or proposal for amendment of the Constitution.
- Subject to the provisions of Art. 368, Constitution Amendment Bills are to be passed by the Parliament in the same way as Ordinary Bills.
- The procedure for joint session is not applicable to Bills for amendment of the Constitution.
- The *previous sanction of the President is not required* for introducing any Bill for amendment of the Constitution.
- The requirement relating to ratification by which the state Legislatures is more liberal than the corresponding provisions in the American constitution. The latter requires ratification by three fourths of the states.
- The amendment of Art. 368 in 1971 has made it obligatory for the President to give his assent to a Bill for amendment of the Constitution, when it is presented to him after its passage by the Legislature {Ref.: 24th Amendment 1971).

Whether Fundamental Rights are Amendable
- Until the case of Golak Nath, Supreme Court held that no part of our Constitution was unamendable.
- In Golak Nath's case(1967) a majority of six judges, in a special bench of eleven, overruled the previous decisions and held that if any of such rights is to be amended, a new Constituent Assembly must be convened for making a new Constitution or radically changing it.
- Constitution (24th Amendment) Act, 1971, held that an amendment of the Constitution passed in accordance with Art. 368, will not be law within the meaning of Art. 13 and the validity of a Constitution Amendment Act shall not be questioned on the ground that it takes away or affects a fundamental right {Ref.: Art. 368(3)}
- Validity of the 24th Constitution Amendment Act itself was challenged in the case of Keshavananda Bharati.
- In the case of Keshvananda Bharati the Supreme court overruled its own decision given in the case of Golak Nath and held that the Parliament could amend any provision of the constitution including fundamental rights.

The Doctrine of Basic Features

- The Supreme court held in the case of Keshavananda Bharati that there are certain *basic features* of the Constitution of India, which cannot be altered by an amendment under Art. 368.
- Article 31C, introduced by 25th Amendment Act provided that if any law seeks to implement the directive principles contained in Art. 39(b)-(c) i.e. regarding socialistic control and distribution of the material resources of the country, such law shall not be void on the ground of contravention of Art. 14 or 19. The Supreme Court later held that Art. 368 did not empower the Parliament to take away judicial review, in the name of 'amending' the Constitution.
- The 42nd Amendment 1976 inserted two clauses in Art. 368 to the effect that Constitution Amendment Act "shall be called in Question in any court on any ground". These clauses were nullified by the Supreme Court in the Minerva Mills case.
- There are three implications of the decision in Keshavananda Bharati's case.
  - Any part of the Constitution may be amended as per the procedure laid down in Art. 368.
  - No referendum or reference to Constituent Assembly is required to amend any provision of the Constitution.
  - Basic features of the Constitution cannot be amended.
- There is no limited list of basic features. In so many decisions the Supreme Court has declared different things as basic features. Prominent among them are the following :
  - Supremacy of the Constitution.
  - Rule of law.
  - The principle of separation of powers.
  - The objectives specified in the Preamble to the Constitution.
- Judicial review; Art. 32.
- Federalism
- Secularism
- The Sovereign, Democratic, Republican structure
- Freedom and dignity of the individual
- Unity and integrity of the Natio.
- The Principle of equality, not every feature of equality, but the quintessence of equal justice.
- The 'essence' of fundamental rights in Part III.
- The concept of social and economic justice to build a Welfare State.
- The balance between fundamental rights and directive principles.
- The Parliamentary system of Government.
- The principle of free and fair elections.
- Limitations upon the amending power conferred by Art. 368.

- Independence of the Judiciary.
- Effective access to justice.
- Powers of the Supreme Court under Arts. 32,136,141,142.

19. Executives of Union Government

The machinery of the Union Government includes:
- The President
- The Vice President
- The Prime Minister
- The Council of Ministers
- The Parliament
- The Supreme Court
- The State Executive
- The Governor
- The State Council of Ministers
- The High Courts

The President

The President of India is the *constitutional head of the parliamentary form of government*, as followed in our country. The President in such a system represents the nation, but doesn't rule it. The real power here is vested in the council of ministers.

Qualifications to be the President of India
- A person must be a citizen of India.
- A person must not be less than 35 years of age.
- A person must be eligible to be a member of Lok Sabha, but he/she should not be a sitting member of the House.
- The person must not be in occupation of any office of the Government of India, except that of the Vice President of India and the Governor.

Process of election of the President of India

The President of India is elected indirectly by the Electoral College comprising the:
- Elected members of both the Houses of Parliament – Lok Sabha and Rajya Sabha
- Elected members of the State Legislatures
- The value of each vote of an MP and MLA is calculated by the following process:
    - Value of vote of an MLA = Total population of a state/total number of elected MLAs ÷ 100
    - Value of vote of an MP = Total value of vote of MLAs of all the states/ total number of MPs (Lok Sabha + Rajya Sabha)
    - After being elected, the President of India takes oath in the presence of Chief Justice of India or senior most judge of Supreme Court.

Tenure and emoluments of the President of India

Tenure: The President of India is elected for five years, but he/she is eligible to be re-elected for any number of terms. There is no upper limit on the number of times a person can become President as per Article 57 of the Indian Constitution.

Emoluments: The President receives an emolument of Rs 1, 50, 000 per month as salary and other benefits in the capacity of the chairman of the Rajya Sabha. An ex – President of India receives a pension of 50 percent of his/her salary.

Powers of the President of India

Executive and Administrative Powers:
The President of India appoints people to senior most offices of India including that of Prime Minister, Comptroller Auditor General, Attorney General, Chief Election Commissioner, members of UPSC, members of Finance Commission, and Ambassadors. Notably, all Union Territories are directly under the President of India.

Legislative Powers:
- President appoints 12 members to Rajya Sabha and two Anglo-Indian members to Lok Sabha.
- President summons sessions of both houses of Parliament
- President addresses first session after general elections and first session of the year.
- Passes only non-money Bills to become laws or sends them back to Parliament for reconsideration, but for once only.
- Can enact laws through Ordinance that has to be passed by Parliament within six weeks.

Financial Powers:
- Causes the Budget to be laid before Parliament
- Sanctions introduction of monetary Bills
- Appoints Finance Commission and distributes revenue between the Centre and the state.

Judicial Powers:
- Appoints judges in the Supreme Court and the High Courts.
- Can pardon, reprieve, remit or suspend the sentences from the accused.

Emergency Powers:
- Under Article 352 of the Constitution, President can proclaim national emergency in case of external aggression or armed rebellion within.
- Article 356 of the Constitution empowers the President to declare emergency due to failure of the constitutional machinery in any state.
- Under Article 360, the President can declare emergency due to threat to financial stability or credit of the country.
- The President cannot be questioned in any court of law for the action taken by him while discharging his duties.

Impeachment of the President:
- The President of India can be impeached on the ground of violation of Constitution.
- Process for the impeachment of President can be initiated in either House of the Parliament.
- If the House, where impeachment process has been initiated passes the resolution by not less than $2/3^{rd}$ majority, the matter will be referred to the other House.
- During the impeachment process, charges are framed by one House and the other House investigates. While the impeachment process is underway, the President has the right to defend either in person or through lawyer.
- After the investigation, if other House passes the resolution by not less than two-third majority, the President stands impeached.

The Vice-President

Qualifications
- He/she must be a citizen of India.
- The person must not be less than the age of 35 years.
- He/she must be eligible to be a member of the Rajya Sabha, but must not be a sitting member of either house of the Parliament.

Election of the Vice-President: The Vice-President is elected by the members of electoral college consisting of members of the Lok Sabha and the Rajya Sabha. Unlike the election of President, members of the Legislative Assemblies have no role to play in the election of the Vice-President.

Functions of the Vice-President
- The Vice-President is the ex-officio chairman of the Rajya Sabha.
- He/she performs functions of the President, when the President is unable to discharge duties due to illness, absence or any other cause.
- The Vice-President holds the office for a term of five years and can be re-elected.

The Prime Minister

The Prime Minister of India is the head or the executive authority of the State heading the council of ministers. The Prime Minister is the head of the political party that wins majority of seats in the Lok Sabha. The Prime Minister is appointed by the President. Generally, the tenure of the Prime Minister of India is for five years, however, a person continues to be in the office as long as he/she enjoys majority in the lower house of Parliament. If the Prime Minister's party looses majority in the Lok Sabha, then he along with his council of ministers has to resign. The salary and emoluments received by the Prime Minister are the same as that of other members of Parliament. In addition to this, the Prime Minister gets a sumptuary allowance of Rs 15,000 per month, free residence and free medical facilities.

The Council of Ministers

The Constitution provides that there shall be a Council of Ministers headed by the Prime Minister. The Council of Ministers, a policy making body is appointed by the President on the advice of the Prime Minister. Any person, who is a member of either House of the Parliament can be appointed as a minister.

20. The Parliament

India has a *parliamentary form of government*. This form of government was borrowed from the Constitution of UK. The Parliament consists of: (i) The President of India (ii) The Council of States also known as the Rajya Sabha or the Upper House (iii) The House of People is known as the Lok Sabha.

The Rajya Sabha/The Council of States:

The Rajya Sabha, also known as the *Upper House of Parliament* comprises members elected from states and members nominated by President, who have achieved distinguished recognition in the field of art, literature, science or social science.

There are 250 members in the Rajya Sabha of which 238 members representing States and Union Territories come through election process, 12 are nominated by the President.

The Vice-President is the ex-officio Chairman of the Rajya Sabha, and the Deputy Chairman is elected from among the members of the Rajya Sabha.

To be a member of the Rajya Sabha, a person must not be less than 30 years of age, and he should be an elector from the state, which he is representing.

Unlike the Lok Sabha, the Rajya Sabha is never dissolved. The tenure of a Rajya Sabha member is for six years and one-third of its members retire after every two years.

Functions of the President: He/she shares with the Lok Sabha the power of amending the constitution. A bill has to be passed in the Rajya Sabha as well to become a law. The Rajya Sabha can't originate a bill, except the *Money Bill*. The elected members are part of the electoral college to elect the President of India.

The Lok Sabha, also known as the *Lower House or the Council of People* consists of *545 members* of which 543 are elected directly by the people from States and Union Territories. Two members belonging to the Anglo-Indian community are nominated by the President.

To conduct the business of the House, the Lok Sabha Speaker is elected from among the members, and the Speaker of the House elects a deputy speaker to discharge functions in his absence.

To be a member of the Lok Sabha, a person must be a citizen of India. He/she must not be less than 25 years of age. The person must not be occupying any government office of profit. He/she must not be of unsound mind or insolvent.

A Lok Sabha member can be disqualified if he/she overrules the whip, remains absent for 60 days without intimation. A member can also voluntarily give up his membership.

Sessions of Parliament
There are normally three sessions of the Parliament in a year.
- *The Budget Session (February to May)*
- *The Monsoon Session (July to August)*
- *The Winter Session (November to December)*

There should not be a gap of six months between the two sessions of the Parliament.

Joint Session of Parliament
There can be a Joint Session of the Parliament in any of the following cases:
- A Bill passed by one House is rejected by another House.
- The Amendment passed in one House is not acceptable to another House.
- A Bill remains pending for more than six months.

The Comptroller and Auditor General of India
- The CAG controls the entire financial system of the Union as well as the States {Ref.: Art. 148 }.
- Though appointed by the President, the Comptroller and Auditor General can be removed only on an address from both Houses of Parliament on the ground of proved misbehaviour or incapacity.
- His salary and conditions of service are laid down by Parliament and can not be varied to his disadvantage during his term of office.
- The term of office of the Comptroller and Auditor-General (CAG) is 6 years from the date on which he assumes office.
- CAG vacates office on attaining the age of 65 years even without completing the 6-year term. He can resign by writing under his hand, addressed to the President of India. He can be removed by impeachment {Ref.: Arts. 148(1); 124(4)}.
- His salary is equal to that of a Judge of the Supreme Court.
- Other conditions of his service are similar to an I. A. S. of the rank of Secretary to the Government of India.
- He is disqualified for any further Government office after retirement.
- The salaries, etc. of the Comptroller and Auditor-General and his staff and the administrative expenses of his office are charged upon the Consolidated Fund of India and thus non-votable {Ref.: Art. 148 (6)}.
- The main duties of the Comptroller and Auditor General are:
    - To audit and report on all expenditure from the Consolidated Fund of India and of each state and each Union Territory having a Legislative Assembly as to whether such expenditure has been in accordance with the law.
    - To audit and report on all expenditure from the Contingency Funds and Public Accounts of the Union and of the states.

- To audit and report on all trading manufacturing profit and loss accounts etc. kept by any department of the Union or a state.
- To see that rules and procedures in that behalf are designed to secure an effective check on the assessment, collection and proper allocation of revenue.
- To audit and report on the receipts and expenditure of all bodies and authorities substantially financed from the Union or State revenues, Government companies; and other corporations or bodies, if so required by the laws relating to such corporations or bodies.

Speaker and Deputy Speaker of the Lok Sabha

- Speaker presides over the Lok Sabha.
- The Speaker or the Deputy Speaker, normally holds office during the life of the House, but his office may terminate earlier in any of the following ways:
  - By his ceasing to be a member of the House.
  - By resignation in writing, addressed to the Deputy Speaker, and *vice versa*.
  - By removal from office by a resolution, passed by a majority of all the then members of the House {Ref.: Art. 94}.
- A resolution to remove the speaker cannot be moved unless at least 14 days notice has been given of the intention to move the resolution.
- While a resolution for his removal is under consideration, the Speaker cannot preside but he can speak in, take part in the proceedings of the House and vote except in the case of equality of votes (Ref.: Art. 96).
- At other meetings of the House the Speaker cannot vote in the first instance, but can exercise a casting vote in case of equality of votes.
- The Speaker has the final power to maintain order within the Lok Sabha and to interpret its Rules of Procedures.
- In the absence of a quorum the Speaker adjourns the House or suspends the meeting until there is a quorum.
- The Speaker's conduct in regulating the procedure or maintaining order in the House cannot be questioned in a Court {Ref.: Art. 122}.
- The Speaker presides over a joint sitting of the two Houses of Parliament {Ref.: Art. 118(4)}.
- When a Money Bill is transmitted from the Lok Sabha to the Rajya Sabha the Speaker may certify that it is a Money Bill (Ref.: Art. 110(4)).
- The decision of the Speaker on whether a Bill is Money Bill is final.
- While the office of Speaker is vacant or the Speaker is absent from a sitting of the House, the Deputy Speaker presides, except when a resolution for his own removal is under consideration.

Chairman and Deputy Chairman of the Rajya Sabha

- Vice-President of India is ex-officio Chairman of the Rajya Sabha and

functions as the Presiding Officer of that House so long as he does not officiate as the President.
- When the Chairman acts as the President of India, the duties of the Chairman are performed by the Deputy Chairman.
- The Chairman may be removed from his office only if he is removed from the office of the Vice-President.
- The powers of Chairman in the Rajya Sabha are similar to those of the Speaker in the Lok Sabha except that the Speaker has certain special powers like certifying a Money Bill, or presiding over a joint sitting of the two Houses.

Privileges of Parliament

- The privileges of each House can be divided into two groups:
  - Those which are enjoyed by the members individually.
  - Those which belong to each House of Parliament, as a collective body.
- The privileges enjoyed by the members individually are:
  - *Freedom from Arrest* exempts a member from arrest during the continuance of a meeting of the House or Committee thereof of which he is a member and during a period of 40 days before and after such meeting or sitting.
  - This immunity is confined to arrest in civil cases and not in criminal cases or under the law of Preventive Detention.
  - A member cannot be summoned, without the leave of the House to give evidence as a witness while Parliament is in session.
  - There is *Freedom of Speech* within the walls of each House.
  - The limitation on freedom of speech is that no discussion can take place in Parliament with respect to the conduct of any judge of the Supreme Court or of a High Court in the discharge of his duties except upon a motion for removal of the judge (Ref.: Art. 121).
- The privileges of the House *collectively* are:
  - The right to publish debates and proceedings and to restrain publication by others.
  - The right to exclude others.
  - The right to regulate internal affairs of the House.
  - The right to publish Parliamentary misbehaviour.
  - The right to punish members and outsiders for breach of its privileges.

Representation of States and Union Territories in the Rajya Sabha

State	No.	State/UT	No.
Uttar Pradesh	31	Jammu & Kashmir	4
Maharashtra	19	Himachal Pradesh	3

State	No.	State/UT	No.
Tamil Nadu	18	Uttarakhand	3
Andhra Pradesh	18	Goa	1
Bihar	16	Manipur	1
Bengal	16	Nagaland	1
Karnataka	12	Sikkim	1
Gujarat	11	Tripura	1
Madhya Pradesh	11	Arunachal Pradesh	1
Rajasthan	10	Mizorarn	1
Odisha (Orissa)	10	Meghalaya	1
Kerala	9		
Assam	7		
Punjab	7	**Union Territories**	
Jharkhand	6	Delhi	3
Chhattisgarh	5	Puducherry	1

Representation of States and Union Territories in the Lok Sabha

State	No.	State/UT	No.
Uttar Pradesh	80	Uttarakhand	5
Maharashtra	48	Himachal Pradesh	4
Andhra Pradesh	42	Tripura	2
West Bengal	42	Manipur	2
Bihar	40	Meghalaya	2
Tamil Nadu	39	Goa	2
Madhya Pradesh	29	Arunachal Pradesh	2
Karnataka	28	Nagaland	1
Gujarat	26	Sikkim	1
Rajasthan	25	Mizoram	1
Odisha (Orissa)	21	**Union Territories**	
Kerala	20	Delhi	7
Jharkhand	14	Puducherry	1
Assam	14	Chandigarh	1
Punjab	13	Lakshadweep	1
Chhattisgarh	11	Dadra & Nagar Haveli	1
Haryana	10	Daman & Diu	1
Jammu & Kashmir	6	Andaman & Nicobar	1

Parliamentary Committees

Parliamentary committees are an important link between the Parliament, the Executive and the general public. These Committees play significant role in a parliamentary form of government.

The need to have Parliamentary Committees arises out of the fact that the work done by the Parliament in modern times is not only varied and complex in nature, but also considerable in volume. The time at its disposal is limited. It cannot, therefore, give close consideration to all the legislative and other matters that come up before it. A good deal of its business is, therefore, transacted in Committees of the House. Also, these Committees are to keep a vigil on the part of the Legislature over the actions of the Executive.

A Parliamentary Committee is appointed or elected by the House or nominated by the Speaker. A Parliamentary Committee works under the direction of the Speaker and presents its report to the House or to the Speaker and the Secretariat.

A Committee dealing with a particular matter deliberates the issue at length. Views are expressed freely by members of the Committee. Significantly, in most of the Committees, public is directly or indirectly associated when memoranda containing suggestions are received, on-the-spot studies are conducted and oral evidence is taken which helps the Committees in arriving at the conclusions.

By nature, Parliamentary Committees are of two kinds : Ad Hoc Committees and Standing Committees and the most powerful of all is the Public Accounts Committee which is headed by the leader of the opposition.

Standing Committees

Parliamentary Standing Committees are permanent and regular committees, which are constituted from time to time in pursuance of the provisions of an Act of Parliament or Rules of Procedure and Conduct of Business in Parliament.

Both the Houses of Parliament have Standing Committees like the Business Advisory Committee, the Committee on Petitions, the Committee of Privileges and the Rules Committee, etc. The work of these Committees is of continuous nature.

Ad hoc Committees

Unlike Standing Committees of the Parliament, the Ad hoc committees are temporary as they are appointed for a specific purpose. The Ad hoc committees cease to exist as soon as they finish the task assigned to them and submit a report. The principal ad hoc committees are — Select and Joint Committees on Bills. Others like the Railway Convention Committee, the Committees on the Draft Five Year Plans and the Hindi Equivalents Committee were appointed for specific purposes.

The Joint Committee on Food Management in Parliament House Complex etc. also come under the category of ad hoc committees.

Civil Services in Inda : Nature and Role

The administration and government of a country is carried on through the civil servants. The civil servants are essential part of a political system. The members of civil service enter into this service through a well defined process. They are trained in their job and inducted in the administrative system. Since they remain in the system for a long time, they gain rich experience at a later stage. Therefore, the senior members of the civil service are actively involved in decision making and policy formulation at the apex level. Every political system of a democratic character tries to attract the best talented personnel for carrying out its administrative responsibility.

The civil servants are also called the Permanent Executive because they enjoy a fixed term of office for a long period. The Political Executive, that is the Council of Ministers is not permanent and has a very short term in the office, which is often unpredictable in nature. It is the Permanent Executive which performs the functions of government on a permanent basis and imparts a sense of permanency in the political system.

In India, the civil service was evolved and developed during the British period with the objective of fulfilling the desires and the interests of the British Empire. After Independence, India has, more or less, adopted the same administrative set-up which was evolved and strengthened during the colonial rule.

The History of Civil Services — The structure and the process of civil service in India was evolved during the British period with the efforts of such eminent persons as Macaulay, Islington etc.

During the rule of East India Company (before 1858) the civil servants appointed in India were appointed by a Selection Committee of Hailybury College and Board of Directors of the Company.

In 1854, the Committee on Indian Civil Services was constituted under the chairmanship of Lord Macaulay to suggest reforms in the civil service. The suggestion of the committee led to the introduction of the principle of merit based-career oriented civil services. In 1892, the minimum and maximum age limit for entering into the civil service was fixed at 18–23 years respectively. The civil services were divided into two categories. First, the covenanted civil service which consisted of British civil servants occupying the higher posts in the administration. Second, the uncovenanted civil service which was introduced to facilitate the entry of Indians at the lower rung of the administration.

Between 1886 to 1923, **three important commissions on Civil services** were appointed to study and make suggestions with respect to civil services in India.

(1) Aitchison Commission (1886) — It recommended formation of Provincial Civil Service in place of Statutory Civil Service. On the basis of its recommendations, the government abolished the covenanted and uncovenanted civil services and in their place, the Imperial Civil Service and the Provincial Civil Services respectively were formed.

1. **Islington Commission (1912)** — The commission recommended the categorisation of civil service into three classes–the first class, the second class and the third class. This classification still continues.

2. **Lee Commission (1923)** — It recommended for the classification of civil services, the establishment of Public Service Commission for recruitment and cadrewise Indianisation of civil services.

The Government of India Act, 1919 is the first legal measure which reorganised the Imperial Civil Service in the present form. Consequently, around 1920, three types of civil services emerged:

(i) **Central Services**—These services were under the direct and permanent control of the British Government in India.

(ii) **Imperial Services**—These were under the control of the Secretary of State for India.

(iii) **Provincial Services**—These were under the control of Provincial Governors.

Under the provisions of the Government of India Act, 1935, the Union Public Service Commission and the Provincial Public Service Service Commission Were established to make recruitment to these services.

The Goals of Civil Service Before Independence:

The civil service was designed to perform mainly three functions during the British period.

(i) Advancement of the interest of the colonial government.

(ii) To maintain law and order and

(iii) To collect government revenues and other dues.

The welfare and the developmental activities were not given priority during colonial rule. The very structure and the role of the administration promoted in civil services such characteristics as generalist, elitist, loyalist, neutralist etc. The evolution and development of specialised services was not encouraged.

Civil Services After Independence

The All India Services, created during the British period were retained under the Constitution of India. The Council of States was given the power of creating new All India Service by passing a resolution to that effect. It was also provided in the Constitution that for making recruitment to the Civil Services, there shall be a Union Public Service Commissions and State Public Service Commission in every state.

Public Service Commissions :

1. There is a Union Public Service Commission for making recruitment to

the All India Services and central services. Similarily there are the State Public Service Commissions at the State level to make recruitment to the provincial civil service. Two or more states, if the parliament provides by law, may have a Joint Public Service Commission.

2. The service conditions of the member of the Union Public Service Commission and the Joint Service Commission, are determined by the President, whereas the service conditions of the members of the State Public Service Commission are determined by the Governor.

3. The members of the Union Public Service Commission and the Joint Public Service commission are appointed by the President in consultation with the Union Council of Ministers. The members of the State Public Service Commission are appointed by the Governor in consultation with the Chief Minister. It is provided in the Constitution that not less than half of the members of a commission shall be persons who have served for not less than 10 years under the government of the Union or the State.

4. The term of office for members of a commission is six years. But if the members of the Union Public Service Commission attain the age of 65 years before the completion of the term of six years, they retire from the office. The maximum age of retirement of a member of the State Public Service Commission is 62 years.

Civil Services in Inda

All India Services
1. Indian Administrative Service
2. Indian Police Service
3. Indian Forest Service

Central Services (Class-I) :
1. Indian Foreign Service
2. Indian Revenue Service
3. Indian Postal Service
4. Indian Railway Accounts Service
5. Indian Audit and Accounts Service
6. Indian Defence Accounts Service
7. Indian Railway Traffic Service
8. Indian Information Service
9. Indian Economic Service
10. Indian Statistical Service

Provincial Services :
1. Provincial Civil Service
2. State Police Service
3. State Education Service
4. State Audit and Accounts Service
5. State Judicial Service
6. State Cooperative Service
7. State Agricultural Service
8. State Forest Service
9. State Service of Engineers
10. State Medical Service
11. State Veterinary Service

However, the members of a Commission may be removed from office before the expiry of the term under the conditions given below.

1. The members of the Union Public Service Commission and Joint Public Service Commission may resign their office by Writing to the President.

The members of the State Public Service Commission may resign from their office by submitting their resignation to the Governor.
2. The members of a Commission may be removed by the President:
   (i) if a member is declared undischarged insolvent or mentally and physically not fit or holds any other office of profit.
   (ii) on the ground of misbehaviour after an inquiry by the Supreme Court and it found guilty of such misbehaviour.

Commissions/Committees Constituted For Administrative Reforms		
Chairman	**Year**	**Report**
N. Gopal Swamy Iyenger	1949	Reorganisation plan for Head Offices.
A. D. Gorwala	1950-51	Examination of public administration for the implementation of development programmes.
A.D. Gorwala	1950-51	Review of administration of public undertakings.
Paul H. Appleby	1952	Survey of Indian Administration
Paul H. Appleby	1956	Review of functional autonomy and policy making in industrial and commercial undertakings.
J.B. Kriplani	1955-57	Review of corruption in Railways.
A. Rama Swamy Muddaliar	1956	Merit and recruitment of public services.
Morarjee Desai and K. Hanumantiah	1966-67 1967-70	Administrative Reforms Commission. It reported comprehensively on all aspects of Administration.
K. Santhanan	1964	Indian and State Public Services and problems of District Administration.
D.S. Kothari	1976	Method and procedure of recruitment with respect to higher civil services in India. This Commission recommended the Preliminary Exams in Civil Services.
Dharamvir	1979	National Police Commission.
Satish Chandra	1989	Review of examination pattern of Civil Services. Recommended Essay paper in the main examination and inclusion of some more subjects in the optional category.

N.N. Vohra	1997	Nexus between politicians and criminals.
P.C. Jain	1998	Review of administrative laws.
Y.K. Alagh	2000	Evaluation of Civil Services Exam. system and suggestions for reforms.
P. C. Hota	2002-04	For improvement in Civil Services
Veerappa Moilly	2005-09	Second Administrative Reforms Commission.

Second Administrative Reform Commission

The Second Administrative Reform Commission was constituted by the Government of India in 2003 under the Chairmanship of Veerappa Moily. The Commission submitted its report on May 31, 2009. The main recommendations made by it are related to :

1. Right to Information — Master key to Government; 2. Unlocking human capital, entitlements and governance; a case study; 3. Crisis management, from despair to hope; 4. Ethics in governance; 5. Public order, justice for all; 6. Local governance; 7. Capacity building for conflict resolution; 8. Combating Terrorism; 9. Social Capital — A shared destiny; 10. Refurbishing of Personnel Administration scaling new heights; 11. Promoting e-governance — the smart way forward; 12. Citizen Centric administration-The heart of governance; 13. Organisational structure of Government of India; 14 Strengthening Financial Management Systems; 15. State and District Administration.

3. The Governor cannot remove the members of the State Public Service Commission. He can suspend them, while inquiry is pending for their removal.

If a member of a Commission becomes concerned or interested in any contract or agreement made by or on behalf of the Government of India or the Government of a State or takes profit there from otherwise than as a common member of an incorporated company, such member shall be deemed to be guilty of misbehaviour.

The Measures to Maintain the Autonomy of the Public Service Commission :

1. The service conditions of the members and the Chairman of a Commission cannot be altered to their disadvantage after their appointment.
2. Expenditure incurred on the functioning of the Union Public Service Commision shall be charged upon the Consolidated Fund of India and that of the State Public Service Commission is charged upon the Consolidated Fund of the State. This means Voting shall not take place in Parliament with respect to such expenditure.

3. The Chairman of the Union Public Service Commission after his retirement, is not eligible for further appointment to any office under the Government of the Union or the State.
4. The Chairman of a State Public Service Commission, after his retirement, is not eligible for further appointment under the government except as a member or Chairman of the Union Public Service Commission and the Chairman of other State Public Service Commission.
5. A member of the Union Public Service Commission, after retirement, is not eligible for any further appointment under the government except as the Chairman of the Union Public Service Commission or of a State Public Service Commission.
6. A member of the State Public Service Commission, after retirement, is not eligible for any further appointment to a post under the government except as the Chairman of the State Public Service Commission or the Chairman or the member of the Union Public Service Commission.

Functions of the Public Service Commission:
The Public Service Commission is an advisory body. It performs the given functions:

1. To conduct the examinations to test the merit of the candidates for making selection to various posts and to recommend the names of the selected candidates for appointment to various posts.
2. The Commission shall be consulted by the government on the following matters:
    (i) On all matters relating to methods of recruitment to civil services,
    (ii) On the principles to be followed in making appointment, promotions and transfer of civil servants,
    (iii) On all disciplinary matters affecting a person serving under the government in a civil capacity,
    (iv) On any claim by a civil servant of the cost incurred by him on legal proceedings in the course of his duties,
    (v) On any claim for the award of the pension in respect of the injuries suffered by a civil servant during the course of his duties.

It is also mentioned in the Constitution that the commission shall not be consulted on the matters related to the reservation of the SC/ST or backward classes in public services.

Also, the Commission performs such other functions which are assigned to it from time to time by the President or the Governor, as the case may be.

Is the Government bound to Accept the Recommendations of the Commission:
The Public Service Commission is an Advisory body and therefore the government is not bound to accept the recommendations of the commission. It is prescribed in the Constitution that the Annual Report of the Commission

is to be presented before the Parliament or the State Legislature as the case may be. If the Government has not accepted the recommendations of the Commission on some specific cases it has to explain in writing the reasons therefore. But, in practice, leaving aside few rare exceptions the report of the Commission is generally accepted by the Government.

Validity of the functions of the Commission:
The functioning of the commission, with respect to the method of recruitment and selection, has been questioned from time to time. Some critics hold the view that the Commission makes the selection only on the basis of theoretical knowledge of the candidates and fails to take into account the practical knowledge required in various job situations. Therefore, the bulk of the recruitment and selection should be made in the departments itself.

The impartiality of the Commission, particularly at the state level, in making selection has also come under the cloud of suspicion. Many cases have been reported from various States that the Commission has buckled down under the pressure of influential politicians. Few years back, it was reported that the question papers of the Union Public Service Commission were leaked before the examination. These incidents mar the validity of the functioning of the Commission.

In spite of the above criticism, the Commission continues to be a very important institution. It has succeeded, to a considerable extent, to check the practices of corruption, nepotism, favouritism, casteism etc. in the selection and recruitment of the civil servants. The departmental appointments are still afflicted by these evils. However, the functioning of the Commission requires further improvement to make it yet more effective.

Fundamental Rights of Public Servants :
In terms of Article 33 of the Constitution, Parliament has the power to restrict the operation of Fundamental Rights with respect to the persons employed in the Armed and Police forces and in the Intelligence or counter Intelligence services. There is no such provision with respect to other public servants who enjoy all Fundamental Rights like any other citizen of India.

Functions of Civil Servants :
The main function of the civil servants is to implement the law of the nation and manage the administrative affairs in relation to such implementation. Their functions include:

1. At higher level, civil servants advise and assist the political executive in policy-making.
2. To advise the political executive (Ministers) on the technical aspect of the departmental administration.
3. To assist the political executive in preparing proposals of law and other such matters because they have specialised knowledge of these matters.
4. To implement the policies and programmes of the government.

5. To act as a link between the people and political leadership because civil servants remain in constant touch with the people in the field. The success or failure of the government depends upon the performance of the civil servants. Infact, the administrative affairs of the government are managed and directed by the civil servants. They impart a sense of continuity and stability in the public administration.

Bureaucracy

The term "Bureaucracy' is used in many senses. First, it means a body of civil servants engaged in the implementation of policies and programmes of the government. Second, it refers to a specific organisational structure of administration based on the principles of hierarchy, anonymity, division of work etc. Third, in popular sense it has some negative connotation as opposed to democracy. Finer terms bureaucracy as 'desk government'. In fact, bureaucracy refers to a type of organisation based on the principle of hierarchy and unity of direction and which is manned by skilled, trained and paid personnels. Max Weber, terms it as the most rational and efficient form of organisation in modern times. According to him, the bureaucracy is based on the rational legal authority.

The bureaucracy has the following characteristics:

1. Permanence
2. Political Neutrality
3. **Hierarchy:** Control of the higher officers on the lower officials.
4. **Unity of Direction:** An employee gets directions and orders from one higher authority.

In the present context, the following are the main behavioural attributes of bureaucracy in India.

1. Red Tapism: The public servants follow all the rules and regulations meticulously while discharging their official responsibilities. This delays the process of decision making. The British scholar, Parkinson remarked that civil servants create work for each other. This is known as Parkinson's Law. The bureaucrats become so much engrossed in procedural details and formalities that they become insensitive to the basic objectives of the administration. Even urgent problems of the people are not taken care of. Red tapism has delayed the implementation of many programmes and policies of the government so much so that their basic purpose has been defeated.

2. Elitist Attitude: The Bureaucracy is self-centred and egoist by nature and develops an elitist and aristrocratic outlook. Administrative officers are selected through a long procedure and well defined methods. They consider themselves superior in the society and try to keep away from the common man. Though, they are called civil servants, yet, infact, they become the effective rulers in a democracy. This tendency is dangerous to a healthy democracy.

3. **Lack of Responsibility:** In fact, the bureaucracy in India was evolved during British period and it was not accountable to people for its activities. The rules and procedures were designed in such a way that they ensured its strong control over the affairs of the government without being accountable to the citizens. This tendency of the bureaucracy continued even after independence. It has defeated the very purpose of democracy. The bureaucracy, instead of being a servant of the people and thus responsible to them, has become the master of law and lord of the people. It is alleged that the Indian democracy is for the bureaucracy, of the bureaucracy and controlled by the bureaucracy. In other words, the nature and structure of Indian democracy is decided by the bureaucracy and its future depends on the civil servants.

4. **Dominance of Generalist and Neglect of Specialists:** The bureaucracy in India is dominated by the Generalist civil servants — those officials who have a general knowledge and training of administrative affairs. It has been realised now that many of the specialized activities of the administration like, medical, education, agriculture etc., if managed by the specialists of these fields, may produce better results. But the higher positions with respect to specialised activities are still occupied and managed by the Generalist officials. This has become more apparent with respect to the development activities which have been organised by the Generalists. The activities related with development work are of specialised nature and hence may be managed better by the specialists. The growing number and the importance of the specialists in the administration, have given rise to the Generalist-Specialist controversy. At present, some space is being created for the specialists at the higher levels of administration.

5. **Dominance of Bureaucracy on the Political Executive:** In a democracy the highest leadership rests with the Political Executive (ministers) but, in Indian context, it has become a distant possibility. On the contrary, the members of bureaucracy have come to dominate the scene even at the higher level. The reasons for this change are not far to seek. The members of the Political Executive (ministers) are temporary and they often come and go, whereas the members of bureaucracy hold office on permanent basis for a long time. Again, the minister is not well versed in the affairs of the department in detail but the bureaucrats are experienced persons having deep knowledge of the administrative affairs. The minister, while deciding any matter with respect to his department depends on the information and advice given by the bureaucrats. The net result of these factors is that the civil servants have come in a position of dominance over the Political Executive.

6. **Political Commitment:** In an ideal situation, the members of bureaucracy are supposed to be politically neutral and indifferent, but it has been observed that the civil servants develop political loyalties and undermine their neutrality. The political leadership also develops close nexus with the civil servants. The transfer, posting, promotion etc. depend

upon the political loyalty of a civil servant. Of late, it has been noticed in some states that the members of the State bureaucracy are divided on caste lines as the political parties are also formed and operate on that pattern. This has undermined the independence, unity, morale and effectiveness of the bureaucracy in general.

7. Lack of Faith on the Subordinates: In the bureaucratic culture prevailing in India, the subordinate officials do not enjoy the confidence and faith of their superior officials. In fact, this tendency is the legacy of the British bureaucratic culture. During the colonial period, the higher officials were invariably British citizens and the lower positions in the administration were occupied by the Indian citizens. The factor led to the erosion of faith and confidence between the two. This results into two effects. First, the process of decision-making is delayed without the assistance of the subordinates and the second, the subordinates do not get the practical knowledge and experience required to manage higher responsibilities in future.

8. Class Consciousness: Like in other countries, the members of bureaucracy in India harbour an elitist attitude vis-a-vis people and function as a distinct class. This is due to the autonomy and powers, perks and facilities and distinct service conditions they enjoy in their career. The class consciousness leads to the negligence of peoples, demands and the increase in the gap between the people and the administration.

Emerging Tendencies of Indian Bureaucracy

In the last 50 years since independence, the bureaucracy in India has displayed two distinct tendencies:
1. Political commitment of bureaucracy, and
2. Bureaucracy as a powerful interest group.

1. Commitment of Bureaucracy: The commitment of bureaucracy is referred to in two contexts; first, the commitment towards the ideals and goals of the Constitution or the policies of the government; and the second, commitment to a political ideology or political party or political leadership.

The commitment to the goals and ideals of the Constitution or the policies of the government is a desirable and even necessary element which ensures the smooth functioning of the administration within the limits of the constitution. This also ensures a sense of purpose and high morals among the members of bureaucracy. The former Prime Minister of India, Mrs. Indira Gandhi believed that this kind of commitment in bureaucracy is essential for the rapid development of the country. But the other kind of commitment i.e., political commitment is dangerous to the Bureaucracy and the administration both. Unfortunately the members of Bureaucracy in India, in the recent period, have displayed the tendency of affiliating with either different political parties or individual political leaders. Political leaders or parties also need such committed civil servants as it serves their partisan interests. The promotion, transfer, posting etc. of civil servants is done on political lines in States. It has been reported that whenever there is a change of political leaders, mass transfers of civil servants are made in order to award the loyal civil servants. Thus, the bureaucracy should be politically neutral in its own long term interests.

2. **A Powerful Interest Group:** The members of every civil service have formed their own associations at various levels. These associations, in order to advance the interests of their members, indulge in manipulation and pressure tactics. Many times, the government comes under the pressure of these associations and concede to their not so justified demands. This kind of organised pressure becomes a hurdle in the process of administrative reforms.

Role of Bureaucracy in Development

The bureaucracy plays an important role in the development of a country, particularly in a country which has recently moved on the path of socio-economic development. Earlier, the development was defined in terms of increase in Gross Domestic product. But, of late it has been felt by economists, planners and social scientists alike that increase in the GDP may not necessarily result in reducing the misery of common man. In this context, the case of Phillippines, Indonesia, Brazil and Mexico can be cited, where, in spite of increase in Gross Domestic Product, the relatively poor section of the society remained unaffected. Therefore, as initiated in Japan, the development is being, now, measured in forms of Gross National Welfare in place of Gross Domestic Product. This new concept of development gives more emphasis to equal distribution specially with respect to the poor sections of society.

Immediately after independence, planning in India, aimed mainly at increasing the rate of the Gross Domestic Product. As long as our objective was to increase the size of GDP, the bureaucratic organisation was appropriate, but it proved inadequate in the changing context and composition of development. It was felt that the common man is left aside in the process of development. The need was, therefore, felt to give opportunity for the involvement and participation of people in the process of development. Consequently more emphasis was placed on the development of the scheduled castes/scheduled tribes and other backward sections. The bureaucratic organisation does not go well with these development programmes; because of its elitist background, authoritative and centralised structures, and lack of sensitivity to the needs of common man.

The bureaucracy is blamed for the poor implementation of development programmes. This allegation against bureaucracy has some amount of truth. It is a known fact that the meritorious and sincere civil servants were kept aside and the corrupt and inefficient ones were involved in the implementation of these development programmes. The corrupt and inefficient public servants forge similar nexus with political leaders and fulfil their own selfish interests at the cost of people's welfare. Its consequences for development are that the objectives of these programmes are not achieved within time and the cost of project keeps on increasing day by day.

Another factor associated with the poor implementation of these programmes is the very structures and procedures of bureaucracy itself. The Indian bureaucracy has not been able so far to shed its colonial attributes. The centralised structures, cumbersome rules and regulations, lack of spirit of initiative and tendency to shirk responsibility etc. are some of the elements, which are not conducive to effective, prompt and timely implementation of these programmes.

The cumulative effect of these factors has been that many of the attractive programmes have remained on paper. It results in the loss of national wealth and resources. Since corrupt and irresponsible civil servants get protection from their political bosses, no effective control can be ensured against erring officials. The usual remedy of the government is to indulge in transfers of officials. As long as this vicious circle is not broken, the stituation is not likely to improve.

It becomes incumbent on the government to fix responsibility for poor performance on those civil servants who are in charge of implementation of various programmes. However, it should be mentioned that the politicians are equally responsible for this sorry state of affairs. The political interference has increased at every level of programme implementation; which has brought down the morale of even sincere officers.

In the light of the above discussion, it appears desirable to develop a new culture of civil servants, which is conducive to the needs of development. More flexible and simplified structures and procedures of administration need to be evolved. In this context, reference to the concept of Development Administration is not out of place. The development administration refers to those new structures, processes and techniques which are designed to conceive and implement the programmes of socio-economic development. We cannot change the system overnight but the process of reform should start right now. There are certain new elements in this scenario. New Panchayati Raj System has been started throughout the country, which intends to galvanise the participation of people in rural areas in the process of development. Under the new arrangement, the Panchayati Raj institutions have been given more powers, functional autonomy, financial independence and durable tenure. This is likely to effect the structure of bureaucracy at lower levels and a new pattern of relationship between people and bureaucracy is likely to emerge. If the bureaucracy becomes more transparent and sensitive, the process of development will have the desired impact. However, the desired success of the Panchayati Raj Institutions needs to be watched in future.

Governance and Good Governance in India

The notions of Governance and good Governance have become the matters of global concern in the present context. The practices of good governances are presented as the prerequisites of democracy and development. International agencies have devised indicators to measure the levels of good governance in different countries. The countries are arranged on the basis of good governance Index. The international donor agencies and rich nations insist on following the practices of good governance while giving aids to developing countries.

What is Governance?

In the late eighties and early nineties, the concept of governance was popularised by multi-national and bilateral aid giving agencies; as a precondition for providing financial assistance to poor countries. The World Bank was the first to use the notion of governance in 1989. Later on other multilateral agencies like United Nations Development Programme (UNDP), Organisation of Economic Cooperation and Development (OECD) and UNESCO also used this concept with the same purpose.

The World Bank defines governance, "as the manner in which power is exercised in the management of country's economic resources by the government."

According to the OECD, "the term governance refers to the use of political authority and exercise of control in society in relation to the management of its resources for Social and economic development." The UNDP defines governance "as the exercise of economic, political and administrative authority to manage a nations affairs at all levels."

Thus, the Governance is what government does or it is the activity of governing. In this way it is distinct from the government as the government is the tool of governance. Alternatively, the governance is the result or impact of government.

The use of the term 'governance' in place of government has certain practical implications. It emphasises on the effectiveness of the government as how decisions are made and implemented. Thus governance focuses on the process of decision making and their implementation in the form of public policies at various levels. Since it is a process, its analysis involves both the formal structure (government) and influence of informal actors in the decision making. Thus, the government is just one actor in governance. It signified the behavioural aspects of government activity in its totality. Governance can be used in several contexts such as corporate governance, international governance, national governance and local governance.

Good Governance in India

While governance is a value neutral notion, the good governance is a special type of governance. The notion of good governance was also used for the first time in 1992 by the World Bank. The Bank has underlined the need of good governance which leads to economic, human and institutional development.

The World Bank has identified the following characteristics of the good governance. These are:

(1) Participation of People in the Process of Governance: The active participation of people is necessary for the practice of good governance. This requires freedom of expression and association and decentralization of government and its structures and processes. In India while people's participation is ensured through representative democracy and political power is decentralized through the local self government agencies, citizens active association at decision-making is not strong as civil society organisations are in nascent stage.

(2) Political Accountability: It means not only the government institutions and public officials but also the private sector and civil service organisation should be accountable to people for their activities. It has been observed that the lines of political and administrative accountability are weak in India.

(3) Legal Framework based on Rule of Law and Independence of Judiciary: While India has adopted both rule of law and independence of judiciary, in actual practice there is biased implementation of rules. Also, the judicial process is delayed and costly, which does not go well with the protection of human rights, social justice and guard against exploitation of marginalised sections of society.

(4) Transparency and Responsiveness in the Administration: India has inherited the British pattern of bureaucracy which was tuned to exclusiveness and secrecy. However, with changing requirement, the administration is gradually being made responsive to the needs and aspirations of people. Also, in order to bring transparency in the administration, the Right to Information Act was passed in 2005 in which, every public authority is obliged to provide public information to an applicant within a period of one month. The effective implementation of the provisions of this act is required to bring about desired level of transparency in the administration.

(5) Efficiency and Effectiveness of Administrative and Political System: It means that the government processes and institutions should produce results which meet the needs of society and citizens. This requires the effective management and use of various resources to achieve desired goals. On this count, India lacks far behind. The public policies are slow in implementation leading to overrun of costs and failure to achieve the desired objectives. The process of decision-making is also not efficient and rationalised with multiple of agencies and overlapping roles.

(6) Cooperation Between the Government and Civil Society Organisations: In India, the growth of civil society organisations is at nascent stage, leaving little scope for effective cooperation between the two. The culture of such cooperation is yet to evolve. However, the government has taken some steps to strengthen and involve civil society organisation in the process of governance. The success of Bhagidari movement in Delhi is a case in point.

(7) Equity and Inclusiveness: This means that the governance should aim at incorporating the weaker sections of society in the mainstream of the development process. The gap between the rich and the poor should be reduced to the minimum. Though the planned development strategy in India has always aimed at the goal of growth with equity', the gap between the rich and poor is still high and about one third of Indian people are still below the poverty line.

(8) Consensus Oriented: There are several actors and different viewpoints in the society. Good governance requires the mediation of different, sometimes conflicting interests to reach a broad consensus about the fundamental goals and methods of governance. In India, while we find a reasonable amount political consensus on external front, the internal policies and development strategy suffers from lack of political consensus. The lack of political consensus mars the effective implementation of the policies and programmes.

21. Executive of the States
The Governor

- The Governor of a state is appointed by the President and holds his office at the pleasure of the President.
- Qualifications for the post of Governor are :
  - Should be a citizen of India.
  - Should be over 35 years of age.
  - Must not hold other office of profit and should not be a Member of the Legislature of the Union or of any State {Ref. : Art. 158}.
- If a Member of a Legislature is appointed Governor, he ceases to be a Member immediately upon such appointment.
- The normal term of a Governor's office is five years, but it may be terminated earlier by :
  - Dismissal by the President {Ref. : Art. 156 (1)};
  - Resignation {Art. 156(2)}.
- There is no bar to a person being appointed Governor more than once.

An appointed Governor
- An appointed governor would save the country from the evil consequences of still another election, run on personal issues.
- If the Governor is elected by direct vote, then he might consider himself superior to the Chief Minister, leading to friction between the two.
- The expenses involved and the elaborate machinery of election would not match the powers of Governor.
- A second rate man of the party may get elected as Governor.
- Through an appointed Governor the Union Government can maintain its control over the states.
- The method of election may encourage separatist tendencies.

Powers of Governor
The Governor has no diplomatic or military powers like the President, but he has executive, legislative and judicial powers analogous to those of the President.

Executive
Governor has the power to appoint Council of Ministers, Advocate General and the members of the State Public Service Commission.
- The Ministers as well as Advocate General hold office during the pleasure of the Governor but the Members of the State Public Service Commission can be removed only by the President on the report of the Supreme Court and in some cases on the happening of certain disqualifications {Ref.: Art. 317}.
- The Governor has no power to appoint Judges of the State High Court but he is entitled to be consulted by the President in the matter {Ref.: Art. 217(1)).
- Like the President the Governor has the power to nominate members of the Anglo-Indian community to the Legislative Assembly of his State.
- To the Legislative Council, the Governor can nominate persons having special knowledge or practical experience of literature, science, art, cooperative movement and social service {Ref.: Art. 171(5)}.
- 'Co-operative movement' is not included in the corresponding list for Rajya Sabha.

Legislative
Governor is a part of the State Legislature and he has the right of addressing and sending messages, and of summoning, proroguing and dissolving the State Assembly.

Judicial
The Governor has the power to grant pardons, reprieves, respites, or remission etc. of punishments {Ref.: Art. 161}.

Emergency
The Governor has no emergency powers to counter external aggression or armed rebellion.
- He has the power to report to the President if Government of the State cannot be carried on in accordance with the Constitution {Ref.:Art. 356}.

Discretionary functions of the Governor
- The functions which are specially required by the Constitution to be exercised by the Governor in his discretion are :
    - The Governor of Assam can determine the amount payable by the State of Assam to the District Council, as royalty accruing from licences for minerals.
    - Where a Governor is appointed administrator of an adjoining Union Territory, he can function as such administrator independently of his Council of Ministers.

- The President may direct that the Governor of Maharashtra or Gujarat shall have a special responsibility for taking steps for the development of Vidarbha and Saurashtra.
- The Governor of Nagaland has similar special responsibility with respect to law and order in that State.
- Governor of Manipur has special responsibility to secure the proper functioning of the Committee of the Legislative Assembly consisting of the members elected from the Hill Areas of that State.
- Governor of Sikkim has special responsibility for peace and equitable arrangement for ensuring the social and economic advancement.
- The Governor has the power to dismiss an individual Minister at any time.
- Governor can dismiss a Council of Ministers or the Chief Minister, only when the Council of Ministers has lost confidence of the Legislative Assembly and the Governor does not think fit to dissolve the Assembly.

Chief Minister and The State Council of Ministers

- Chief Minister is the head of the State Council of Ministers.
- The Chief Minister is appointed by the Governor.
- The other Ministers are appointed by the Governor on the advice of Chief Minister.
- Any person may be appointed a minister but he must become member of the legislature within six months of such appointment.
- The Council of Ministers is collectively responsible to the Legislative Assembly of the state but individually responsible to the Governor.
- The relation between the Governor and his Ministers is similar to that between the President and his Ministers.

Governor's Power of Veto

- When a Bill is presented before the Governor after its approval by the Houses of the Legislature, the Governor can :
  - Declare his assent to the Bill, in that case it would become law at once.
  - Declare that he withholds his assent to the Bill, such a Bill fails to become a law.
  - Declare that he withholds his assent to the Bill (other than a Money Bill) and the Bill is returned with a message.
  - Reserve a Bill for the consideration of the President. Such reserving is compulsory where the law in question would derogate the powers of the High Court.

Power of Governor to Promulgate Ordinances

- The Governor can promulgate Ordinance only when the Legislature, or both Houses there of, are not in session.
- It must be exercised with the aid and advice of the Council of Ministers.
- The Ordinance must be laid before the State Legislature when it reassembles.

- An Ordinance ceases to have effect after 6 weeks from the date of reassembly, unless disapproved earlier by that Legislature.
- The Governor himself is competent to withdraw the Ordinance at any time.
- The scope of the Ordinance : promulgating power of the Governor is confined to the subjects in Lists II and III of the Seventh Schedule.
- Governor cannot promulgate Ordinances without instructions from the President if :
  - A Bill containing the same provisions would require previous sanction of the President.
  - Bill is required to be reserved for consideration of the President.

22. Inter-State Relations

- Art. 131 provides for the judicial determination of disputes between states by vesting the Supreme Court with exclusive jurisdiction in the matter, while Art. 262 provides for the adjudication of one class of such disputes by an extra judicial tribunal.
- Art. 263 provides for the prevention of inter State disputes by investigation and recommendation by an administrative body. Under Art. 262 Parliament has constituted the Inter-State Water Disputes Tribunal for adjudication of disputes between States for the waters of any inter-State river or river valley.
- Inter-State river water disputes are excluded from the jurisdiction of all Courts including the Supreme Court.
- An Inter-State Council has been constituted for co-ordinating in Inter-State disputes {Ref. : Art. 263 (a)}.
- Six Zonal Councils have been established to discuss and advise on matters of common interest. These are :
  - **The Central Zone :** Uttar Pradesh, Madhya Pradesh, Uttarakhand and Chhattisgarh.
  - **The Northern Zone :** Haryana, Himachal Pradesh, Punjab, Rajasthan, Jammu & Kashmir, and the Union Territories of Delhi & Chandigarh.
  - **The Western Zone :** Gujrat, Maharashtra, Goa and the Union Territories of Dadra & Nagar Haveli and Daman & Diu.
  - **The Southern Zone :** Andhra Pradesh, Karnataka, Tamil Nadu, Kerala, and the Union Territory of Puducherry.
  - **The Eastern Zone :** Bihar, Jharkhand, West Bengal and Odisha.
  - **The North-Eastern Council :** Arunachal Pradesh, Assam, Manipur, Mizoram, Tripura, Meghalaya, Nagaland and Sikkim.
- Each Zonal Council consists of the Chief Minister and two other Ministers of each of the States in the Zone and the Administrator in the case of a Union Territory.
- The Union Home Minister has been nominated to be the common chairman of all the Zonal Councils.

The Advocate General
- Each state has an Advocate-General, an official corresponding to the Attorney-General of India and having similar functions for the State.
- He is appointed by the Governor of the state and holds office during the pleasure of the Governor.
- Only a person who is qualified to be a judge of a High Court can be appointed Advocate-General. He receives such remuneration as the Governor may determine.
- He has the right to speak and to take part in the proceedings of, but no right to vote in, the Houses of the Legislature of the state {Ref. : Art. 177}.

The Strength of Legislative Councils	
State	Total seats
Andhra Pradesh	90
Bihar	75
Jammu & Kashmir	36
Karnataka	75
Maharashtra	78
Uttar Pradesh	99

The State Legislature
- Some states have bi-cameral Legislature (having two Houses). The Six States having two Houses are Andhra Pradesh, Bihar, Karnataka, Maharashtra, Uttar Pradesh and Jammu & Kashmir.
- In the remaining States, the Legislature is uni-cameral and has the Legislative Assembly only.
- For creation or abolition of Legislative Council, the Legislative Assembly of the State should pass a resolution by a special majority followed by an Act of Parliament {Ref. : Art. 169}.
- The size of the Legislative Council may vary, but its membership should not be more than 1/3 of the membership of the Legislative Assembly but not less than 40.
- Legislative Council is a partly nominated and partly elected body.
- Election to the Legislative Council is indirect and in accordance with proportional representation by single transferable vote.
- 5/6 of the total number of members of the Council is indirectly elected and 1/6 is nominated by the Governor.
- 1/3 of the total members of the Council is elected by local bodies such as municipalities, district boards.
- 1/12 is elected by graduates of three years' standing residing in the State.
- 1/12 is elected by teachers of secondary schools or higher educational institutions.
- 1/3 is elected by members of the Legislative Assembly from amongst persons who are not members of the Assembly.
- The remainder is nominated by the Governor from persons specialised in literature, science, art, co-operative movement and social service.

- The Court cannot question the *bona fides* or propriety of the Governor's nomination in any case.
- The Legislative Assembly of each State is directly elected on the basis of adult suffrage from territorial constituencies.
- The Number of members of the Assembly can not be more than 500 nor less than 60.
- The Assembly in Mizoram and Goa have only 40 members each. While the Assembly in Sikkim has only 32 members.
- Governor can nominate one member of the Anglo-Indian community in the Assembly {Ref.: Art. 333}.
- The duration of the Legislative Assembly is five years. It may be dissolved sooner than five years, by the Governor.
- The term of five years may be extended by the Parliament in case of a Proclamation of Emergency by the President for not more than one year at a time {Ref.: Art. 172(1).}
- Legislative Council (Vidhan Parishad) is a permanent body like the Council of State (Rajya Sabha).
- The Legislative Council is not dissolved. One-third of the members of Legislative Council retire on the expiry of every second year {Ref.: Art. 172(2)}.
- A Legislative Assembly has its Speaker and Deputy Speaker and a Legislative Council has its Chairman and Deputy Chairman, and the provisions relating to them are analogous to those relating to the corresponding officers of the Union Parliament.
- Qualifications for membership of State Legislature are :
  - Should be a citizen of India;
  - For Legislative Assembly, not less than twenty-five years of age and for Legislative Council not less than thirty years of age;
  - Should possess other qualifications prescribed in that behalf by or under any law made by Parliament {Ref.: Art. 173}.

The Strength of Legislative Assembly in States/U.Ts

State/U.T.	Strength	State/U.T.	Strength
Uttar Pradesh	403	Haryana	90
West Bengal	294	Jharkhand	81
Andhra Pradesh	294	Jammu-Kashmir	76
Maharashtra	288	Uttarakhand	70
Bihar	243	Delhi (NCT)	70
Tamil Nadu	234	Himachal Pradesh	68
Madhya Pradesh	230	Arunachal Pradesh	60
Karnataka	224	Manipur	60

Rajasthan	200	Meghalaya	60
Gujarat	182	Nagaland	60
Orissa	147	Tripura	60
Kerala	140	Goa	40
Assam	126	Mizoram	40
Punjab	117	Sikkim	32
Chhattisgarh	90	Puducherry	30

Comparison of Legislative Procedures between a Bi-cameral State Legislature and the Parliament

- For Money Bills, the position is the same.
- For other Bills the only power of the Council is to interpose a delay of 3 months. In case of disagreement, the Bill is second time referred to the Legislative Council and this time the Council has no power to withhold the Bill for more than a month {Ref.: Art. 197(2)(b)}.

Privileges of State Legislature

- Privileges of State Legislature are similar to those of Union Parliament.
- Each House of the State Legislature can punish for breach of its privileges or for contempt.
- Each House is the sole judge of the question whether any of its privileges has been infringed. Court has no jurisdiction to interfere with the decision of the House on this point.
- No House of the Legislature can create any new privilege for itself. Court can determine whether the House possesses a particular privilege.

23. Special Position of Jammu & Kashmir

- The jurisdiction of the Parliament in relation to Jammu & Kashmir is confined to the Union List, and the Concurrent List.
- Residuary power belongs to the Legislature of Jammu & Kashmir.
- Proclamation of Emergency under Art. 352 on the ground of internal disturbance has no effect in the State of Jammu & Kashmir, without the concurrence of the Government of the State.
- No decision affecting the disposition of the State can be made by the Government of India, without the consent of the Government of the State.
- The Union has no power to suspend the Constitution of the State on the ground of failure to comply with the directions given by the Union under Art. 365.
- Arts. 356-357 relating to suspension of constitutional machinery have been extended to Jammu & Kashmir by the Amendment Order of 1964. But "failure" would mean failure of the constitutional machinery of Jammu & Kashmir.
- The Union has no power to make a Proclamation of Financial Emergency with respect to the State of Jammu & Kashmir under Art. 360.

- Directive Principles of States Policy do not apply to the State of Jammu & Kashmir.
- Jammu & Kashmir has its own Constitution made by a separate Constituent Assembly and promulgated in 1957.
- The Constitution of Jammu & Kashmir (accepting the provisions relating to the relationship of the State with the Union of India), can be amended by an Act of the Legislative Assembly of the State, passed by not less than 2/3 majority.
- No alteration of the area or boundaries of Jammu & Kashmir can be made by Parliament without the consent of the Legislature of the State.
- The jurisdictions of the Comptroller and Auditor-General, the Election Commission, and the Special Leave jurisdiction of the Supreme Court have been extended to Jammu & Kashmir.

Temporary Provisions for Different State

1. The provisions of Art. 238 shall not apply to the State of Jammu and Kashmir.
2. The power of Parliament to make laws with respect to Jammu and Kashmir shall be limited to:
   (a) those matters in the Union List and the Concurrent List, which in consultation with the Government of the State, are declared by the President to correspond to matters specified in the Instruments of Accession governing accession of the State to the Dominion of India;
   (b) Such other matters in the said lists as, with the concurrence of the State Government, the President may by order specify.
3. The provisions of Article 1 and of this Article shall apply in relation to that State.
4. Such of the other provisions of this constitution shall apply to that State, which the President may by order specify, provided no such order shall be issued except in consultation with the Government of that State.
5. The Art. 370, making special provisions with respect to the State of Jammu and Kashmir became operative on Nov. 17, 1952 by an order of the President.
6. The President may by public notification declare that this Article shall cease to be operative from such date as specified by him, provided no such notification shall be issued by the President except on the recommendation of the Constituent Assembly of Jammu and Kashmir, which was constituted to frame the separate Constitution of that State. (Art. 370)

Special Provisions with Respect to the States of Maharashtra and Gujarat
The President may by order provide for special responsibility of the Governor for the establishment of separate Development Boards for Vidarbha (Maharashtra), Marathwada, Saurashtra and Kutch, the equitable distribution of funds for such boards and an equitable arrangement providing facilities for technical education, vocational training and adequate opportunities for employment in services of the State with respect to all the said areas. (Art. 371)

Special Provision with Respect to the State of Nagaland
No act of parliament shall apply to the State of Nagaland unless the Legislative Assembly so decides with respect to:
(a) religious or social practices of Nagaland;
(b) Naga customary law and procedure;
(c) administration of civil and criminal justice involving decisions according to Naga customary law;
(d) ownership and transfer of land and its resources. (Art. 371A)

Special Provisions with Respect to the State of Assam
The President may by order provide for the constitution and functions of a Committee of the Legislative Assembly of the State consisting of members of that Assembly elected from tribal areas of the State. (Art. 371B)

Special Provisions with Respect to the State of Manipur
1. The President may by order provide for the constitution and functions of a Committee of the Legislative Assembly of the State consisting of members of that Assembly elected from the Hill Areas of the State.
2. The Governor shall make an annual report to the President regarding administration of Hill Areas of Manipur and the executive power of the Union shall extend to the giving of directions to the State as to the administration of the said areas. (Art. 371C)

Special Provisions with Respect to the State of Andhra Pradesh
1. The President may by order provide, having regard to the requirements of the State as a whole, for equitable opportunities and facilities for the people belonging to different parts of the State in matters of public employment and education.
2. The President may, by order, provide for the constitution of an Administrative Tribunal for the State of Andhra Pradesh. (Art. 371D)
3. Parliament may by law provide for the establishment of a university in the State of Andhra Pradesh. (Art. 371E)

Special Provisions with Respect to the State of Sikkim
1. The Legislative Assembly of the State of Sikkim shall consist of not less than thirty members.
2. There shall be allotted to the State of Sikkim one seat in the House of the people.
3. There are other special provisions which relate to the property rights, High Court and administration of the State of Sikkim. (Art. 371F)

Special Provisions with Respect to the State of Mizoram
No Act of parliament in respect of:
(a) religious and social practices of Mizos;
(b) Mizo customary law and procedure;
(c) administration of civil and criminal justice involving decisions according to Mizo customary law;
(d) ownership and transfer of land, shall apply to the State of Mizoram unless the Legislative assembly of Mizoram so decides. (Art. 371G)

(e) The Legislative Assembly of the State of Mizoram shall consist of not less than forty members.

Special Provisions with Respect to the State of Arunachal Pradesh
1. The Governor of Arunachal Pradesh shall have special responsibility with respect to the law and order in the State. In this regard, he shall exercise his individual judgement after consulting the Council of Ministers.
2. The decision of the Governor shall be final as to what matters fall in the category of individual judgement. The validity of anything done by the Governor in the exercise of his individual judgement shall not be questioned in any Court.
3. The Legislative Assembly of the State of Arunachal Pradesh shall consist of not less than thirty members. (Art. 371H)

Special Provisions with Respect to the State of Goa
The Legislative Assembly of Goa shall consist of less than thirty members. (Art. 371-I)

24. Panchayats

- Part IX of the Constitution envisages a three tier system of Panchayats:
  - Panchayat at the village level;
  - The District Panchayat at the district level;
  - The Intermediate Panchayat in States where the population is above 20 lakhs.
- All the seats in a Panchayat are filled by direct election.
- The electorate is named 'Gram Sabha'.
- The Chairperson of each Panchayat is elected according to the law-passed by a State.
- Seats are reserved in Panchayat for Scheduled Castes, and Scheduled Tribes in proportion to their population [Art. 243D].
- Out of the reserved seats, 1/3 is reserved for women belonging to Scheduled Castes and Scheduled Tribes. 1/3 of the total seats to be filled by direct election in every Panchayat is reserved for women.
- A State can make similar reservation for Chairpersons in the Panchayats.
- Every Panchayat can continue for 5 years from the date of its first meeting. It can be dissolved earlier in accordance with State law.
- A Panchayat reconstituted after premature dissolution, continues only for the remainder of the period. But if the remainder of the period is less than 6 months it is not necessary to hold elections.
- All persons above 21 years of age and qualified to be a member of the State Legislature are qualified as a member of a Panchayat [Art. 243F].
- Panchayats can be entrusted to prepare and implement plans for economic development and social justice.
- A State can authorise a Panchayat to levy, collect and appropriate taxes, duties, tolls etc.
- After the 73rd amendment of the Constitution (25th April, 1993), every 5 years the States appoint a Finance Commission to review the financial position of the Panchayats and make recommendations.

- State Election Commission consisting of a State Election Commissioner is appointed by the Governor for superintendence, direction and control of elections to Panchayats [Art. 243K].
- The Community Development Programme was launched on Oct. 2, 1952.
- The Democratic Decentralisation was implemented for the first time in 1958 in some areas of Andhra Pradesh on experimental basis.
- The Panchayati Raj was introduced for the first time on Oct. 2, 1959 in Nagur District of Rajasthan by the Prime Minister Jawahar Lal Nehru.
- Rajasthan is the first state in India, where Panchayati Raj was implemented in the whole state.

25. Municipalities

- PART IXA gives a constitutional foundation to the local self government units in urban area.
- Most provisions for municipalities are similar to those contained in PART IX, e.g. Structure, Reservation of Seats, Functions, Sources of Income etc.
- *Nagar Panchayat* is for an area being transformed from a rural area to an urban area.
- *Municipal Council is* for a smaller urban area.
- *Municipal Corporation* is for a larger urban area. The municipal corporation is the topmost urban local government.
- The members of a municipality are generally elected by direct election.
- The Legislature of a State can provide for representation in municipalities of:
  - Persons having special knowledge or experience in municipal administration,
  - Members of Lok Sabha, State Assembly, Rajya Sabha and Legislative Council.
  - The Chairpersons of Ward Committees.

Note : *If the population is 3 lacs or more Ward Committees are constituted.*

- Two Committees constituted for preparing development plan are :
  - A District Planning Committee at the district level
  - A Metropolitan Planning Committee at the metropolis level

26. Union-State Relations

These relations are divided into three categories as per the Constitution.
- *Union List* (100 subjects)
- *State List* (66 subjects)
- *Concurrent List* (47 subjects)

Union List: The Parliament has exclusive authority over subjects mentioned in the Union List of the Constitution. The Union List contains subjects like defence, foreign affairs, currency, communication, citizenship, inter–state trade and commerce, banking, atomic energy, post and telegraph, etc.

State List: State governments have exclusive power over subjects mentioned in the State List. The State List contains subjects on which ordinarily the

States alone can make laws. It includes subjects such as public order, police, administration of justice, prisons, local government, agriculture, public health and sanitation, irrigation, etc. However, under certain conditions the Constitution authorises the Central Government to extend its jurisdiction over matters formally included in the State List. Also, on the proclamation of Emergency, the Parliament can legislate on matters enumerated in all the three lists.

Concurrent List: Both Parliament and state legislatures can legislate on subjects mentioned in the Concurrent List. Subjects enumerated in Concurrent List are - criminal and civil law, forest, education, marriage and divorce, drugs, trade unions, labour welfare, newspapers, books and printing press, population control and family planning, etc.

The federal structure in India is tilted in favour of the Centre as *Residual powers* (i.e., subjects not included in any of the lists) rests with the union government.

Article 200 of the Constitution authorises the Governor to reserve a Bill passed by the State Legislature for the consideration of the President, if the Governor is of the opinion that the Bill passed into law, would derogate the powers of the High Court.

27. The Supreme Court and the High Courts

The Supreme Court: The Supreme Court of India came into existence on January 26, 1950. On January 28, 1950, two days after India became a Sovereign Democratic Republic, the Supreme Court held its first sitting. The Supreme Court of India is the highest judicial forum standing at the top of the Indian judiciary. The Supreme Court also known as the apex court is the final court of appeal.

The Supreme Court consists of the Chief Justice of India and 25 other judges. The President of India appoints the Chief Justice of the Supreme Court. Other judges of Supreme Court are also appointed by the President in consultation with the Chief Justice.

To be appointed as the Judge of the Supreme Court, a person must be a citizen of India and must have been, for at least five years, a Judge of a High Court or an Advocate of a High Court for at least ten years, or the person must be, in the opinion of the President, as a distinguished jurist.

The Judges of the Supreme Court can hold office upto the age of 65. After retirement, a judge of the Supreme Court shall not plead or act before any authority in India.

The removal of the judge of the Supreme Court is a tough process. A judge of the Supreme Court can only be removed by an order of the President after an address by each House of the Parliament supported by a majority of a total membership of the House and not less than two-third members present and voting.

A judge of Supreme Court can be removed on the grounds of: (i) proven misbehaviour and (ii) incapacity to act as a judge.

The Supreme Court generally sits in Delhi. However, it can hold sittings anywhere in India. Decision to hold sittings outside Delhi are taken in consultation with President of India.

Functions of the Supreme Court: a) The Supreme Court decides cases of dispute between the Union government and the State governments. B) It hears appeals of civil and criminal cases from High Court. c) The President of India can refer any question of law of fact of sufficient importance to the Supreme Court for its opinion. D) The Supreme Court can issue directions or writs to enforce fundamental rights as enshrined in the Constitution of India.

The High Courts

India has a *unitary judicial system*, with the Supreme Court at the apex of this judicial court. In this judicial system, High Court is the highest judicial body in the state. Presently, there are *21 High Courts in India*, with each court having jurisdiction over a state and Union Territory or a group of states and Union territories. Below the High Court, there is a hierarchy of courts in a state, such as the district courts and the civil courts.

The High Court consists of the Chief Justice and other judges appointed by the President in consultation with the Chief Justice of India and the Governor of respective states.

To be appointed as a judge of the High Court, a person must have been an advocate in one or more high courts in succession for a minimum period of 10 years or he should have held a judicial office in India for minimum 10 years.

A High Court judge retires on at the age of 62. He can tender his resignation to President or can be removed by President on the grounds of proven misbehavior.

A judge of a High Court can be removed from office by an order after an impeachment process involving both the Houses of Parliament.

National Judicial Appointments Commission (NJAC)

The National Judicial Appointments Commission Act, 2014 and 99th Constitutional Amendment Act, 2014 provides for the setting up of the National Judicial Appointments Commission (NJAC), a six member panel headed by the Chief Justice of India, and includes two senior most Supreme Court Judges, the Union Minister of Law and Justice and two eminent persons nominated by a Committee Comprising the Prime Minister, the Chief Justice of India and the leader of the Opposition.

The appointments and Transfers of the judges in Supreme Court and High Courts, shall be on the recommendation of the National Judicial Appointments Commission.

National Judicial Appointments Commission* (NJAC)

Chairperson: The Chief Justice of India, *ex officio;*

Members: Two other senior Judges of the Supeme Court next to the Chief Justice of India, *ex officio;*

The Union Minister in charge of Law and Justice, *ex officio;*

Two eminent persons to be nominated by the committee consisting of the Prime Minister, the Chief Justice of India and the Leader of Opposition in the House of the People or where there is no such Leader of Opposition, then, the Leader of single largest Opposition Party in the House of the People-Members :

Provided that one of the eminent person shall be nominated from amongst the persons belonging to the Scheduled Castes, the Scheduled Tribes. Other Backward Classes, Minorities or Women :

Provided further that an eminent person shall be nominated for a period of three years and shall not be eligible for renomination.

* The Constitution Bench of the Supreme Court has rejected the NJAC Act as 'unconstitutional and void' on October 16, 2015 and the older collegium system will remain in practice.

28. The Political Processes in India

India has a constitutional democracy form of political system. It follows a parliamentary form of government and holds fairs and free elections to determine:

- composition of the government
- the membership of two Houses of Parliament
- the membership of State and Union Territory as well as the Legislative Assemblies
- membership and composition of local bodies at the district and the panchayat levels

The Indian political system follows a multi-party system, unlike a bi-party system in the United Kingdom and United States. In India, there are several parties that take part in electoral fray. Presently, there are six national parties and several regional parties that take part in elections at various levels.

General Elections in India

General elections or Lok Sabha elections are held once in five years if the Lok Sabha or Lower House of Parliament is not dissolved beforehand.

Elections in India are conducted by the Election Commission, which supervises the most complex of tasks in the world's largest democracy.

In India, the first general elections were conducted in 1951. The current Lok Sabha is 16th Lok Sabha for which elections were held in 2014.

The elections in India, which have become a model for many democracies in the world reveal much about the Indian society. Candidates from varied spectrum of backgrounds including former royalty, farmers, cinema personalities, former sportspersons take part in the elections.

Candidates in fray are allowed to campaign following a strict model code of conduct prescribed by the Election Commission to ensure free and fair elections.

29. Order of Precedence

The Order of Precedence in India is the protocol list or hierarchy of functionaries and officials listed according to their rank and office in the Government of India. In this Order of Precedence, the President is at the top, followed by the Vice-President, the Prime Minister and other functionaries as follows:

- The President of India
- The Vice-President of India
- The Prime Minister of India
- Governors of States (within their respective states)
- Former Presidents of India, Deputy Prime Minister of India
- Chief Justice of India, Speaker of the Lok sabha
- Former Prime Ministers of India, Cabinet Ministers of the Union, Leader of the Opposition in the Rajya Sabha and Lok Sabha, Deputy Chairman of the Planning Commission of India, Chief Ministers of States (within their respective states)
- Ambassadors, Extraordinary and Plenipotentiary, and the High Commissioners of the Commonwealth of Nations accredited to India, Governors of States (outside their respective states), Chief Ministers (outside their respective states)
- Judges of the Supreme Court of India, Comptroller and Auditor General of India, Chief Election Commissioners of India
- Deputy Chairman of the Rajya Sabha, Deputy Speaker of the Lok Sabha, Members of the Planning
- Commission, Deputy Chief Ministers of States, Ministers of State of the Union Government
- Attorney General of India, Cabinet Secretary, Lieutenant Governors within their respective territories
- Chiefs of staff holding the rank of full Governor or equivalent rank
- Envoys : Extraordinary and Ministers Plenipotentiary accredited to India
- Chairman and Speakers of State Legislatures within their respective states and the Chief Justices of High Courts within their respective jurisdictions
- Cabinet Ministers in States within their respective states, Chief Ministers of Union Territories and Chief Executive Councillors of Delhi, within their respective Union Territories, Deputy Ministers of the Union
- Officiating Chiefs of staff holding the rank of Lieutenant General or equivalent rank
- Chairman of the Administrative Tribunal, Chairman of the Minorities Commission, Chairman of the Scheduled Castes and Scheduled Tribes Commission, Chairman of the Union Public Service Commission, Chief Justice of High Courts outside respective jurisdiction
- Cabinet Ministers of States outside their respective states, Chairman and Speaker of the State Legislatures outside their respective states, Deputy Chairman and the Deputy Speaker of State Legislatures within their respective states.

- Minister of State Governments within their respective states, Minister of Union Territories within their respective Union territories.
- Chief Commissioners of Union Territories not having Council of Ministers within their respective Union Territories
- Deputy Chairman and Deputy Speakers of State legislatures outside their respective states, Ministers of State in states outside their respective states, Judges of High Court outside their respective states
- Members of Parliament
- Army Commanders/Vice Chief of Army Staff or equivalent in other services, Chief Secretaries to State governments within their respective states.

30. Offices under the Government of India

Following are the major departments or offices under the Government of India:
- Agriculture Department
- Central Government
- Controller and Auditor General of India
- Indian Passport
- Meteorological Department
- National Commission on Population
- Planning Commission
- Telecom Regulatory Authority of India
- Visa
- CBI
- Central Vigilance Commission
- Election Commission of India
- Indian Railways
- National Commission for Women
- National Human Rights Commission
- State Governments
- Union Public Service Commission

31. Inter-State Council

- Inter-State Council was constituted in April, 1990 under Art. 263.
- Inter-State Council consists of Prime Minister, 6 Union Cabinet Ministers, the Chief Ministers of all the States and administrators of all UTs.
- The Sarkaria Commission recommended the constitution of a permanent Inter-State Council for co-ordination among States and with the Union. (Justice R.S. Sarkaria died in 2007)
- Inter-State Council is chaired by the Prime Minister and it meets thrice a year.

32. Finance Commission

- The Constitution provides for the establishment of a Finance Commission (Art. 270, 273, 275 and 280) by the President. The first Finance Commission was constituted in 1951.

Finance Commissioners of India

Sl.	Year of Constitution	Chairman	Report Implementation Year
1.	1951	K. C. Niyogi	1952-1957
2.	1956	K. Santhanam	1957-1962
3.	1960	A. K. Chanda	1962-1966
4.	1964	Dr. P. V. Rajamannar	1966-1969
5.	1968	Mahavir Tyagi	1969-1974
6.	1972	Brahmanand Reddy	1974-1979
7.	1977	J. M. Schelet	1979-1984
8.	1983	Y. B. Chavan	1984-1989
9.	1987	N. K. P. Salve	1989-1995
10.	1992	K. C. Pant	1995-2000
11.	1998	A. M. Khusro	2000-2005
12.	1st Nov., 2002	C. Rangarajan	2005-2010
13.	Nov., 2007	Dr. Vijay L. Kelkar	2010-2015
14.	2nd Jan. 2013	Y. V. Reddy	2015-2020

➪ The Finance Commission consists of a Chairman and four other members.
➪ According to the qualifications prescribed by the Parliament, the chairman is selected among persons who have had experience in public affairs, while the members are selected among persons who :
- are or have been or are qualified to be appointed judges of the High Court; or
- have special knowledge of the finance and accounts of government; or
- have had wide experience in financial matters and in administration; or
- have special knowledge of economics.

➪ The members of the commission hold office for such period as may be specified by the President in his orders and are eligible for reappointment.
➪ The main functions or *duties* of the Finance Commission are :
- To recommend to the President the basis for distribution of the net proceeds of taxes between the centre and states.
- To recommend the principles which should govern the grants in-aid to be given to states out of the consolidated Fund of India.
- To tender advice to the President on any other matter referred to the Commission in the interest of sound finance.
- To suggest amounts to be paid to the states of Assam, Bihar, Odisha and West Bengal in lieu of the assignment of system of export duty on Jute products.

- The commission submits its recommendations to the President which are generally accepted by the Central Government. The recommendations of the Commission are applicable for a period of five years.

33. NITI Aayog

- NITI Aayog (National Institution for Transforming India) has been established by the Narendra Modi government in place of the Planning Commission.
- NITI Aayog is an economic advisory body set up by a resolution of the Union Cabinet in 1950.
- At present, the NITI Aayog consists of the Chairman, four Ministers as part time members and seven full-time members.
- Prime Minister is the Chairman of Planning Commission.
- *Main functions* of the NITI Aayog are :
  - To prepare an integrated Five Year Plan for the most effective and balanced utilisation of the country's resources for economic and social development.
  - To act as an advisory body to the Union Government and State Governments.

34. National Development Council (NDC)

- The National Development Council was formed in 1952, to associate the States in the formulation of the Plans.
- All members of the Union Cabinet, Chief Ministers of States, the Administrators of the Union Territories and member of the Planning Commission are members of the NDC.
- Functions of the NDC are :
  - Review working of national plan.
  - Recommend measures to meet targets of national plan.
- It is an extra constitutional and extra legal body.

35. National Integration Council

- National Integration Council was set-up in 1986, to deal with welfare measures for the minorities on an All-India basis.
- It includes Union Ministers, Chief Ministers of State, representatives of National and Regional political parties, labour, women, public figures and media representatives. NDC is a non-constitutional body.

36. Public Service Commissions

- Constitution provides a Public Service Commission for the Union, a Public Service Commission for each State or a Joint Public Service Commission for a group of States.
- A Joint Public Service Commission can be created by Parliament in pursuance of a resolution passed by the State Legislatures concerned.
- The Union Public Service Commission can serve the needs of a State, if so requested by the Governor of that State and approved by the President {Ref.: Art. 315}.

- The appointment, determination of number of members of the Commission and their conditions of service is done by :
  - The President in the case of the Union or a Joint Commission, and
  - The Governor of the State in the case of a State Commission.
- Conditions of service of a member of the Public Service Commission can not be varied to his disadvantage after his appointment [Art. 318].
- Half of the members of a Commission should be persons who have held office under the Government of India or of a State for at least 10 years {Art. 316}.
- The term of service of a member of a Commission is 6 years from the date of his entering upon office, or until the age of retirement, which ever is earlier.
- Age of retirement for a member of UPSC is 65 years.
- Age of retirement for a member of PSC of a State or a Joint Commission is 62 years.
- Services of a member of a Public Service Commission can be terminated by:
  - Resignation in writing addressed to the President (to the Governor in the case of a State Commission).
  - Removal by the President.
- President can remove a member if he :
  - is adjudged insolvent; or
  - engages himself in paid employment outside the duties of his office; or
  - is infirm in mind or body; or
  - found guilty of misbehaviour by the Supreme Court.
- Even in the case of a State Commission, only the President can remove a member, while Governor has only the power to pass an interim order of suspension.
- The expenses of the Commission are charged on the Consolidated Fund of India or of the State (as the case may be) {Ref.: Art. 322}.
- Disabilities imposed upon the Chairman and members of the Commission for future employment under the Government are :
  - The Chairman of the UPSC is ineligible for further employment either under the Government of India or under the Government of a State.
  - The Chairman of a State Public Service Commission is eligible for appointment as the Chairman or member of the Union Public Service Commission or as the Chairman of any other State Public Service Commission, but not for any other employment either under the Government of India or under the Government of a State.
- A member of a State Public Service Commission is eligible for appointment as the Chairman of a State Public Service Commission and Chairman or member of UPSC, but not for any other employment either under the Government of India or under the Government of a State.

- The Public Service Commissions are advisory bodies. Government can accept its recommendation or depart from it.
- **Functions of Public Service Commission :**
  - To conduct examination for appointments to the services of the Union and States.
  - To advise on any matter so referred to them and on any other matter which the President or the Governor of a state may refer to the appropriate Commission [Art. 320].
  - To exercise such additional functions as may be provided for by an act of Parliament or of the Legislature of a State.

37. Election Commission

- The general election is held on the basis of adult suffrage.
- Every person who is a citizen of India and is not less than 18 years of age is entitled to vote at the election, provided he is not disqualified by law.
- Election to Parliament or the Legislature of a State can be called in question only by an election petition in the High Court, with appeal to the Supreme Court [Art. 329].
- The exclusive forum for adjudicating disputes relating to the election of the President and Vice-president is the Supreme Court [Art. 71].

Election Commission
- In order to supervise the entire procedure and machinery for election and for some other ancillary matters, the Constitution provides for this independent body [Art. 324].
- The Election Commission is independent of executive control to ensure a fair election.
- The Election Commission consists of a Chief Election Commissioner and two other Election Commissioners.
- President can determine the number of Election Commissioners [Art. 324(2)].

Chief Election Commissioner (CEC)
- The President appoints the Chief Election Commissioner who has a tenure of 6 years, or up to the age of 65 years, whichever is earlier.
- The CEC enjoys the same status and receives the same salary and perks as available to judges of the Supreme Court.
- The Chief Election Commissioner can be removed from his office only in a manner and on the grounds prescribed for removal of judge of the Supreme Court.
- Other Election Commissioners can be removed by the President on the recommendation of the Chief Election Commissioner.
- The Election Commission has the power of superintendence, direction and conduct of all elections to Parliament and the State Legislatures and of elections to the offices of the President and Vice-President {Ref.: Art. 324(1)}.
- Regional Commissioners can be appointed by the President in consultation with the Election Commission for assisting the Election Commission {Ref.: Art. 324(4).

Chief Election Commissioner of India

SN.	Name	Tenure
1.	Sukumar Sen	21st March, 1950–19th Dec, 1958
2.	K. V. K. Sundaram	20th Dec, 1958–30th Sept., 1967
3.	S. P. Sen Verma	01st Oct., 1967–30th Sept., 1972
4.	Dr. Nagendra Singh	01st Oct., 1972–06th Feb., 1973
5.	T. Swaminathan	7th Feb., 1973–17th June, 1977
6.	S. L. Shakdhar	18th June, 1977–17th June, 1982
7.	R. K. Trivedi	18th June, 1982–31st Dec, 1985
8.	R. V. S. Peri Shastri	01st Jan., 1986–25th Nov., 1990
9.	Smt. V. S. Rama Davi	26th Nov., 1990–11th Dec, 1990
10.	T. N. Seshan	12th Dec, 1990–11th Dec, 1996
11.	M. S. Gill	12th Dec, 1996–13th June, 2001
12.	J. M. Lyngdoh	14th June, 2001–07th Feb., 2004
13.	T. S. Krishna Murthy	8th Feb., 2004–15th May, 2005
14.	B. B. Tandon	16th May, 2005–07th Feb., 2006
15.	N. Gopalaswami	08th Feb., 2006–19th April, 2009
16.	Naveen Chawla	20th April, 2009–29th July, 2010
17.	S. Y. Quraishi	30th July, 2010–10th June, 2012
18.	V. S. Sampath	11th June, 2012–15th Jan., 2015
19.	H.S. Brahma	16th Jan., 2015–18th April 2015
20.	Nasim Zaidi	19th April 2015–till present

⇨ The main functions of the Election Commission are :
  (i) The preparation of electoral rolls before each general election and registration of all eligible voters.
  (ii) The delimitation of constituencies.
  (iii) The recognition of various political parties and allotment of election symbol to these parties.
  (iv) The preparation of a code of conduct for the political parties.
  (v) The tendering of advice to the President regarding disqualification of the members of the parliaments etc.
  (vi) The appointment of election officers to look into disputes concerning election arrangements.
  (vii) The preparation of roster for central broadcasts and telecasts by various political parties.
  (viii) Keep voters lists up-to-date at all times.
  (ix) To issue identity cards to the voters.

38. Delimitation Commission of India

- Delimitation Commission or Boundary Commission of India is a Commission established by Government of India under the provisions of the Delimitation Commission Act.
- The main task of the Commission is to redraw the boundaries of various assembly and Lok Sabha Constituencies based on a recent census (Art. 82).
- The representation from each state is not changed during this exercise. However, the number of SC and ST seats in a state are changed in accordance with the census.
- The Commission in India is a high power body whose order have the force of law and cannot be called in question before any court.
- These orders come into force on a date to be specified by the President of India in this behalf. The copies of its orders are laid before the House of the People and the state Legislative Assembly concerned, but no modifications are permissible there in by them.
- In India, such Delimitation Commissions have been constituted 4 times- in 1952, 1963, 1973 and in 2002.
- The recent Delimitation Commission was set up on 12th July 2002 (after 2001 census) with Justice Kuldip Singh (retd. Judge of Supreme Court of India) as its Chairperson.
- The recommendation of this commission was approved by the then President Pratibha Patil on 19th February 2008.
- The Constitution of India was specifically amended in 2002 (84th Amendment Act, 2001, which amended the provisions 170 (3) of Art. 82) not to have delimitation of constituencies till the first census after 2026.
- The recent delimitation has been done on the basis of census 2001.
- Election Commissioners of all the States and Union Territories, along- with the Chief Election Commissioner (CEC) of India are the members of the Delimitation Commission.

No. of Reserved Seats after Delimitation

Category	Present seats	Seats after new delimitation
SC	79	85
ST	41	48
Unreserved	423	410
Total Seats in Lok Sabha	**543**	**543**

N.B. : Assam, Manipur, Arunachal Pradesth, Nagaland and Jharkhand are such states which could not be covered by the Delimitation Commission 2002.

39. The Official Languages

- The Official language of the Union is Hindi in Devanagri script [Art. 343]. English was to continue to be used as principal official language of the Union and Hindi till 1965 as well.

- The first Official Language Commission was appointed in 1955 under Shri B.G. Kher as Chairman and it recommended that a rigid date line for change over of language should not be prescribed. This recommendation was accepted.

Language of the State/Link Language :
- Article 345 seeks to tackle the issue of the official language for each state and the language for intra-State official transactions.
- The Legislature of a State can adopt any one or more languages used in the State or Hindi for the official purposes of that State. There is also a provision for the recognition of any other language for the official purpose of a State or any part thereof, upon a substantial popular demand for it being made to the President {Ref. : Art. 347}.

Language of the SC and HCs and authoritative text of laws :
- Until Parliament by law provides otherwise, English is the language of authoritative text of:
  - All proceedings in the Supreme Court and in every High Court.
  - All Bills or amendments thereto moved in either House of Parliament or the State Legislature.
  - All acts passed by Parliament or the Legislature of a State.
  - All Ordinances promulgated by the President or the Governor of a State.
  - All orders, rules, regulations and by-laws issued under Constitution or under any law made by Parliament or the legislature of a State.
- A State Legislature can prescribe the use of any language other than English for Bills and Acts passed by itself or Subordinate Legislation made thereunder.
- The languages included in the 8th Schedule of the Constitution are: Assamese, Bengali, Gujrati, Hindi, Kannada, Kashmiri, Konkani, Malyalam, Manipuri, Marathi, Nepalese, Oriya, Punjabi, Sanskrit, Sindhi, Tamil, Telugu, Urdu, Maithili, Santhali, Dogri and Bodo.
- Sindhi was inserted by the Constitution (21st Amendment) Act, 1967.
- Konkani, Manipuri and Nepali were inserted by the Constitution (71st Amendment) Act, 1992.
- Maithili, Dogri, Bodo and Santhali were inserted by the Constitution (92nd Amendment) Act, 2003.
- The only privileges gained by the languages included in the 8th Schedule are:
  - To have a member in the Official Language Commission.
  - To be considered for contribution towards the development of Hindi language.

40. National Symbols

National Flag
- The National flag is a horizontal tricolour of deep saffron *(Kesaria)* at the top, white in the middle and dark green at the bottom in equal proportion. The ratio of width of the flag to its length is two to three. In

the centre of the white band is a navy-blue wheel which represents the *chakra*. Its design is that of the wheel which appears on the abacus of the Sarnath Lion Capital of Ashoka. Its diameter approximates to the width of the white band and it has 24 spokes. The design of the National Flag was adopted by the Constituent Assembly of India on 22nd July 1947.

- Apart from non-statutory instructions issued by the Government from time to time, display of the National Flag is governed by the provisions of the Emblems and names (Prevention of Improper Use) Act, 1950 (No.12 of 1950) and the Prevention of Insults to National Honour Act, 1971 (No. 69 of 1971).
- The Flag Code of India, 2002, took effect from 26th January 2002 which brings together all such laws, conventions, practices and instructions for the guidance and benefit of all concerned.
- In an important judgement in January, 2004 the Supreme Court (under the chairmanship of the Chief Justice B. N. Khare) pronounced that unfurling (hoisting) of National Flag is a fundamental right under Article 19 (1) (A).

Note: For the first time the National Flag of India was hoisted in the midnight of 14th August, 1947.

State Emblem

- The state emblem is an adaptation from the Sarnath Lion Capital of Ashoka. In the original, there are four lions, standing back to back, mounted on an abacus with a frieze carrying sculptures in high relief of an elephant, a galloping horse, a bull and a lion separated by intervening wheels over a bell-shaped lotus. Carved out of a single block of polished sandstone, the Capital is crowned by the Wheel of the Law (Dharma Chakra).
- In the state emblem, adopted by the Government of India on 26th January 1950 only three lions are visible, the fourth being hidden from view. The wheel appears in relief in the centre of the abacus with a bull on right and a horse on left and the outlines of other wheels on extreme right and left. The bell-shaped lotus has been omitted. The words *Satyameva Jayate* from Mundaka Upanishad, meaning 'Turth Alone' Triumphs, are inscribed below the abacus in Devanagari script.
- The use of the state emblem of India, as the official seal of the Government of India, is regulated by the State of India (Prohibition of Improper Use) Act, 2005.

National Anthem

- The song *Jana-gana-mana*, composed originally in Bengali by Rabindranath Tagore, was adopted in its Hindi version by the Constituent Assembly as the National Anthem of India on 24th January 1950. It was first sung on 27th December, 1911 at the Kolkata Session (Chairman– Pt.Vishan Narayan Dutt) of the Indian National Congress. The complete song consists of five stanzas.
- Rabindranath Tagore had published it in *'Tatvabodhini'* in 1912 with the title *'Bharat Bhagya Vidhata'* and translated it into English in 1919 with

the title 'Morning song of India'. The credit of composing the present tune (Music) of our national anthem goes to Captain Ram Singh Thakur (an INA sepoy)
- Playing time of the full version of the national anthem is approximately 52 seconds. A short version of the first and last lines of the stanza (Playing time approximately 20 seconds) is also played on certain occasions.

National Song
- The song *'Vande Mataram'*, composed in Sanskrit by Bankimchandra Chatterji, was a source of inspiration to the people in their struggle for freedom. It has an equal status with *Jana-gana-mana*. The first political occasion when it was sung at the 1896 session (Chairman-Rahimtulla Sayani) of Indian National Congress.
- The song was published in the novel *'Anandmath'*, authored by Bankimchandra Chatterji and was adopted as the National Song on 26th January, 1950.
- Playing time of this song is one minute and five i.e. seconds (65 seconds). No body can be forced to sing the National Song.

Note : Session of Parliament begins with *'Jana-gana-mana'* and concludes with *'Vande Mataram.'*

National Calendar
- The National Calendar based on the Saka Era, Chaitra as its first month and a normal year of 365 days was adopted from 22nd March 1957 along with the Gregorian calendar for the following official purposes: (i) Gazette of India, (ii) news broadcast by All India Radio, (iii) calendars issued by the Government of India and (iv) Government communications addressed to the members of the public.
- Dates of the National Calendar have a permanent correspondence with dates of the Gregorian calendar, 1 *Chaitra* falling on 22nd March normally and on 21st March in leap year.

  National Animal: The magnificent tiger, *Panthera tigris*.
  National Bird : The Indian peacock, *Pavo cristatus*.
  National Flower : Lotus *(Nelumbo Nucipera Gaertn)*.
  National Tree : The Banyan Tree *(Ficus benghalensis)*.
  National Fruit: Mango *(Manigifera indica)*.
  National Aquatic Animal: The mammal Ganges River Dolphin (Platanista gangetica).

41. Glossary of Constitutional Terms
- *Act of God* is a direct, violent, sudden and irresistible act of nature, which could not be by any reasonable care have been foreseen or resisted.
- *Act of Parliament* means a bill passed by the two Houses of Parliament and assented to by President and in the absence of an express provision to the contrary, operative from the date of notification in the Gazette.
- *Act of State* means the act of sovereign power of a country or its agent (if acting intra-vires). By its very nature such an act cannot be questioned by any Court of Law.

- *Address of President* is the prepared speech delivered by the President of India to both Houses of Parliament assembled together at the commencement of the first Session after each general election to Lok Sabha and at the commencement of the first Session of each year informing Parliament of the causes of its summons which is later laid before and discussed on a formal Motion of Thanks in each House of Parliament or an address by the President of India to either House of Parliament of both Houses, assembled together on any other occasion.
- *Adjournment Motion* if Speaker gives his consent after satisfying himself that the matter to be raised is definitely urgent and of public importance and holds that the matter prepared to be discussed is in order, he shall call the member concerned who rise in his place and ask for leave to move the adjournment of the House. If objection to leave being granted is taken, the Speaker shall request those members who are in favour of leave being granted to rise in their places, and if not less than fifty members rise accordingly, the Speaker shall intimate that leave is granted, if not, he shall inform the House that the members have not to leave the House,
- *Adjournment of House* in Lok Sabha the Speaker determines when sitting of House is to adjourn *sine die* or to a particular day or to an hour or part of same day while in Rajya Sabha it is the Chairman who determines.
- *Admonition* is a judicial or ecclesiastic censure or reprimand.
- *Advocate-General* the Attorney-General and after him, the advocate-General of a State have precedence over other advocates.
- *Affirmation* is a solemn declaration without oath.
- *Amendment* is a device to alter a motion moved or question under discussion in the legislature, includes omission, substitution, addition and insertion of certain words, figures or marks to the clause of a bill, a resolution or a motion or to an amendment made thereof.

> Amendment is a structural improvement.

- *Anglo-Indian* is of a British birth but living or having lived long in India.
- *Appeal* is the judicial examination of the decision by a higher court of the decision of an inferior court.
- *Appropriation Bill* is the act of devoting or reserving for special or distinct purpose or of destining to a particular end; anything set aside especially money for a specific use.
- *Arrest* is the restraining of the liberty of a man's person in order to compel obedience to the order of a court of justice, or to prevent the commission of a crime, or to ensure that a person charged or suspected of a crime may be forthcoming to answer it.

> Arrest is when one is taken into custody and restrained from his liberty.

- *Assent to Bill,* is ratification, sovereign's formal acquiescence in a measure passed by legislature.

- *Attorney-General* is the Chief Law Officer of a country, legal adviser to the Chief Executive.
- *Backward Classes* the list of OBCs are prepared by the Central Government and are revised after the expiry of every 10 years.

> Backward Classes are the classes slow in development.

- *Ballot*, is a small ball ticket or paper used in secret voting.
- *Begar*, is a labour or service exacted by court or a person in power without giving remuneration.
- *Bill* is a draft of a law proposed to a lawmaking body.

> Bill is the draft or form of an Act presented to a legislature but not enacted.

- *Breach of privilege* disregard of any of the privileges, rights and immunities either of the members of Parliament individually or of either House of Parliament in its collective capacity or of its committees, also includes action which obstructs the House in the performance in its functions and thereby lower its dignity and authority such as disobedience of its legitimate order or libel upon itself, or its member or officers which are called contempt of the House.
- *Budget* refers to the statement of the estimated receipts and expenditure of the Government of India known as annual financial statement; it is caused to be laid before both Houses of Parliament by the President in respect of every financial year on such day as he may direct.
- *Bulletin* is an official notice of a public transaction or matter of public importance.
- *Business to the House* is the relative order of the items of business in the House of a legislature to be taken up on a particular day.
- *Cabinet* is a private and confidential assembly of the most considerable minister of State of concert measures for the administration of public affairs.
- *Censure Motion* is a motion moved against the government censuring its policy in some direction or an individual minister or minister of the Government.
- *Certiorari* is a writ of High Court to an inferior court to call up the records of a case therein depending that conscionable justice may be therein administered.

> Certiorari is issued by the superior Court to inferior judicial or quasi-judicial body, grounds for invoking are excess of jurisdiction, violation of natural justice, fraud and terms on the face of the record. Conditions for issuing this writ are: (i) a body of persons having legal authority, (ii) to determine questions altering rights of subjects, (iii) having the duty to act judicially, (iv) act in excess of their legal authority, (v) issued on constitutional grounds also.

- *Chief whip* is the chief of the whips of different political parties in Parliament (generally the Minister of Parliamentary Affairs).

- *Citizen* is a member of a State or nation, especially one with a republican form of government, who owes allegianes to it by birth or naturalisation and is entitled to full civil rights.
- *Closure* is the Parliamentary Procedure by which debate is closed and the measure under discussion brought up for an immediate vote.

  Closure is the procedure in deliberative assemblies whereby debate is closed.
- *Coalition* usually takes place in multi-party system in which no single party is able to command support of a working majority.
- *Comptroller and Auditor-General* is the officer who is responsible for the auditing of all public accounts.
- *Concurrent List* is a list of subjects appended to a federal Constitution in respect of which the federal legislature and the State of regional legislatures have power to make laws, federal law prevailing in case of conflict.
- *Consolidated fund* is a repository of public money which now comprises the produce of customs, excise, stamps and several other taxes, and some small receipts from the royal hereditary revenue surrendered to its public use.
- *Constituent Assembly* is a legislative body charged with task of framing or revising a Constitution, set up for India after it became independent in 1947 for the purpose of framing its Constitution.
- *Constitution* is the system of fundamental laws and principles of a government written or unwritten.

  Constitution is the basic law defining and delimiting the principal organs of Government and their jurisdiction as well as the basic rights of men and citizens.
- *Contempt of court* is a disobedience to or disregard of the rules, orders, process, or dignity of a court, which has power to punish for such offence by committal.
- *Contingency fund* is placed at the disposal of the executive to meet the unforeseen expenditure.
- *Court* is a place where justice is judicially administered.
- *Debate* is a Parliamentary discussion.
- *Defection* is abandonment of loyalty, duty, principle etc.,
- *Delegated legislation* is rules and regulations with the effect of law made by the executive under statutory sanction by Parliament.
- *Deprivation* is a loss of dismissal from office.

  Deprivation refers to property taken under the power of eminent domain.
- *Deputy Speaker* is the Officer of the House of a legislature who takes the Chair during the absence of the Speaker and performs his duties in relation to all proceedings in the House.
- *Directive Principles of State Policy* lay down guidelines which can be implemented only by passing legislation.

- *Discrimination* is a difference in treatment of two or more persons or subjects.

  Discrimination is an act of depriving an individual or a group of equality of opportunity. Dissolution, is the civil death of Parliament.

- *Doctrine of severability* is a rule of interpretation; it means that where some particular provision of statute offends against a constitutional limitation, but that provision is severable from the rest of the statute, only the offending provision will be declared void by the court and not the entire statute.
- *Double jeopardy* is subjection of an accused person to repeated trial for the same alleged offence.
- *Due process of law* is the law in conformity with due process a concept adopted by the American Constitution; the process of law which hears before it condemns; judiciary can declare a law bad, if it is not in accordance with due process even though the legislation may be within the competence of the legislature concerned.
- *Election* is an act of selecting one or more persons for a political office or other position.
- *Election Commission* is a constitutional body created for the purpose of holding elections to Parliament, State Legislatures and Offices of President and Vice-President.
- *Electoral college* is an intermediary body chosen by electors to choose the representatives in an indirect election.
- *Electoral roll* is known as voter's list in common parlance; is the basic document on which the whole electoral process is founded.
- *Equal protection* all individuals and classes will be equally subjected to the ordinary law administered by the law courts.
- *Equality* is the state of being equal in political, economic and social rights.
- *Existing law* is the law in force at the passage of an Act.
- *Expulsion* is the unseating of members for offences committed against the House or for grave misdemeanours.
- *Extradition* is the surrender by a foreign State of a person accused of a crime to the State where it was committed.
- *Financial memorandum* is a memorandum required to accompany all bills involving expenditure.
- *Fundamental duties* are certain obligations on the part of a citizen which he or she owes towards the State so that the individual may not overlook his duties to the community while exercising his fundamental right or commit wanton destruction of public property or life.
- *Fundamental rights* is protected and guaranteed by the written Constitution of a State.
- *Gazette* is the official newspaper of the Government.

  Gazette is known as the Gazette of India or the Official Gazette of a State.

- *Government* is an established system of political administration by which State is governed.
- *Habeas corpus* commands a Judge of the inferior court to produce the body of the defendant with a statement of the cause of his detention, to do and to receive whatever the higher court shall decree.
- *Hung Parliament* is a Parliament wherein no part has won a working majority.
- *Impeachment* a person found guilty may be removed from his office.
- *Joint sitting* is a joint sitting of both Houses of a bicameral legislature for setting a disagreement between them.
- *Judgment* order or sentence given by a judge or law court.
- *Judicial review* is the power of the court to review statutes or administrative acts and determine their constitutionality. The examination of federal and State legislature statutes and the acts of executive officials by the Courts to determine their validity according to written Constitutions.
- *Judiciary* is the body of officers who administer the law.
- *Law* all the rules of conduct established and enforced by the authority.
- *Legislative relations* in case of conflict the union law prevails.
- *Legislature* is the body of persons in a State authorised to make, alter and repeal law. It may consist of one or two Houses with similar or different powers.
- *Liberty* is something which results from a permission given to or something enjoyed under sufferance by a particular person or body or persons as opposed to enjoyment by all and sundry.
- *Locus standi* means a place for standing, right to be heard.
- *Maiden speech* is one's first or earliest speech especially in Parliament.
- *Martial law* is arbitrary in its decisions and is not built on any settled principles.
- *Migration* means coming to India with the intention of residing here permanently.
- *Minority* is racial, religious or political groups smaller than and differing from larger, controlling group of which it is a party.
- *Money Bill* is a bill which contains only provisions dealing with the imposition, repeal, remission, alteration or regulation of taxes etc.
- *Motion* is a proposal made in the House of a legislature to elicit its decision on a subject.
- *Oath* is a ritualistic declaration, based on an appeal to God or some revered person or object that one will speak the truth, keep a promise, remain faithful etc.
- *Office of profit* is an employment with fees and emoluments attached to it; where pay or salary is attached to an office, it immediately and indisputably makes the office and "office of profit".
- *Official gazette* means the Gazette of India or the Official Gazette of a State.
- *Ordinance* is a State paper operative as a fundamental law, yet not describable as either a Constitution or a statute.

- *Personal liberty* consists in the power of locomotion, of changing situation or moving one's person to whatever place one's own inclination may direct, without imprisonment or restraint unless by due course of law.
- *Petition* is a solemn, earnest supplication or request to a superior or to a person or group in authority.
- *Pith and substance* is a doctrine relating to the interpretation of statutes, evolved by the Privy Council, to solve the problem of two competing legislatures.
- *Preamble* is an introduction, especially one to a constitutional statute etc., stating its reason and purpose.
- *President* is Chief executive of a Republic.
- *Presumption of constitutionality* is an assumption made failing proof of the contrary that an enactment is in accordance with the Constitution. The presumption is always in favour of the constitutionality of an enactment and the burden is upon him who attacks it to show that there has been a clear transgression of the constitutional principles.
- *Privilege* is an exceptional right or advantage.
- *Privy purse* was the sum fixed by the Government of India for covering the expenses of each of the rulers of former Indian States and their families in consideration of their agreement of merger in the Indian Union.
- *Probationer* is one who is on probation or trial.
- *Procedure established by law* is the procedure prescribed by the law of the State. It does not mean the due process of law.
- *Prohibition*, is a remedy provided by the Common Law against the encroachment of jurisdiction.
- *Proportional representation* is a method of representation designed to secure the election of candidates in proportion to the numerical strength of each section of political opinion, thus accurately reflecting the political feeling of the country in Parliament.
- *Question hour* is the time fixed for asking and answering oral questions in a sitting in a legislature; it is fixed under the rules of the House or standing orders.
- *Qua warranto* is a writ ordering a person to show by what right he exercises an office, franchise or privilege.
- *Quorum* is a minimum number required to be present at an assembly before it can validly proceed to transact business.
- *Reasonable restriction* is restrictions imposed by State on the enjoyment of the fundamental rights.
- *Religion* is the specific system of belief, worship, conduct involving a Code of ethics and philosophy.
- *Repugnancy* is contradictory of each other, set of clauses in statutes, will, etc,.
- *Res judicata* is final judgment already decided between the same parties or their privies on the same questions by a legally constituted court having jurisdiction is conclusive between the parties, and the issue cannot be raised again.

- *Rule* is an established guide or regulation for action, conduct.
- *Rule of law* is absolute supremely or predominance of regular law as opposed to the influence of arbitrary power's equality before the law or the equal subjection of all classes to the ordinary law court; Constitution is the result of the ordinary law of the land.
- *Session* connotes the sitting together of the legislative body for the transaction of business.
- *Shadow cabinet* is a body of opposition leaders meeting from time to time and ready to take office.
- *State* comprises people, territory, government through which its policies are implemented and sovereignty having authority to make final legal decisions and having physical power to enforce them.
- *State Act* is an Act passed by Legislature of a State established or continued by the Constitution.
- *Statute* is synonymous with Act of Parliament.
- *Subordinate legislation* is a making of statutory instruments or orders by a body subordinate to the legislature in exercise of the power within specific limits conferred by the legislature, also covers statutory instruments themselves.
- *Swear* is to make a solemn declaration or affirmation with an appeal to God or to someone or something held sacred for confirmation.
- *Untouchability* is social disabilities historically imposed on certain classes of people by reason of their birth in certain castes.
- *Vote* is a decision by one or more persons on a proposal, resolution expressed by ticket, ballot, or voice.
- *Vote on account* is estimate of an advance payment to enable Government Departments to carry on their work from beginning of financial year till the passing of Appropriation Act.
- *Walk out* is a strike, an informal or unauthorised strike, an action of leaving a meeting or organisation as an expression of disapproval; continued absence from the meetings of an organisation as an expression of disapproval.
- *Zero hour* is a time set for the beginning of an attack or other military operation; any crucial or decisive moment.

Zero hour is usually noisy interregnum between the Question Hour and the beginning of the rest of day's business in a legislature; members raise often without notice various matters during this period.

1. Indian Economy

The Indian government supports a mixed economy, most of which is in the control of private enterprise. Under a policy announced in 1956, the government undertook a plan to nationalise the entire segments of the economy, while leaving other sectors subject to varying degrees of government planning and control. Nearly 250 corporations are owned by the state today.

2. Characteristics of Indian Economy

Agriculture

Agriculture is the mainstay of the majority of the population in India. A far-seeing agricultural policy initiated in the 60s resulted in a Green Revolution in India. With extensive cultivable regions, a comprehensive network of irrigation facilities, and valuable stands of timber, today India is not only self-sufficient in food grains, but also exports its crops. India has the largest area in the world under *pulse crops* and is also the first in the world to evolve a *cotton hybrid*.

Banking

India has a well developed banking system that is *government-regulated* and largely *government-owned*. **The Reserve Bank of India**, founded in **1935** and nationalised in 1949, is India's principal banking institution. It regulates the circulation of bank notes, manages the country's reserves of foreign exchange and operates the currency and credit system. Fourteen of the country's largest commercial banks were nationalised in 1969 and by 1980, most of the country's commercial banking passed into the public sector. Other banks have been established by the central government to provide credits promoting various types of industry and foreign trade. Many foreign banks maintain branch offices in India, and Indian banks maintain offices in numerous foreign countries. The *Rupee*, India's basic monetary unit, is divided into *100 paisa* (approx. 43 rupees equal U.S.$1).

Manufacturing

India's manufacturing sector is highly diversified and includes a range of heavy and high-technology industries, largely under government ownership. Consumer-goods industries are more commonly privately owned. The country's chief manufactures include textiles, iron and steel, cement, fertilizers, other chemicals, automotive vehicles, ships, bicycles, textile and other machinery, electrical appliances and electronics, and pharmaceuticals. Electricity is generated mainly by thermal and secondarily by hydroelectric installations. Labour unions, generally affiliated with various political parties, are important in the modern sectors of the economy. India's chief trading partners include the *United States, Japan, the United Kingdom, Russia, Germany*, and *Saudi Arabia*.

Mining

Domestically supplied minerals form an important underpinning for India's diversified manufacturing industry, as well as a source of modest export revenues. The nationalization of many foreign and domestic enterprises and the government initiation and management of others have given the Indian government a predominant role in the mining industry. India ranks among the world leaders in the production of iron ore, coal and bauxite and produces significant amounts of manganese, mica, dolomite, copper, petroleum, chromium, lead, limestone, phosphate rock, zinc, gold, and silver.

Trade

Initially, stock exchanges did not play the prominent role in India in the way that they do in more affluent capitalist societies. However, today one can find vibrant stock exchanges in most of the largest Indian cities and they facilitate the flow of capital in the form of securities under rules set down by the Ministry of Finance. India's trade links are worldwide. The *United States* and the former *Soviet Union* have been the principal destinations for India's exports (often, in the latter case, under barter arrangements), while Japan and the countries of the European Community (EC), especially Germany and the United Kingdom, have also been important. The main import sources have been Japan, the United States, the EC, the Middle East and the former Soviet Union. Today, the United States is India's leading trading partner, receiving about 16 percent of India's yearly exports and supplying about 10 percent of its imports.

Transportation

India, at independence, had a superior transportation system. In the decades that followed, she built steadily on that base, and railroads in particular formed the sinews that initially bound the new nation together. Although railroads have continued to carry the bulk of goods traffic, there has been a steady increase in the relative dependence on roads and motorised transport. India has a broad network of railroad lines, the largest in Asia and the fourth largest in the world, all of which are publicly controlled. The major Indian ports, including Calcutta (Kolkata), Bombay(Mumbai), Madras(Chennai), and Vishakhapatnam, are reached by cargo carriers and passenger liners operating to almost all the parts of the world. A comprehensive network of Indian-operated air routes connects the major cities and towns of the country. International connections are maintained by Air India, Indian Airlines and foreign air-transport services.

3. Types of Economies in the World

Basically, there are three types of economic systems that exist, each with their own drawbacks and benefits; the *Market Economy*, the *Planned Economy* and the *Mixed Economy*. An economic system is loosely defined as country's plan for its services, goods produced, and the exact way in which its economic plan is carried out. In general, there are three major types of economic systems prevailing around the world.

Market Economy

In a market economy, national and state governments play a minor role. Instead, consumers and their buying decisions drive the economy. In this type of economic system, the assumptions of the market play a major role in deciding the right path for a country's economic development. Market economies aim to reduce or eliminate entirely the subsidies for a particular industry, the pre-determination of prices for different commodities, and the amount of regulation controlling different industrial sectors. The absence of central planning is one of the major features of this economic system. Market decisions are mainly dominated by supply and demand. The role of the government in a market economy is to simply make sure that the market is stable enough to carry out its economic activities properly.

Planned Economy

A planned economy is also sometimes called a *command economy*. The most important aspect of this type of economy is that all major decisions related to the production, distribution, commodity and service prices, are all made by the government. The planned economy is government directed, and market forces have very little say in such an economy. This type of economy lacks the kind of flexibility that is present in a market economy, and because of this, the planned economy reacts slower to the changes in consumer needs and fluctuating patterns of supply and demand. Basically, a planned economy aims at using all available resources for developing production instead of allotting the resources for advertising or marketing.

Mixed Economy

A mixed economy combines elements of both the planned and the market economies in one cohesive system. This means that certain features from both market and planned economic systems are taken to form this type of economy. This system prevails in many countries where neither the government nor the business entities control the economic activities of that country — both sectors play an important role in the economic decision-making of the country. In a mixed economy there is flexibility in some areas and government control in others.

Mixed economies include both capitalist and socialist economic policies and often arise in societies that seek to balance a wide range of political and economic views. Examples of countries following a Mixed Economy are: The United States, Canada, Australia, Japan, Germany, the United Kingdom, Italy, etc... Examples in the developing world include Mexico, Slovenia, South Africa, etc. India is also a mixed economy where public private partnership co-exists.

4. Agriculture and Land Development

Agriculture is the mainstay of the Indian economy.

- ▷ The share of agricultural sector's capital formation in GDP declined from 1.92% in the early 1990s to 1.28% in early 2000s. This has improved to 2.12% in 2006-07.
- ▷ Agriculture and allied sectors contribute nearly 18% of national income (GNI of India), while about 60% of the population is dependent on agriculture for their livelihood.
- ▷ The agricultural output, depends on monsoon as nearly 60% of area sown in is dependent on rainfall.
- ▷ Land utilisation data is available for 92.9% of total geographical area of 3,287.3 lakh hectares.
- ▷ Agriculture accounts only for about 10.6% of the total export earnings in 2009-10.

Share of Agricultural Sector in Total Gross Domestic Product

(At 1999-00 prices, in percentage terms)

Year	Agriculture*
1950-51	56.5
1970-71	45.9
1990-91	34.0
2007-08	17.8
2008-09 (Q) (2004-05 Prices)	15.7
2009-10 (R) (2004-05 Prices)	14.6

* Agriculture includes agriculture, forestry and fishing.
[Source: Economic Survey 2007-08, Statistical Abstract of India 2008. CSO, National Accounts Statistics, 2010, (2004-05 prices)].

- Figures provided by the Central Statistical Organisation reveal that between 1950-51 to 1960-61, the share of agriculture in GDP has been in the range of 55 to 52%. The share of agriculture indicated a sharp decline and reached a level of 14.6% in 2009-10.
- Importance of agriculture in the national economy is indicated by many facts, e.g.- agriculture is the main support for India's transport systems, secure bulk of their business from the movement of agricultural goods. Internal trade is mostly in agricultural products.
- Agricultural growth has direct impact on poverty eradication. It is also an important factor in containing inflation raising agricultural wages and employment generation.
- But, since 2002-03, Indian agricultural sector is almost going through a crisis — huge food grains surplus wiped out, large imports of wheat being planned and farmers' suicides more frequent all over the country.
- Besides, the allied sectors like horticulture, animal husbandry, dairy and fisheries have an important role in improving the overall economic conditions and nutrition of the rural masses.
- To maintain ecological balance, there is need for sustainable and balanced development of both agriculture and the allied sectors.
- The Tenth Plan asserts emphatically that the agricultural sector acts as a bul-work in maintaining food security and, in the process, national security as well.
- Agricultural growth rate achieved in 9th Plan was 2.1%, while the target for the 10th Plan (2002-07) was 4% and for 11th plan (2007-12) is also 4%.
- Commercial crops are those crops which are produced for trade purpose and not for self consumption by the farmers. It includes Oilseeds crops, Sugar crops, Fibre crops, Narcotic crops, Beverage crops.
- To encourage the agricultural products, the government announces to minimum support price for important agricultural crops.
- The function of Agriculture Cost and Price Commission (ACPC) is to decide the minimum support prices on behalf of the government.
- Minimum Support Price (MSP) announced by the government is that price at which government is ready to purchase the crop from the farmers directly, if crop price falls below the MSP.
- For providing facilities relating to storage of agriculture products, "National Co-operative Development and Warehousing Board" was established in 1956 and "Central Warehousing Corporation" was established in 1957. Thereafter in states also the State Warehousing Corporations were established.
- The programme of High Yielding Variety Seeds was combined with a guiding project I.A.D.P. and a target was set to extend this system of development in entire country.

- The credit of green revolution in India is given to the Agriculture Scientist Dr. Norman Borlaug. However, the contribution of Dr. M.S. Swaminathan is not less. But, its termed name is the contribution of American scientist Dr. William Gande.
- Due to horrible famine during 1965-66 and 1966-67, the government implemented the new agriculture policy of high yielding seeds so as to increase agriculture production.
- India is the largest milk producing country in the world.
- There is significant increase in the milk production to the level of 108.5 million tonnes in the year 2008-09 as compared to 53.9 million tonnes in 1990-91.
- Speedy increase in the field of milk production is called White Revolution.
- To increase the pace of White Revolution, the Operation Flood was started.
- In milk production of the country, the share of buffalo, cow and goat is 50%, 46% and 45% respectively.
- The *Father of Operation Flood* was Dr. Verghese Kurien.
- The Operation Flood was the largest integrated dairy development programme of the world. It was started by National Dairy Development Board in 1970.
- The increase in oil seeds production was due to "Yellow Revolution".
- The progress in increase of fish production was called "Blue Revolution".
- Assam is the biggest tea producer in the country.
- India ranks sixth in world coffee production and contributes only 4% of world coffee production.
- Cuba is known as the Sugar Bowl of the world. Here, sugar is made of Beetroot.
- India holds first position in the world in the production of sugar-cane and sugar.
- The importance of agriculture in the industrial sector is not only for supply of raw material, but it provides foodgrains for the people working in that sector and market for industrial products.

Agricultural Production
- Indian agriculture still depends upon monsoon.
- Agricultural production can be divided into two parts – Foodgrains and Non-foodgrains, in which the share of foodgrains is two-third and non-foodgrains is one-third.

Pattern of Government Outlay on Agriculture in the Plans

Five Year Plans	Total Plan Outlay	Outlay on Agriculture and Irrigation	Percent of total outlay
First Plan (1951-56)	1,960	600	31
Second Plan (1956-61)	4,600	950	20
Third Plan (1961-66)	8,600	1,750	21
Fourth Plan (1969-74)	15,780	3,670	23
Fifth Plan (1974-79)	39,430	8,740	22
Sixth Plan (1980-85)	1,09,290	26,130	24
Seventh Plan (1985-90)	2,18,730	48,100	22
Eighth Plan (1992-97)	4,85,460	1,02,730	21
Ninth Plan (1997-2002)	8,59,200	1,76,217	20.5
Tenth Plan (2002-07)	15,25,639	3,05,055	20
Eleventh Plan (2007-12)	36,44,718	6,74,105	18.5

Note : 1. Agricultural sector is composed of agriculture and allied activities, rural development, special area programmes and irrigation and flood controls.
2. Tenth and Eleventh Plan figures are at 2006-07prices.

Source : Various Five-Year Plan Documents *(Courtsey: Indian Economy)*

- The percentage of plan outlay on agriculture and allied sectors to total plan outlay varied between 31% and 14.9% from the First Plan to Tenth Plan.
- Actual outlay on the agricultural sector ranged between 18 and 24% of the total Plan outlay (except during the First Plan, it was as high as 31%).
- During Eleventh Plan (2007-12) the plan outlay on agriculture has declined to only 18.5%.
- **Food grains Ploduction:** This was at a record high of 259.32 million tonnes in 2011-12 in India.
- During the first decade of planning (1951-61) when the First and Second Five Year Plans were implemented, the annual rate of growth in agriculture was 3.3%.
- During the next two decades of planning in 1961-81, despite spectacular progress achieved under the new agricultural strategy and IADP and HYVP, the overall progress in agriculture was dismal; the annual average rate of growth declined to 2.2% and 1.7% respectively, mainly because of bad weather and poor monsoon conditions.
- The growth rate in the 1980's was highly respectable (3.9%).

- The Tenth Plan had fixed a target rate of growth of 4% in agriculture to achieve 8% rate of growth in GDP.
- During the Eleventh Plan also, the Planning Commission fixed the target of 4% rate of growth in agriculture.
- The Tenth Plan was the first plan which did not fix targets of crop production.
- Actual production of rice ranged between 82 and 93 million tonnes in between 1997 and 2007.
- The production of wheat which stood at 11 million tonnes in 1960-61 rose to 76 million tonnes in 1999-2000, but declined to 72 million tonnes in 2003-04.
- Actual production of wheat ranged between 69 and 75 million tonnes in between 1997-2007.
- Even now the production of pulses fluctuates between 13 and 15 million tonnes per year.
- Green revolution did not cover barley, ragi and minor-millets.
- The Green revolution was confined only to High Yielding Varieties (HYV) mainly rice, wheat, maize and *jowar*.
- National Agriculture Insurance Scheme was implemented in Oct. 1999.
- On 28th July 2000, the Central government fixed target for rate of growth in agriculture sector at more than 4% by 2005 under the National Agriculture Policy.

Land Reforms Programmes in India include:
- Elimination of intermediaries
- Tenancy Reforms
- Determination of ceiling of holdings per family
- Distribution of surplus land among landless people
- Consolidation of holdings (Chakbandi)

- By the end of first five year plan, middlemen had been removed (except small areas).
- The following measures were made effective for the betterment of farmers :
  (i) Regulation of tax (ii) Security for the rights of farmers (iii) Right of land ownership for the farmers
- For the reorganisation of agriculture land holding mainly two measures were taken – (i) Land ceiling and (ii) *Chakbandi*.
- Land ceiling determines the maximum land which can be held by a farmer. Holding more than that area will be illegal.
- *Chakbandi* of land means to aggregate the divided and broken land.

- The land within area less than 1 hectare, is called marginal land holding, 1 to 4 hectare area is called small land holding and the land within area more than 4 hectare, is called large land holding.
- Chakbandi was implemented first time in India in the year 1920 in Baroda.
- The irrigation potential in India in 2000-01 was 9.47 crore hectare.
- Green Revolution was started in the Third Five Year Plan.
- The most positive effect of Green Revolution was on wheat. There was 500% increase in crop production.
- Unorganised sources of agriculture finance are money-lenders, money-dealers, relatives, businessmen, landlords and commission agents.
- Organised sources of agriculture finance are Co-operative Committees, Co-operative Banks, Commercial Banks, Regional Rural Banks, the Government etc.
- Co-operative Credit Organisation started first time in 1904.
- Primary Co-operative Committees provide credit for short period.
- State Co-operative Agriculture and Rural Development Banks provide credit for long period.
- Land Development Bank provides long-term loans.
- Land Development Bank was established in the year 1919 in the form of Land Mortgage Bank.
- *National Bank for Agriculture and Rural Development* (NABARD) is the apex institution of Rural Credit. It was established on 12th July, 1982 by the merger of Agriculture Credit department and reconstruction of Agriculture and Development Corporation of the Reserve Bank of India. Its establishment is based on the recommendations of Shivraman Committee.
- Authorised share capital of NABARD was Rupees 500 crore. However, after an amendment its authorized share increased upto 5000 crore with effect from 1st February, 2001.
- Food stocks are maintained by the central government for 3 purposes:
    (i) Maintaining prescribed buffer stock norms for food security,
    (ii) Monthly supply through Public Distribution System (PDS),
    (iii) Market intervention to stabilise open market prices.
- Buffer stock on January 1, 2002 was a 58 million tonnes.

Two Major Crops of India

(a) *Kharif Crops :* Sown in July and harvested in October. They include Rice, Jowar, Bajra, Maize, Cotton, Soyabean, Groundnut.

(b) *Rabi Crops:* Sown in October and harvested in March/ April. They include Wheat, Barley, Gram, Tur, Rapeseed, Mustard.

(c) *Zayad Crops:* Sown during March to June. It includes Watermelons, Vegetables, Moong etc.

MSP for Rabi Crops of 2015-16 Season

The Cabinet Committee on Economic Affairs (CCEA), chaired by the Prime Minister Shri Narendra Modi, has given its approval for the Minimum Support Prices (MSPs) for Rabi Crops of 2015-16 season to be marketed in 2016-17. The decision is based on recommendations of Commission for Agricultural Costs and Prices (CACP) for the Price Policy for Rabi Crops for the Marketing Season 2016-17. The CACP, which is an expert body, takes into account the cost of production, overall demand-supply, domestic and international prices, inter-crop price parity, terms of trade between agricultural and non-agricultural sectors, the likely effect of the Price Policy on the rest of economy, besides ensuring rational utilization of production resources like land and water, while recommending MSPs.

The CCEA has decided to give a bonus of ₹ 75 per quintal for Rabi pulses over and above the recommendations of the CACP. It is expected to give a strong price signal to farmers to increase acreage and invest for increase in productivity of pulses.

The Minimum Support Prices (MSPs) for all Rabi Crops of 2015-16 seasons to be marketed in 2016-17 have been increased and are given in table below:

Commodity	MSP for 2014-15 season (₹ per quintal)	MSP for 2015-16 season (₹ per quintal)	Increase in MSP over 2014-15		Bonus* (₹ per quintal)
			Absolute	%	
Wheat	1450	1525	75	5.2	—
Barley	1150	1225	75	6.5	—
Gram	3175	3425	250	7.9	75
Masur (Lentil)	3075	3325	250	8.1	75
Rapeseed/Mustard	3100	3350	250	8.0	—
Safflower	3050	3300	250	8.2	—

Note* Bonus on Rabi pulses is payable over and above the MSP.

The prices would be effective from the Rabi marketing season 2016-17. The higher MSPs would increase investment and production through assured remunerative prices to farmers.

Sugarcane FRP Raised for 2015-16

The Cabinet Committee on Economic Affairs on January 16, 2015 raised the central government's recommended Fair and Remunerative Price (FRP) for sugar mills' purchase of cane for the 2015-16 season by ₹ 10 a quintal, to ₹ 230 a quintal. The season will start from October 2015 and end in September 2016. The FRP for 2014-15 is ₹ 220 a quintal. FRP is the minimum price that mills will have to pay to cane farmers.

As per government announcement, the (price) will be linked to a basic recovery rate of 9.5 per cent, subject to a premium of ₹ 2.42 a quintal for every 0.1 percentage point increase in recovery above that level.

Millers say even such a small increase will be a payment challenge, unless ex-factory price of sugar, which is set by the government, increases significantly in the next few months. It is evident that almost all sugar mills were unable to pay even at ₹ 220 a quintal for cane in the current season.

5. National Income

➪ National income is the measurement of flow of services and goods in economic system.

➪ *Comparison between National income with National wealth :* The national wealth is the measurement of present assets available on a given time, while the National income is the measurement of the production power of economic system in a given time period.

➪ The figures of National income are based on the financial year (i.e. from 1st April to 31st March).

➪ The base of one year is taken for calculating National income, as all the seasons come in a year.

➪ The data of estimation of India's National income are issued by Central Statistical Organisation (CSO).

Relationship among different forms of National Products

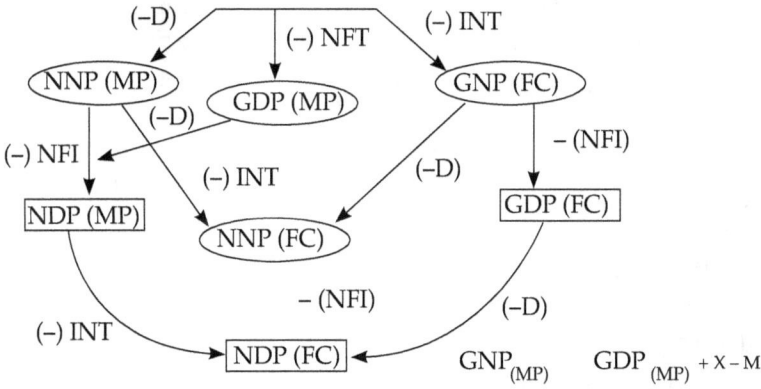

$GNP_{(MP)} = GDP_{(MP)} + X - M$

Where:
X = Income earned and received by nationals within the boundaries.
M = Income received by foreign nationals within the country.
NFI → Net Foreign Income.

Where:
GNP → Gross National Product
NNP → Net National Product
NDP → Net Domestic Product
GDP → Gross Domestic Product
MP → Market Price
FC → Factor Cost
D → Depreciation
INT → Indirect Net Tax

NNP at Factor Cost = NNP at market prices – Indirect Taxes + Subsidies
= GNP at market prices – Indirect Taxes + Subsidies = National Incomes

India's GDP Growth Seen Accelerating to 7.6% in FY' 16

According to the estimates released by Central Statistics Office (CSO), the growth estimate of India has exceeded China's growth. Indian economy is expected to grow at a 5 year high of 7.6 per cent in 2015-16 on improved performance in manufacturing and farm sectors, faster than the 6.9 per cent growth in China. The Gross Domestic Product (GDP) or economic growth is estimated at 7.3 per cent in October-December quarter of the fiscal year 2015-16.

The CSO estimate of 7.6 per cent growth in current fiscal is higher than the projection by RBI, finance ministry and IMF. While RBI projected a growth rate of 7.4 per cent, finance ministry's mid-year economic review had estimated the growth to be between 7-7.5 per cent. Besides, IMF had said India will clock 7.3 per cent growth in 2015-16 and Asian Development Bank projected it at 7.4 per cent.

	Growth%
Q 1 2014–15	6.7
Q 2 2014–15	8.4
Q 3 2014–15	6.6
Q 4 2014–15	7.5
Q 1 2015–16	7.6
Q 2 2015–16	7.7
Q 3 2015–16	7.3

Positive Trend	
Year	GDP Growth (%)
2012–13	5.6
2013–14	6.6
2014–15	7.2
2015–16*	7.6

* Advance estimates for FY 16

POSITIVE SIGNALS

Data projected a growth of 7.6% in 2015-16 against the government's more modest expectation of 7-7.5% growth. This is despite growth decelerating to 7.3% in the quarter ended December from 7.7% in the previous quarter. Economists were surprised by the spurt in manufacturing both in the third quarter (12.6%) as well as in 2015-16 (9.5%)

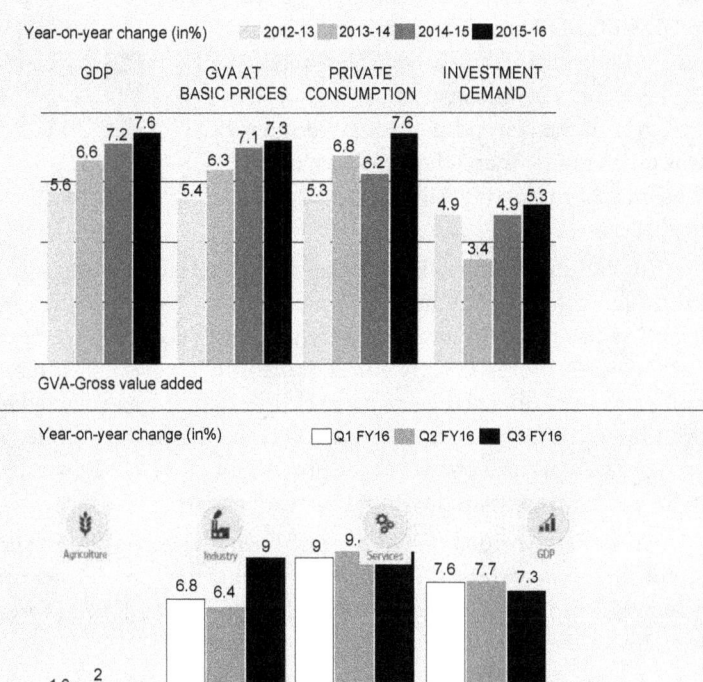

Source: Central Statistics Office

The CSO has also revised upwards the GDP growth estimates for April–June and July-September quarters to 7.6 per cent and 7.7 per cent from earlier calculation of 7 per cent and 7.4 per cent, respectively. At 7.6 per cent, India would be growing at the fastest pace in the last five years. The previous high was recorded at 8.9 per cent in 2010-11.

The manufacturing sector is estimated to grow at 9.5 per cent in 2015-16, up from 5.5 per cent a year ago. Similarly, in case of agriculture sector, the growth has been projected at 1.1 per cent as against decline of 0.2 per cent a year ago.

GDP Growth Revised Down to 7.2%) for FY' 15

According to the official data, India's economy grew 7.2 per cent in 2014-15, a shade lower than an earlier estimate of 7.3 per cent. Among various segments, agriculture and manufacturing growth was revised down for FY15. The official data also showed that in 2013-14, GDP grew at 6.6 per cent, significantly lower than the earlier calculation of 6.9 per cent. This means that growth in the first year of the Narendra Modi government was much higher than what was seen during the United Progressive Alliance government in 2013-14.

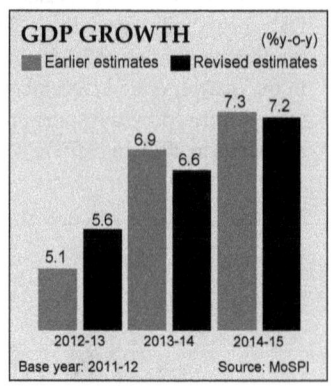

Sunil Kumar Sinha, Principal Economist, India Ratings & Research, said, "Lower GDP growth in FY14 means lower base. Yet, the revised GDP for FY 15 has come down marginally instead of going up. In a nutshell, the data released by the CSO (Central Statistics Office) suggest that economy in the past two financial years grew slower than it was believed earlier and even though GDP growth may have bottomed out, the path to recovery is going to be slow and painful." The growth rate for 2012-13 was also revised to 5.6 per cent, compared with 5.1 per cent earlier.

Gross Value Added (GVA) has also been revised on almost similar lines. According to new data, GVA for 2014-15 now grew by 7.1 per cent against previous estimates of 7.2 per cent. Similarly, GVA for 2013-14 rose by 6.3 per cent, lower than earlier calculation of 6.9 per cent.

The 2014-15 GVA estimate was revised downwards as agriculture contracted 0.2 per cent against the previous estimates of 0.2 per cent growth. Similarly, manufacturing was shown growing at 5.5 per cent against the earlier calculation of 7.1 per cent.

The size of the economy has now been projected at ₹ 124.9 lakh crore against earlier estimate of ₹ 1.25 lakh crore for 2014-15. Similarly, the economy size stood at ₹ 112.7 lakh crore for 2013-14 against earlier calculation of ₹ 113.4 lakh crore. Per capita income stood at ₹ 86,879 in 2014-15, lower than the earlier calculation of ₹ 87,748.

India to be Fastest Growing Economy at 7.3% in 2016 : UN Report

According to United Nations World Economic Situation and Prospects 2016 report, India will be the world's fastest growing large economy at 7.3 per cent in 2016, improving further to 7.5 per cent in the following year. India's economy, which accounts for over 70 per cent of South Asia's GDP, has been projected to grow by 7.3 per cent in 2016 and 7.5 per cent in 2017, slightly up from an estimated 7.2 per cent in 2015. The report is produced annually by the UN Department of Economic and Social Affairs (UN/DESA), the UN Conference on Trade and Development (UNCTAD), the five UN regional commissions and the World Tourism Organisation.

The report said South Asia is expected to be the world's fastest-growing region in 2016 and 2017. UN report sees majority of the countries in South Asia to see accelerated growth over the next two years on the back of strong private consumption as the main driver of growth, offsetting relatively tight fiscal policies and sluggish exports.

Highlighting the challenges for South Asia, the UN report said countries like India, Bangladesh, Iran and Nepal have narrowed their fiscal deficits in 2015, however, weaknesses are there.

Growth Rates as Shown in World Economic Situation and Prospects Report 2016 (UN Report)

Country	Expected Growth Rate %	
	2016	2017
India	7.3	7.5
China	6.4	6.5
Brazil	–0.8	2.3
USA	2.6	2.8
EU	2.0	2.2
Africa	4.4	4.4
Japan	1.3	0.6
Whole World	2.9	3.2

National Income Statistics at a Glance

(in crore Rs.)

Country	At Current Prices		At Constant 2011-12 Prices	
	2014-15 (First RE)	2015-16 (AE)	2014-15 (First RE)	2015-16 (AE)
GDP (Gross Domestic Produce)	1,24,88,205 (10.8)	1,35,67,192 (8.6)	1,05,52,151 (7.2)	1,13,50,692 (7.6)
NDP (Net Domestic Produce)	1,11,55,025 (10.7)	1,21,18,824 (8.6)	93,59,476 (7.1)	1,00,71,224 (7.6)
GVA at Basic Prices	1,14,72,409 (10.5)	1,22,52,306 (6.8)	97,27,490 (7.1)	1,04,37,579 (7.3)

GNI (Gross National Income)	1,23,40,722 (10.8)	1,34,09,892 (8.7)	1,04,27,701 (7.3)	1,12,14,077 (7.5)
NNI (Net National Income)	1,10,07,592 (10.8)	1,19,61,524 (8.7)	92,35,026 (7.2)	99,34,339 (7.6)
Per Capita Income (In ₹)	86,879 (9.4)	93,231 (7.3)	72,889 (5.8)	77,431 (6.2)

Note :
1. Data in brackets show per cent growth over the past year.
2. For calculating per capita income, population has been taken in 2014-15 and 2015-16 as 126.7 crore and 128.3 crore respectively.

6. Planning in India

Planning without an objective is like driving without any destination. There are generally two sets of objectives for planning, namely the short-term objectives and the long-term objectives. While the short-term objectives vary from plan to plan, depending on the immediate problems faced by the economy, the process of planning is inspired by certain long term objectives. In case of our Five Year plans, the long-term objectives are:

- A high rate of growth with a view to improvement in standard of living.
- Economic self-reliance
- Social justice
- Modernisation of the economy
- Economic stability
- High Rate of growth

Five-Year Plans of India

The economy of India is based on the planning through its five-year plans, which are developed, executed and monitored by the **Planning Commission**. The eleventh plan completed its term in March 2012 and the twelfth plan is currently underway. Prior to the fourth plan, the allocation of state resources was based on schematic patterns rather than a transparent and objective mechanism, which led to the adoption of the Gadgil Formula in 1969. Revised versions of the formula have been used since then to determine the allocation of central assistance for state plans.

First Five-Year Plan (1951–1956)

The first Indian Prime Minister, Pandit Jawaharlal Nehru presented the first five-year plan to the Parliament of India on December 8, 1951.This plan was based on the *Harrod-Domar model*. The plan addressed, mainly, the agrarian sector, including investments in dams and irrigation. The agricultural sector was hit hardest by the *Partition of India* and needed urgent attention. The total planned budget of INR 2069 crore was allocated to seven broad areas:

irrigation and energy (27.2 percent), agriculture and community development (17.4 percent), transport and communications (24 percent), industry (8.4 percent), social services (16.64 percent), land rehabilitation (4.1 percent), and for other sectors and services (2.5 percent). The most important feature of this phase was active role of state in all economic sectors. Such a role was justified at that time because immediately after independence, India was facing basic problems — deficiency of capital and low capacity to save.

The target growth rate was about 2.1% annual gross domestic product (GDP) growth; the achieved growth rate was 3.6%. The net domestic product went up by 15%. The monsoon was good and there were relatively high crop yields, boosting exchange reserves and the per capita income, which increased by 8%. National income increased more than the per capita income due to rapid population growth. Many irrigation projects were initiated during this period, including the Bhakra Dam and Hirakud Dam. The World Health Organisation(WHO), with the Indian government, addressed children's health and reduced infant mortality, indirectly contributing to population growth.

At the end of the plan period in 1956, five Indian Institutes of Technology (IITs) were started as major technical institutions. The University Grant Commission was set up to take care of funding and take measures to strengthen the higher education in the country. Contracts were signed to start five steel plants, which came into existence in the middle of the second five-year plan. The plan was successful.

Target Growth: 2.1%   Actual Growth: 3.6%

The Second Five-Year Plan (1956 – 1961)

The second five-year plan focussed on industry, especially heavy industry. Unlike the First Plan, which focussed mainly on agriculture, domestic production of industrial products was encouraged in the Second Plan, particularly in the development of the public sector. The plan followed the *Mahalanobis Model*, an economic development model developed by the Indian statistician, *Prasanta Chandra Mahalanobis* in 1953. The plan attempted to determine the optimal allocation of investment between productive sectors in order to maximise long-run economic growth. It used the prevalent state of art techniques of operations research and optimisation as well as the novel applications of statistical models developed at the Indian Statistical Institute. The plan assumed a closed economy in which the main trading activity would be centred on importing capital goods.

Hydroelectric power projects and five steel mills at *Bhilai, Durgapur,* and *Rourkela* were established. Coal production was increased. More railway lines were added in the North-east.

The **Atomic Energy Commission** was formed in 1958 with **Homi J. Bhabha** as the first chairman. The **Tata Institute of Fundamental Research** was established as a research institute. In 1957, a talent search and scholarship program had begun to find talented young students to train for work in nuclear power.

The Third Five-Year Plan (1961–1966)
The third plan stressed on agriculture and improvement in the production of wheat, but the brief *Sino-Indian* War of 1962 exposed weaknesses in the economy and shifted the focus towards the Defence industry or the Indian Army. In 1965–1966, India fought a 'Indo-Pak' War with Pakistan. Due to this, there was a severe drought in 1965. The war led to inflation and the priority was shifted to price stabilisation. The construction of dams continued. Many cement and fertilizer plants were also built. Punjab began producing an abundance of wheat.

Many primary schools had been started in rural areas. In an effort to bring democracy to the grassroot level, Panchayat elections had been started and the states had been given more development responsibilities.

State electricity boards and state secondary education boards were formed. States were made responsible for secondary and higher education. State road transportation corporations were formed and local road building became a state responsibility.

Target Growth: 5.6%   Actual Growth: 2.4%

The Fourth Five-Year Plan (1969 – 1974)
At this time, Indira Gandhi was the Prime Minister. The Indira Gandhi government nationalised 14 major Indian banks and the Green Revolution in India advanced agriculture. In addition, the situation in East Pakistan (now Bangladesh) was becoming dire as the Indo-Pakistani War of 1971 and Bangladesh Liberation War took funds earmarked for the industrial development had to be diverted for the war effort. India also performed the Smiling Buddha underground nuclear test in 1974, partially in response to the United States deployment of the Seventh Fleet in the Bay of Bengal. The fleet had been deployed to warn India against attacking West Pakistan and extending the war.

Target Growth: 5.7%   Actual Growth: 3.3%

Fifth Five-Year Plan (1974–1979)
Stress was laid on employment, poverty alleviation, and justice. The plan also focused on self-reliance in agricultural production and defence. In 1978, the newly elected Morarji Desai government rejected the plan. *The Electricity Supply Act* was enacted in 1975, which enabled the Central Government to

enter into power generation and transmission. *The Indian national highway system* was introduced and many roads were widened to accommodate the increasing traffic. Tourism was also expanded.

Target Growth: 4.4%   Actual Growth: 5.0%

Sixth Five-Year Plan (1980–1985)

Rajeev Gandhi was the Prime Minister during this period. The sixth plan also marked the beginning of economic liberalization. Price controls were eliminated and ration shops were closed. This led to an increase in food prices and an increase in the cost of living. This was the end of *Nehruvian Socialism*.

Family planning was also expanded in order to prevent overpopulation. In contrast to China's strict and binding one-child policy, the Indian policy did not rely on the threat of force. More prosperous areas of India adopted family planning more rapidly than less prosperous areas, which continued to have a high birth rate. The sixth five year plan was a great success.

Target Growth: 5.2%   Actual Growth: 5.4%

Seventh Five-Year Plan (1985–1990)

The Seventh Plan marked the comeback of the Congress Party to power. The plan laid stress on improving the productivity level of industries by upgrading of technology. The main objectives of the 7th Five-year Plan were to establish growth in areas of increasing economic productivity, production of food grains, and generating employment.

As an outcome of the Sixth Five-Year Plan, there had been a steady growth in agriculture, control on rate of inflation, and favourable balance of payments which had provided a strong base for the Seventh Five-Year Plan to build on the need for further economic growth. The 7th Plan had strived towards socialism and energy production at large. The thrust areas of the 7th Five year plan have been enlisted below:

- Social Justice
- Removal of oppression of the weak
- Using modern technology
- Agricultural development
- Anti-poverty programs
- Full supply of food, clothing and shelter
- Increasing productivity of small and large-scale farmers
- Making India an Independent Economy

Based on a 15-year period of striving towards steady growth, the 7th Plan was focussed on achieving the pre-requisites of self-sustaining growth by the year, 2000. The Plan expected a growth in labour force of 39 million people and employment was expected to grow at the rate of 4 percent per year.

Some of the expected outcome of the Seventh Five Year Plan of India are given below:

- Balance of Payments (estimates): Export – INR 33,000 crore (US $ 6 billion), Imports – (-)INR 54,000 crore (US $ 9.8 billion), Trade Balance – (-)INR 21,000 crore (US $ 3.8 billion)
- Merchandise Exports (estimates): INR 60,653 crore (US $ 11 billion)
- Merchandise Imports (estimates): INR 95,437 crore (US $ 17.4 billion)
- Projections for Balance of Payments: Export – INR 60,700 crore (US $ 11 billion)
- Imports – (-)INR 95,400 crore (US $ 17.4 billion), Trade Balance– (-) INR 34,700 crore (US $ 6.3 billion)

Under the Seventh Five Year Plan, India strove to bring about a self-sustained economy in the country with valuable contributions from voluntary agencies and the general populace.

Target Growth: 5.0%   Actual Growth: 5.7%

Eighth Five-Year Plan (1992–1997)

1989 – 91 was a period of economic instability in India and hence no five-year plan was implemented. Between 1990 and 1992, there were only **Annual Plans**. In 1991, India faced a crisis in **Foreign Exchange (Forex) reserves**, left with reserves of only about US $ 1 billion. Thus, under pressure, the country took the risk of reforming the socialist economy. P.V. Narasimha Rao was the twelfth Prime Minister of the Republic of India and head of the Congress Party, and led one of the most important administrations in India's modern history overseeing a major economic transformation and several incidents affecting national security. At that time, Dr. Manmohan Singh launched India's free market reforms that brought the nearly bankrupt nation back from the edge. It was the beginning of privatisation and liberalisation in India.

Modernisation of industries was a major highlight of the Eighth Plan. Under this plan, the gradual opening of the Indian economy was undertaken to correct the burgeoning deficit and foreign debt. Meanwhile, India became a member of the World Trade Organisation on January 1, 1995. This plan can be termed as Rao and Manmohan model of Economic Development. The major objectives included controlling population growth, poverty reduction, employment generation, strengthening the infrastructure, institutional building, tourism management, human resource development, involvement of the Panchayat Raj, Nagar Palikas, NGOs and Decentralisation and people's participation. Energy was given priority with 26.6% of the outlay. An average annual growth rate of 6.78% against the target 5.6% was achieved.

Ninth Five-Year Plan (1997–2002)

The Ninth Five Year Plan of India runs through the period from 1997 to 2002 with the main aim of attaining objectives like speedy industrialisation, human development, full-scale employment, poverty reduction and self-reliance on domestic resources.

The Ninth Five Year Plan was formulated amidst the backdrop of India's Golden Jubilee of Independence.

The main objectives of the Ninth Five Year Plan of India were:
- to prioritise agricultural sector and emphasise on the rural development
- to generate adequate employment opportunities and promote poverty reduction
- to stabilise the prices in order to accelerate the growth rate of the economy
- to ensure food and nutritional security
- to provide for the basic infrastructural facilities like education for all, safe drinking water, primary health care, transport, energy, etc.
- to check the growing population increase
- to encourage social issues like women empowerment, conservation of certain benefits for the Special Groups of the society
- to create a liberal market for increase in private investments

During the Ninth Plan period, the growth rate was 5.35 percent, a percentage point lower than the target GDP growth of 6.5 per cent.

Tenth Five-Year Plan (2002–2007)

The main objectives were:
- To attain 8% GDP growth per year.
- Reduction of poverty ratio by 5 percentage points by 2007.
- Providing gainful and high-quality employment at least to the addition to the labour force.
- Reduction in gender gaps in literacy and wage rates by at least 50% by 2007.
- 20 point program was introduced.
  Target growth: 8.1%   Growth achieved: 7.7%

Eleventh Five-Year Plan (2007–2012)

The Eleventh Plan had the following objectives:
- Income and Poverty: Accelerate GDP growth from 8% to 10% and then maintain at 10% in the 12th Plan in order to double per capita income by 2016–17.
- Increase agricultural GDP growth rate to 4% per year to ensure a broader spread of benefits

- Create 70 million new work opportunities.
- Reduce educated unemployment to below 5%.
- Raise real wage rate of unskilled workers by 20 per cent.
- Reduce the headcount ratio of consumption poverty by 10 percentage points.

Education	• Reduce dropout rates of children from elementary school from 52.2% in 2003–04 to 20% by 2011–12. • Develop minimum standards of educational attainment in elementary school, and by regular testing monitor effectiveness of education to ensure quality. • Increase literacy rate for persons of age 7 years or above to 85%. • Lower gender gap in literacy to 10 percentage point.
Health	Reduce infant mortality rate to 28 and maternal mortality ratio to 1 per 1000 live births.
Reduce Total Fertility Rate to 2.1 percent	• Provide clean drinking water for all by 2009 and ensure that there are no slip-backs. • Reduce malnutrition among children of age group 0–3 to half its present level. • Reduce anaemia among women and girls by 50% by the end of the plan.
Women and Children	• Raise the sex ratio for age group 0 – 6 to 935 by 2011 – 12 and to 950 by 2016–17. • Ensure that at least 33 percent of the direct and indirect beneficiaries of all government schemes are women and girl children. • Ensure that all children enjoy a safe childhood, without any compulsion to work.
Infrastructure	• Ensure electricity connection to all villages and BPL households by 2009 and round-the-clock power. • Ensure all-weather road connection to all habitation with population 1000 and above (500 in hilly and tribal areas) by 2009, and ensure coverage of all significant habitation by 2015. • Connect every village by telephone by November 2007 and provide broadband connectivity to all villages by 2012. • Provide homestead sites to all by 2012 and step up the pace of house construction for rural poor to cover all the poor by 2016–17.

| Environment: | • Increase forest and tree cover by 5 percentage points.
• Attain WHO standards of air quality in all major cities by 2011–12.Treat all urban waste water by 2011–12 to clean river waters. Increase in energy efficiency by 20%.
• Target growth: 8.33% and Growth achieved:7.9%. |

Basically, all the **Indian Five Year Plans** have given primary importance to higher growth of real national income. During the British rule, the Indian economy was stagnant and the people were living in a state of abject poverty. The Britishers exploited the economy both through foreign trade and colonial administration. While the European industries flourished, the Indian economy was caught in a vicious circle of poverty. The pervasive poverty and misery were the most important problem that had to be tackled through the Five Year Plan.

Vision of 12th Five Year Plan (2012-17)

National Development Council has finally approved Draft 12th Five Year Plan in its meeting under the Chairmanship of Prime Minister Dr. Manmohan Singh on December 27, 2012. As per approved Draft 12th Five Year Plan twenty-five core indicators that are listed below reflect the vision of rapid, sustainable and more inclusive growth.

1. Real GDP Growth Rate of 8.0 per cent.

Key Parameters of 12th Five Year Plan	
■ Gross Domestic Savings (as % of GDP at current prices)	33.6%
■ Investment Rate (as % of GDP at current prices)	38.8%
■ Total Consumption Expenditure (as % of GDP at current prices)	69.3%
■ Merchandise Export (as % of GDP at current prices)	16.0%
■ Merchandise Import (as % of GDP at current prices)	25.2%
■ Merchandise Trade Deficit (as % of GDP at current prices)	(–) 9.2%
■ Net Service Export (as % of GDP at current prices)	3.5%
■ Current Account Balance (as % of GDP at current prices)	(–) 3.4%
■ Capital Account Balance (as % of GDP at current prices)	3.9%

Economic Growth

2. Agriculture Growth Rate of 4.0 per cent.
3. Manufacturing Growth Rate of 7.1 per cent.
4. Industrial Sector Growth Rate of 7.6 per cent.
5. Service Sector Growth Rate of 9.0 per cent.
6. Every State must have a higher average growth rate in the Twelfth Plan than that achieved in the Eleventh Plan.

Poverty and Employment

7. Head-count ratio of consumption poverty to be reduced by 10 percentage points over the preceding estimates by the end of Twelfth Five Year Plan.
8. Generate 50 million new work opportunities in the non-farm sector and provide skill certification to equivalent numbers during the Twelfth Five Year Plan.

Education

9. Mean Years of Schooling to increase to seven years by the end of Twelfth Five Year Plan.
10. Enhance access to higher education by creating two million additional seats for each age cohort aligned to the skill needs of the economy.
11. Eliminate gender and Social gap in school enrolment (that is, between girls and boys, and between SCs, STs, Muslims and the rest of the population) by the end of Twelfth Five Year Plan.

Health

12. Reduce IMR to 25 and MMR to 1 per 1000 live births, and improve Child Sex Ratio (0-6 years) to 950 by the end of the Twelfth Five Year Plan.
13. Reduce Total Fertility Rate to 2.1 by the end of Twelfth Five Year Plan.
14. Reduce under-nutrition among children aged 0–5 years to half of the NFHS-3 levels by the end of Twelfth Five Year Plan.

Infrastructure, Including Rural Infrastructure

15. Increase investment in infrastructure as a percentage of GDP to 9 per cent by the end of Twelfth Five Year Plan.
16. Increase the Gross Irrigated Area from 90 million hectare to 103 million hectare by the end of Twelfth Five Year Plan.
17. Provide electricity to all villages and reduce AT&C losses to 20 per cent by the end of Twelfth Five Year Plan.
18. Connect all villages with all-weather roads by the end of Twelfth Five Year Plan.
19. Upgrade national and state highways to the minimum two-lane standard by the end of Twelfth Five Year Plan.
20. Complete Eastern and Western Dedicated Freight Corridors by the end of Twelfth Five Year Plan.
21. Increase rural teledensity to 70 per cent by the end of Twelfth Five Year Plan.
22. Ensure 50 per cent of rural population has access to 55 LPCD piped drinking water supply and 50 per cent of *gram panchayats* achieve the Nirmal Gram Status by the end of Twelfth Five Year Plan.

Environment and Sustainability

23. Increase green cover (as measured by satellite imagery) by 1 million hectare every year during the Twelfth Five Year Plan.
24. Add 30000 MW of renewable energy capacity in the Twelfth Plan.
25. Reduce emission intensity of GDP in line with the target of 20 per cent to 25 per cent reduction by 2020 over 2005 levels.

Service Delivery

26. Provide access to banking services to 90 per cent Indian households by the end of Twelfth Five Year Plan.
27. Major subsidies and welfare related beneficiary payments to be shifted to a direct cash transfer by the end of the Twelfth Plan, using the Aadhar platfo with linked bank accounts.

Sectoral Allocation for Public Sector Resources
Twelfth Plan (2012-17) Projections

S. No.	Heads of Development	Total Outlay Centre		States and Uts		Total Centre, States and Uts	
		Twelfth Plan		Twelfth Plan		Twelfth Plan	
		Amount	% share	Amount	% share	Amount	% share
1.	Agriculture & Allied	134636	3.11	228637	6.85	363273	4.74
2.	Rural Development	267047	6.16	190417	5.71	457464	5.96
3.	Special Area Programme	0	0.00	80370	2.41	80370	1.05
4.	Irrigation & Flood Control	17212	0.40	404800	12.13	422012	5.50
5.	Energy	1085997	25.06	352468	10.57	1438466	18.75
6.	Industry & Minerals	292090	6.74	85212	2.55	377302	4.92
7.	Transport	819482	18.91	384690	11.53	1204172	15.70
8.	Communication	80984	1.87	0	0.00	80984	1.06
9.	Sc. Tecno & Environment	130054	3.00	37296	1.12	167350	2.18
10.	Economic Services	181476	4.19	124136	3.72	305612	3.98
11.	Social Services	1274261	29.40	1390582	41.68	2664843	34.74
12.	General Services	50500	1.17	57459	1.72	107959	1.41
	Total	4333739	100.00	3336068	100.00	7669807	100.00

7. Unemployment

⇨ In common parlance anybody who is not gainfully employed in any productive activity is called unemployed. However, it can be of two kinds (i) voluntary unemployed and (ii) involuntary unemployed. Here we are concerned with the second category of unemployed persons.

- Hence, unemployment can be defined as a situation when persons able and willing to work are seeking jobs at the prevailing wage level but they are unable to get the same.
- Unemployment in developing economies like India is not the result of deficiency of effective demand in the Keynesian sense, but a consequence of shortage of capital equipment or other complementary resources.'
- In India unemployment is structural in nature due to lack of productive capacity and resources.

Types of Unemployment

(i) **Cyclical unemployment:** It is the result of depression in an economy.

(ii) **Frictional unemployment:** This kind of unemployment is temporary. It is the result of a situation when new industries drive out old ones and workers change over to better jobs.

(iii) **Open unemployment :** It refers to those who have no work to do even though they are able and willing to do work.

(iv) **Seasonal unemployment :** This occurs at certain period of the year when work load is comparatively less, and hence people are rendered jobless. For example, in the period between past harvest and next sowing, agricultural labourers are unemployed,

(v) **Educated unemployed :** This is mainly found in urban areas. Those educated persons who are unable to get work come under this category.

(vi) **Under-employment (Disguised unemployment) :** It results when a person contributes to production less than what he or she is capable of, for example, an engineer working as a clerk is under-employed.

(vii) **Compulsory unemployment:** It means the labour power which is ready to work on the current rate but does not get the work.

- During Ninth Plan, total 3.6 crore fresh unemployed began to look for employment.
- The Planning Commission collected data of unemployment on the basis of 'Lakadawala Formula' effective from 11th March, 1997 and prior to this the process to collect data was on the basis of surveys of National Sample Survey Organisation (NASO).
- In 8th Plan, the aim was to create one crore employment. During Ninth Plan the additional requirement of work opportunities was approximately 5 crore 30 lakhs.
- In India, the data relating to unemployment are collected by National Sample Survey Organisation (NASO). This Organisation has the following concepts with regard to unemployment:

1. **General status of unemployment :** In this category, generally, those who are unemployed for more than one year are included. As such it is a long-term unemployment.
2. **Weekly-unemployment :** The persons who have not got work for even one hour in a week are included in this category.
3. **Daily unemployment :** It is considered the best concept of unemployment.

▷ The main reasons for unemployment in India are slow economic development, population explosion, outdated technique, improper education system and limited effect of government planning.

Labour Force Growth and Employment Requirements during Tenth Plan

▷ Job opportunities will need to be created for 53 million persons during 1997-2002 as a consequence of labour force increase, for 58 million during 2002-07 and thereafter for 55 million during 2007-12.

▷ Out of the projected increase of employment of the order of 50 million during the Ninth Plan, 24.2 million employment opportunities – 48.2% would be created in agriculture alone.

Employment Requirements during the 11th Plan (2007-12)

▷ On account of the increasing participation of females, the total increase in labour force will be around 65 million during the 11 Plan. To this may be added the present backlog of about 35 million. Thus, the total job requirements of the 11th Plan work out be 100 million.

▷ The planners aims to provide 65 million additional employment opportunities.

▷ According to the Approach paper of the 11th plan:
- Average daily status unemployment rate, which had increased from 6.1% in 1993-94 to 7.3% in 1999-00 increased further to 8.3% in 2004-05.
- Among agricultural labour households, which represent the poorest groups, there was a sharp increase in unemployment from 9.3% in 1993-94 to a high level of 15.3% in 2004-05.
- Non-agricultural employment expanded robustly at an annual rate of 4.7% during 1999-2005.
- Employment in the organized sector actually declined by 0.38% per annum during 1994-2000.

Unemployment Rates between 1993-94 and 2004-05

▷ The results of the 61st Round of NSSO survey, Employment and Unemployment are based on a sample size which is neither large nor small by standards of previous NSSO rounds.

- The unemployment rates based on current daily status in 2004-05 for males was 8.0% (up from 7.2% in 1993-94) in rural areas and at 7.5% percent (up from 7.3% in 1993-94) in urban areas.
- The corresponding figure for females was 8.7% (up from 7.0% in 1993-94) in rural areas and 11.6% (up from 9.4% in 1993-94) in urban areas.

Employment Opportunities
- Instead of achieving an employment elasticity of 0.38 as projected in the Ninth Plan, the actual employment elasticity achieved during 1993-94 to 1999-2000 was 0.15.
- The employment projections reveal that with 6.5% GDP growth, employment will increase from a level of 397 million in 1999-2000 to 468 million in 2012 – an increase of 71 million in a period of 12 years, giving an annual average growth of 5.9 million.

Development and employment programmes at a glance

S. No.	Programme/Plan/ Institution	Year of beginning	Objective/Description
1.	Community Development Programme (CDP)	1952	Over all development of rural area with people's participation.
2.	Intensive Agriculture Development Programme (IADP)	1960-61	To provide loan, seeds, fertilizer tools to the farmers.
3.	Intensive Agriculture Area Programme (IAAP)	1964-65	To develop the Special harvests.
4.	High Yielding Variety Programme (HYVP)	1966-67	To increase productivity of food grains by adopting latest varieties of inputs for crops.
5.	Indian Tourism Development Corporation (ITDC)	Oct. 1966	To arrange for the construction of Hotels and Guest houses at various places of the country.
6.	Green Revolution	1966-67	To increase the foodgrains, specially wheat production (Credit goes to Dr. M.S. Swaminathan in India and Nobel laureate Dr. Norman Borlaug in the world).
7.	Nationalisation of 14 Banks	19 July 1969	To provide loans for agriculture, rural development and other priority sectors.
8.	Employment Guarantee Scheme of Maharashtra	1972-73	To assist the economically weaker sections of the rural society.

9.	Accelerated Rural Water Supply Programme (ARWSP)	1972-73	For providing drinking water in the villages.
10.	Small Farmer Development Agency (SFDA)	1974-75	For technical and financial assistance to small farmers.
11.	Command Area Development Programme (CADP)	1974-75	To ensure better and rapid utilisation of irrigation capacities of medium and large projects.
12.	Twenty Point Programme (TPP)	1975	Poverty eradication and raising the standard of living.
13.	National Institution of Rural Development (NIRD)	1977	Training, investigation and advisory organisation for rural development.
14.	Desert Development Programme (DDP)	1977-78	For controlling the desert expasion and maintaining environmental balance.
15.	Food for Work Programme (FWP)	1977-78	Providing foodgrains to labour for the works of development.
16.	Antyodaya Yojana	1977-78	To make the poorest families of the village economically independent (only in Rajasthan State).
17.	Training Rural Youth for Self-Employment (TRYSEM)	August 15, 1979	Programme of training rural youth for self-employment.
18.	Intergrated Rural Development Programme (IRDP)	October 2, 1980	All-round development of the rural poor through a programme of asset endowment for self-employment.
19.	National Rural Employment Programme (NREP)	1980	To provide profitable employment opportunities to the rural poor.
20.	Development of Women and Children in Rural Areas (DWCRA)	Sept. 1982	To provide suitable opportunities of self-employment to the women belonging to the rural families who are living below the poverty line.
21.	Rural Landless Employment Guarantee Programme (RLEGP)	August 15, 1993	For providing employment to landless farmers and labourers.

22.	Self-Employment to the Educated Unemployed Youth (SEEUY)	1983-84	To provide financial and technical assistance for self-employment.
23.	Farmer Agriculture Service Centre's (FASC's)	1983-84	To popularise the use of improved agricultural instruments and tool kits
24.	National Fund for Rural Development (NFRD)	February 1984	To grant 100% tax rebate to donors and also to provide financial assistance for rural development projects.
25.	Industrial Reconstruction Bank of India	March 1985	To provide financial assistance to sick and closed industrial units for their reconstruction.
26.	Comprehensive Crop Insurance Scheme	April 1, 1985	For insurance of agricultural crops.
27.	Council for Advancement of People's Actionand Rural Technology (CAPART) (H.Q.- New Delhi)	Sep.1, 1986	To provide assistance for rural Prosperity
28.	Self-Employment Programme for the Urban Poor (SEPUP)	Sep. 1986	To provide self-employment to urban poor through provision of subsidy and bank credit.
29.	Formation of Securities and Exchange Board of India (SEBI)	April 1988	To safeguard the interest of investors in capital market and to regulate share market.
30.	Jawahar Rozgar Yojana	April 1, 1989	For providing employment to rural unemployed.
31.	Nehru Rozgar Yojana	October 1989	For providing employment to urban unemployed.
32.	Agriculture and Rural Debt Relief Scheme (ARDRS)	1990	To exempt bank loans upto Rs.10,000 of rural artisans and weavers.
33.	Scheme of Urban Micro Enterprises (SUME)	1990	To assist the urban poor people for small enterprise.
34.	Scheme of Urban Wage Employment (SUWE)	1990	To provide wages employment after arranging the basic facilities for poor people in the urban areas where population is less than one lakh.

35.	Scheme of Housing and Shelter Upgradation (SHASU)	1990	To provide employment by means of shelter upgradation in the urban areas where population is between 1 to 20 lakh.
36.	Supply of Improved Toolkits to Rural Artisans	July 1992	To supply modern toolkits to the rural craftsmen except the weavers, tailors, embroiders and tobacco labourers who are living below the poverty line.
37.	Employment Assurance Scheme (EAS)	October 2, 1993	To provide employment of at least 100 days in a year in villages.
38.	Members of Parliament Local Area Development Scheme (MPLADS)	December 23, 1993	To sanction Rs. 5 crore per year to every Member of Parliament for various development works in their respective areas through DM of the district.
39.	District Rural Development Agency (DRDA)	1993	To provide financial assistance for rural development.
40.	Mahila Samridhi Yojana	October 2, 1993	To encourage the rural women to deposit in Post Office Savings Account.
41.	Child Labour Eradication Scheme	August 15, 1994	To shift child labour from hazardous industries to schools.
42.	Prime Minister's Integrated Urban Poverty Eradication Programme (PMIUPEP)	November 18, 1995	To attack urban poverty in an integrated manner in 345 towns having population between 50,000 to 1 lakh.
43.	Group Life Insurance Scheme in Rural Areas	1995-96	To provide insurance facilities to rural people on low premium
44.	National Social Assistance Programme	1995	To assist people living below the poverty line.
45.	Ganga Kalyan Yojana	1997-98	To provide financial assistance to farmers for exploring and developing ground and surface water resources.

46.	Kasturba Gandhi Education Scheme	August 15, 1997	To establish girls' schools in districts having low female literacy rate.
47.	Swarna Jayanti Shahari Rozgar Yojana (SJSRY)	December, 1997	To provide gainful employment to urban unemployed and under employed poor through self employment or wage employment.
48.	Bhagya Shree Bal Kalyan Policy	Oct. 19, 1998	To uplift the girls conditions.
49.	Rajrajeshwari Mahila Kalyan Yojana (RMKY)	Oct. 19, 1998	To provide insurance protection to women.
50.	Annapurna Yojana	March 1999	To provide 10 kg. foodgrains to senior citizens (who do not get pension).
51.	Swarna Jayanti Gram Swarozgar Yojana (SJGSY)	April 1999	For eliminating rural poverty and unemployment and promoting self employment.
52.	Jawahar Gram Samridhi Yojana (JGSY)	April 1999	Creation of demand driven community village infrastructure.
53.	Jan Shree Bima Yojana	Aug. 10, 2000	Providing Insurance Security to people living below the poverty line.
54.	Pradhan Mantri Gramodaya Yojana	2000	To fulfill basic requirements in rural areas.
55.	Antyodaya Anna Yojana	Dec. 25, 2000	To provide food security to the poor.
56.	Ashraya Bima Yojana	June 2001	To provide compensation to labourers who have lost their employment.
57.	Pradhan Mantri Gram Sadak Yojana (PMGSY)	Dec. 25, 2000	To line all villages with *Pucca* Road.
58.	Khetihar Mazdoor Bima Yojana	2001-2002	Insurance of Landless Agricultural workers.
59.	Shiksha Sahyog Yojana	2001-2002	Education for Children below Poverty Line.
60.	Sampurna Gramin Rojgar Yojana	Sept. 25, 2001	Providing employment and food security to rural people.

61.	Jai Prakash Narain Rojgar Guarantee Yojana	Proposed in 2002-03 Budget	Employment Guarantee in most poor districts.
62.	Swajaldhara Yojana	2002	Started in Dec. 2002, for ensuring drinking water supply to all villages by 2004.
63.	Hariyali Pariyojana	2003	Inaugurated on January 27, 2003 by the Prime Minister. It aims at tackling the problems of irrigation and drinking water, along with boosting tree plantation programme and fisheries developments in rural areas.
64.	Social Security Pilot Scheme	Jan. 23, 2004	Scheme for labourers of unorganised sector for providing family pension, insurance and medical.
65.	Vande Matram Scheme	Feb. 9, 2004	Major initiative in public-private partnership during pregnancy check-up.
66.	National Food for Work Programme	November 14, 2004	Inaugurated by the Prime Minister on November 14, 2004. This programme is to be implemented initially in 150 districts of the country. It aims at providing 100 days' employment in a year to all able bodied unemployed rural folk.
67.	Janani Suraksha Yojana	April 12, 2005	Takes the place of National Maternity Benefit Scheme. It will be a part of the National Rural Health Mission (NRHM).
68.	Bharat Nirman Yojana	Dec. 16, 2005	Development of Rural infrastructure including six components: Irrigation, Water supply, Housing, Road, Telephone and Eelectricity.

69.	National Rural Employment Guarantee Programme (NREGP)	Feb. 2, 2006	The provisions are the 'same as for food for work programme. The scheme was enforced in 200 districts of the country to begin with. To provide atleast 100 days wages employment in rural areas in a year. The scheme is 100% centrally sponsored.

Bharat Nirman Yojana

▷ The Union Government launched a new comprehensive scheme, named 'Bharat Nirman Yojana' on December 16, 2005.
▷ This scheme aims at developing rural infrastructure.
▷ The duration of implementing this scheme has been fixed for four years with an expected expenditure of Rs. 174000 crore.
▷ The major six sectors and their targets for next four years are :
- **Irrigation :** To ensure irrigation for additional one crore hectare of land by 2009.
- **Roads :** To link all villages of 1000 population with main roads and also to link all ST and hilly villages upto 500 population with roads.
- **Housing :** Construction of 60 lakh additional houses for the poor.
- **Water supply :** To ensure drinking water to all remaining 74000 villages.
- **Electrification :** To supply electricity to all remaining 1,25,000 villages and to provide electricity connections to 2.3 crore houses.
- **Rural Communication :** Toprovide telephone facility to all remaining 66,822 villages.

Mahatma Gandhi National Rural Employment Guarantee Act (MNREGA)

▷ The National Rural Employment Guarantee Bill was passed by Parliament on September 7, 2005. It secured Presidential assent later in 2005 itself and became an Act.
▷ The Act provides for at least 100 days of employment to one able bodied person in every rural household every year.
▷ The wages admissible are around Rs. 120 per day.
▷ The Act (NREGA) came into force from Feb. 2, 2006. Initially 200 districts have been selected for the enforcement of the scheme.
▷ Works under the NREGA generated 90 crore (nearly one billion) person 10 days of employment in 2006-07, at a cost of about Rs. 9,000 crore.
▷ The Government has extended the NREGA to all 604 districts of the country, with a total budget outlay of Rs. 16,000 crore for the extended scheme for 2008-09 (April 1, 2008).

Note: *The Govt. of India, October 2, 2009 renamed the NREGA as the Mahatma Gandhi National Rural Employment Guarantee Act (MNREGA).*

Employment guarantee act, 2005

The Government, on the advice of the National Advisory Council, has passed the National Rural Employment Guarantee Act. The main features of the Act are :

1. Every household in rural India will have a right to at least 100 days of guaranteed employment every year for at least one adult member. The employment will be in the form of casual manual labour at the statutory minimum wage, and the wages shall be paid within 7 days of the week during which work was done.
2. Work should be provided within 15 days of demanding it, and the work should be located within 5 kilometer distance.
3. If work is not provided to anybody within the given time, he/she will be paid a daily unemployment allowance, which will be at least one third of the minimum wages.
4. Workers employed on public works will be entitled to medical treatment and hospitalization in case of injury at work, alongwith a daily allowance of not less than half of the statutory minimum wage. In case of death or disability of a worker, an ex-gratia payment shall be made to his legal heirs as per provisions of the Workmen Compensation Act.
5. 5% of wages may be deducted as contribution to welfare schemes like health insurance, accident insurance, survivor benefits, maternity benefits and social security schemes.
6. For non-compliance with rules, strict penalties have been laid down.
7. For transparency and accountability, all accounts and records of the programme will be made available for public scrutiny.
8. The District Collector/Chief Executive Officer will be responsible for the programme at the district level.
9. The Gram Sabha will monitor the work of the Gram Panchayat by way of social audit.

Some Development and Employment Programmes

⇨ During the Seventh Five-Year Plan, a scheme called 'Jawahar Rozgar Yojana' was introduced from April 1989 to solve the problem of unemployment in the rural sector. The former ongoing two main rural employment programmes — National Rural Employment Programme (NREP) and Rural Landless Employment Guarantee Programme (RLEGP) were merged with Jawahar Rozgar Yojana.

- The total expenditure on Jawahar Rozgar Yojna was shared by the Centre and the State Government in the ratio of 80 : 20.
- Under the Jawahar Rozgar Yojana, 30% employment opportunities was reserved for women.
- Under the Jawahar Rozgar Yojana, it was made compulsory to spend 60% of the total expenditure on labour used in the works completed under the scheme.
- A sub-plan of Jawahar Rozgar Yojana – 'Indira Awas Yojana' was made an independent scheme in itself on January 1, 1996.
- The Employment Assurance Scheme (EAS), was introduced on October 2, 1993, in selective rural areas. The aim of this scheme is to provide work in the form of unskilled physical labour to all the employment seeking men and women (of ages between 18 years to 60 years) in rural areas. The expenditure on this scheme is shared by the Centre and the States in the ratio of 80:20. From maximum of 2 members from one family can be benefitted under this scheme. Since January 1, 1996, the Integrated Jawahar Rozgar Yojana (IJRY) has been merged with Employment Assurance Scheme (EAS).
- The Integrated Rural Development Programme (IRDP) was started on an experimental basis in 1978-79. This programme was launched in the whole country on October 2, 1980. The basic aim of IRDP was to provide assistance to rural poor families living below the poverty line.
- The Integrated Rural Development Programme is financially assisted by the Centre and States in the ratio of 50 : 50.
- Under the Integrated Rural Development Programme, targeted group includes atleast 50% families belonging to scheduled caste and scheduled tribe. Apart from this, among the beneficiaries, 50% were females and 3% physically handicapped persons.
- *Development of Women and Children in Rural Areas* (DWCRA) and *Training Rural Youth for Self-Employment* (TRYSEM) were the sub plans of Integrated Rural Development Programme (IRDP).
- The objective of TRYSEM was to provide training to those rural youth (age 18-35 years) who belong to the families living below the poverty line. This programme was started on August 15, 1979.

Development of Women and Children in Rural Area Programme (DWCRA) was started in September 1982. Under this programme, a group of 10-15 women was taken, who belong to the families living below the poverty line and they were given training for starting any economic activity. Every group was given the economic assistance of Rs. 25,000.

Swarn Jayanti Shahari Rozgar Yojana (SJSRY)
- The Urban Self-employment Programme and Urban Wage-Employment

Programmes of the Swaran Jayanti Shahari Yojana, which substituted (in December 1997) various programmes operated earlier for poverty alleviation.

- SJSRY is funded on 75:25 basis between the Centre and the States.
- During the 3-year period (1997-98 and 1999-2000), a total of Rs. 353 crores were spent on SJSRY generating 21.8 million mandays of employment.

Swarnajayanti Gram Swarozgar Yojana (SGSY): The Government has introduced Swarna Jayanti Gram Swarozgar Yojana on April 1, 1999 and the previous six ongoing schemes have been merged with this scheme, they are: 1. IRDP 2. TRYSEM 3. DWCRA 4. MWS 5. SITRA 6. Ganga Kalyan Yojana. The SGSY is a holistic programme covering all the aspects of self employment. The scheme is funded on 75 : 25 basis by the centre and states.

- The *Drought-prone Area Programme* was started in 1973 with the objective of developing the drought-prone area and also re-establishing the environmental balance. This programme is financially assisted by the Centre and the concerned State Governments in the ratio of 50 : 50.
- The *Desert Development Programme* was started in 1977-78 to end the ill-effects of drought in desert areas and also to stop the process of desert expansion. This programme is implemented on the basis of cent-per cent financial assistance rendered by the Central Government.
- The Rural Landless Employment Guarantee Programme (RLEGP) began on August 15, 1993 and National Rural Employment Programme (NREP) on October 2, 1980. During Seventh Five-Year Plan, these programmes were merged with Jawahar Rozgar Yojana.
- *Council for Advancement of Peoples Action and Rural Technology* (CAPART) is an independent section of the Rural Development Department of the Government of India; which was established on September 1, 1986. For rural development works, 'CAPART' provides grants to voluntary organisations. The head office of CAPART is at New Delhi.
- Following programmes are being implemented by the Ministry of the Urban Development to eradicate Urban Poverty – (i) Nehru Rozgar Yojana (ii) Urban Basic Services for the Poor (iii) Programme of Environment Improvement of Urban Slums.
- The Nehru Rozgar Yojana began on October 1989 which was revised in March 1990. Under this Yojana following schemes were included: (i) Scheme of Urban Micro Enterprises-SOME (ii) Scheme of Urban Wage Employment – SUWE (iii) Scheme of Housing and Shelter Upgradation – SHASU.
- The *Prime Minister's Rozgar Yojana* (PMRY) was started on October 2, 1993 for the educated unemployed youth and initially was in operation in urban areas. From April 1, 1994 onwards the scheme is being implemented throughout the country. Its objective was to give employment

to 10 lakhs educated unemployed urban youth by establishing 7 lakh micro enterprises during the Eighth Five Year Plan. During 1993-94, this yojana was implemented in urban areas only but since April 1, 1994 it was extended to the whole country.

- SHGs (Self-Help Groups) are considered eligible for financing under the PMRY, effective from December 8, 2003 (terms modified on July 30, 2004) provided all members individually satisfy the eligibility criteria laid down and total membership does not exceed twenty (20). There is also a ceiling on the loan amount.

PM Launched 3 Social Security Schemes

After providing bank accounts to 15 crore unbanked people under Jan Dhan Yojana, Prime Minister Mr. Narendra Modi has launched three social security schemes, including a Re. 1 per day insurance cover.

The schemes — Pradhan Mantri Jeevan Jyoti BimaYojana (PMJJBY), Pradhan Mantri Suraksha Bima Yojana (PMSBY) and Atal Pension Yojana (APY) — were simultaneously launched at 115 locations throughout the country.

PMSBY will offer a renewable one year accidental death-cum-disability cover of ₹ 2 lakh for partial/permanent disability to all savings bank account holders in the age group of 18-70 years for a premium of ₹ 12 per annum per subscriber.

PMJJBY, on the other hand, will offer a renewable one year life cover of ₹ 2 lakh to all savings bank account holders in the age group of 18-50 years, covering death due to any reason, for a premium of ₹ 330 per annum per subscriber.

Atal Pension Yojana will focus on the unorganised sector and provide subscribers a fixed minimum pension of ₹ 1000, R 2000, ₹ 3,000, ₹ 4000 or ₹ 5000 per month, starting at the age of 60 years, depending on the contribution option exercised on entering at an age between 18 and 40 years.

Pradhan Mantri Kaushal Vikas Yojana

The Cabinet on March 21, 2015 cleared a scheme to provide skill training to 1.4 million youth, with an Overall outlay of 1,120 crore. The Pradhan Mantri Kaushal Vikas Yojana, to be implemented by the new Ministry of Skill Development and Entrepreneurship through the National Skill Development Corporation, will focus on fresh entrants to the labour market, especially Class X and Class XII dropouts.

The target for skilling would be aligned to demands from other flagship programmes launched in recent times such as Make in India, Digital India, National Solar Mission and Swachh Bharat Abhiyan.

Training under this scheme will include soft skills, personal grooming, behavioural change for cleanliness, good work ethics, etc. Sector Skill Councils and the State Governments would closely monitor skill training that will happen under PMKVY.

Under the scheme, a monetary reward of about ₹ 8,000 will be given to trainees upon certification by third-party assessment bodies.

Skill training would be done on the basis of demand assessed by the NSDC for the period 2013-17. For assessment of demand of Central Ministries/Departments/State Governments, industry and business would be consulted.

ROSHNI : Skill Development Scheme for Tribals

Ministry of Rural Development, GoI, launched on June 7, 2013 a new 'Skill Development Scheme' aimed at providing employment to Tribal youth in 24 Naxal affected districts. The scheme called "Roshni" will provide training and employment to an estimated 50,000 youth in the 10-35 years age group, over a period of 3 years. 50% of the beneficiaries of the scheme will be women. The scheme will follow the 'Himayat' project model, which was launched in Jammu and Kashmir, and has been implemented in Sukma (Chhattisgarh) and West Singhbhum (Jharkhand) on a pilot basis over the last 18 months.

₹ 100 crore project will be jointly funded by the Union and State Governments, with the centre providing 75% of the funding. Further, the scheme will be implemented on a Public Private basis, with private agencies providing job training and employment.

Free LPG Connections to BPL Rural Households

A proposal for providing one-time financial assistance to BPL households for acquiring new LPG connections is under consideration of the Government. Under the proposed scheme, the Government and Oil Marketing Companies would provide one-time assistance of ₹ 1400 for acquiring a new LPG connection to a BPL family. The scheme would cover all eligible house-hold in the BPL list of the State Government/Union Territory. About 32—40 lakh new LPG connections are to be released annually under this scheme.

The annual financial implication of the scheme is estimated to be ₹ 490 crore. The proposed budgetary support has been restricted to the extent of 50 per cent of the total funds required. The remaining 50 per cent would be partly drawn from the Corporate Social Responsibility Funds (CSRFs) of the six major oil companies, namely ONGC, IOCL, BPCL, HPCL, OIL, and GAIL and partly borne by the three oil marketing companies (OMCs) namely IOCL, HPCL, and BPCL in the ratio of LPG connections released to BPL households by each company. It is expected that the OMCs will incur ₹ 6.00 crore during the current financial year.

₹ 1 Lakh Crore to be Disbursed Under MUDRA for Micro-Entrepreneurs

To promote very small businesses, the Centre aims to facilitate credit up to ₹ 1 lakh crore under the MUDRA scheme in the 2015-16. It was proposed that for 2015-16, the target under 'Shishu' category would be 40,000 crore, for 'Kishor' ₹ 35,000 crore, and 'Tarun' ₹ 25,000 crore. The Centre has already made it clear that it would facilitate more credit to the first category as it promotes not only self entrepreneurship but also more employment opportunities.

The whole concept is promoting entrepreneurship at micro level through funding the un-funded. MUDRA (Micro Units Development and Refinance Agency Ltd) was launched by the Prime Minister on April 8, 2015.

Funding Small Businesses (₹ crore)				
Catagories	Loan amount disbursed in 2014-15*	% share in total amount	Target for loan amount in 2015-16	% share in total amount
Shishu	4,075	6.57	40,000	40
Kishor	32,877	52.91	35,000	35
Tarun	25,105	40.52	25,000	25
Total	62,057	100	1,00,000	100

* Classification based on loan size

Under the new scheme, there are three categories of loans — 'Shishu' (loan up to ₹ 50,000) 'Kishor' (loan above ₹ 50,000 up to ₹ 5 lakh) and 'Tarun' (above ₹ 5 lakh up to ₹ 10 lakh) — that will be disbursed by the banks. The amount will be refinanced through the new scheme which is being implemented by a subsidiary of SIDBI.

The MUDRA concept is based on National Sample Survey Organisation's (NSSO) 2013 study which talked about 5.77 crore informal enterprises. They are unincorporated, single person or two person enterprises. They get just 4 per cent of their credit requirements from the institutional mechanism, while 96 per cent comes from informal sources even while they give employment to about 12 crore people.

8. Trade and Commerce

- Indian Trade was extremely developed during ancient time.
- After the British East India Company was established in 1600, the trade between India and Britain was in India's favour till 1757.
- At that time East India Company used to purchase clothes and spices in exchange for costly metals.
- The British Government decided to impose heavy Duty on the clothes to destroy the structure of Industries.

- During the later part of 18th Century, after Industrial revolution in Britain there was heavy production of cheap items. To sell those cheap items in world market, the tradition of colonisation began.
- British Companies established monopoly on the sale of cotton. As a result, the Indian weaver got costly raw material and thus Indian products became costly. By 1813, Indian Handloom business was completely ruined.
- In the later part of 19th Century, the establishment of modern industries on the basis of power machines started. First time in India, the textile industries came into being.
- *First Factory of Cotton Textile* in India was established in 1818 at Ghughari near Kolkata, which failed.
- The Second Factory of Cotton Textile was established by a businessman Kawas Ji Nana Bhai in Mumbai in 1853.
- In 1855, first Jute Factory was established in Rishara (West Bengal).
- In 1853, after the establishment of railway in India, industrial development got momentum here. Rapid expansion of Indian industries started due to development of the means of communication.
- Jamshedji Tata established first Steel Factory in Jamshedpur in 1907.

9. New Economic Policy

- New Economic Policy is related to economic reforms. Its aim is to bring about reforms in production pattern, to obtain new technology and to use full capacity expeditiously and in toto.
- The New Economic Policy was devised and implemented, for the first time in the year 1985 during the period of Prime Minister Rajiv Gandhi.
- The second wave of new economic reforms came in the year 1991 during the period of the P.V. Narsirnha Rao government.
- The main reason to start new economic policy (1991) was Gulf-War and problem of balance of payment in India.
- Three main objectives of new economic policy were – Liberalisation Privatisation, and Globalisation.
- Main sectors of new economic reform policy, 1991 were – Fiscal Policy, Monetary Policy, Value Fixation Policy, Foreign Policy, Industrial Policy, Foreign Investment Policy, Business Policy and Public Sector Policy.
- The following four main steps were taken under the Fiscal Policy, 1991:
    (i) To control public expenditure strictly
    (ii) To expand Tax Net
    (iii) To observe discipline in management of funds of Central and State governments.
    (iv) To curtail grants (subsidy)

- Under the Monetary Policy, steps were taken to control inflation.
- Measures implemented under the Industrial Reforms Policy, 1991 were :
  (i) Delicencing of industries except the list of 18 industries.
  (ii) M.R.T.P. norms were relaxed for disinvestment.
  (iii) The areas reserved for public sector were opened to private sector.
- The objectives fixed for reforms in the Foreign Investment Policy, 1991 were:
  (i) Direct foreign investment upto 50% was given automatic approval, in many industries.
  (ii) Foreign companies, involved in export activities were allowed to invest upto 51% capital.
  (iii) The government gave automatic approval for Technology Agreement in the industries of high priorities.
- Under the Trade Policy 1991, steps were taken to abolish the excessive protection given to many industries, for the promotion of international integration of economy.
- The measures implemented to bring efficiency and market discipline under the Public Sector Policy 1991 were as under:
  (i) Number of reserved industries decreased to 8. Presently these are only four.
  (ii) The work of rehabilitation of sick industries handed over to Board of Industrial Financial Reconstruction.
  (iii) Industries were made powerful with the help of Memorandam of Understandings (MoU).
  (iv) Voluntary Retirement Schemes started to cut down the size of work force.

Economic Reforms

- Economic Reforms were introduced in 1991 in India. First Generation Reforms were aimed at stabilisation of Indian economy and were macro level in nature. It includes liberalisation and deregulation of industry, financial sector reforms, taxation reforms etc. Second Generation Reforms aimed at structural changes and are micro level in nature. It will include labour reforms, land reforms, capital market reforms, expenditure reforms and power sector reforms etc.
- Since economic reform, poverty has been declining from 36% in 1993 to 26% by the end of 10th plan. But as far as inequality is concerned it has increased. A World Bank Report 1999-2000 confirms this rise in inequality.
- The New Economic Reforms Policy, by making progress from 1991 to 2005-06 has become more open, liberal and global.

- Disinvestment means to decrease the share of government in the industries.
- In 1996, Disinvestment Commission was constituted to review, give suggestions and make regulations on the issue of disinvestment.
- Shri G.V. Ramkrishna was the first Chairman of Disinvestment Commission.
- In the year 1992, National Renewal Fund was constituted for rehabilitation of displaced labourers of sick industrial units affected due to industrial modernization, technological development etc.
- "Navratna" is a company which is rising at world level. To encourage these companies, the government has given them complete autonomy.
- In the second phase of economic reforms programme, the main aim is to eradicate poverty from the country and development at the rate of 7 to 8%.

Terminology Related to the New Economic Reforms Policy
- **Privatisation :** To increase participation of private sector in the public sector companies by capital investment or by management or both or to hand over a public sector unit to a private company is called Privatisation.
- **Liberalisation :** Liberalisation is the process by which government control is relaxed or abolished. In this process privatisation is also included.
- **Globalisation :** The process of amalgamation of an economy with world economy is called Globalisation. It is signified by lower duties on import and export. By doing so, that sector will also get private capital and foreign technology.
- **Disinvestment :** To reduce the government share in the public sector is called disinvestment.

10. The Policy of Liberalisation

In the early **1990s**, the then **Prime Minister, Narasimha Rao** and his government embarked on a policy of liberalisation, licensing a small number of private banks. These came to be known as New Generation tech-savvy banks, and included Global Trust Bank (the first of such new generation banks to be set up), which later amalgamated with Oriental Bank of Commerce, UTI Bank (since renamed Axis Bank), ICICI Bank and HDFC Bank. This move, along with the rapid growth in the economy of India, revitalized the banking sector in India, which has seen rapid growth with strong contribution from all the three sectors of banks, namely, government banks, private banks and foreign banks.

The next stage for the Indian banking has been set up with the proposed relaxation in the norms for Foreign Direct Investment, where all Foreign Investors in banks may be given voting rights which could exceed the present cap of 10%, at present it has gone up to 74% with some restrictions.

The new policy shook the Banking sector in India completely. Bankers, till this time, were used to the 4-6-4 method (Borrow at 4%; Lend at 6%; Go home at 4%) of functioning. The new wave ushered in a modern outlook and tech-savvy methods of working for traditional banks.All this led to the retail boom in India. People not just demanded more from their banks but also received more.

Currently, Banking in India is generally fairly mature in terms of supply, product range and reach — even though reach in rural India still remains a challenge for the private sector and foreign banks. In terms of quality of assets and capital adequacy, Indian banks are considered to have clean, strong and transparent balance sheets relative to other banks in comparable economies in its region. The Reserve Bank of India is an autonomous body, with minimal pressure from the government. The stated policy of the Bank on the Indian Rupee is to manage volatility but without any fixed exchange rate and this has mostly been true.

In March 2006, the Reserve Bank of India allowed Warburg Pincus to increase its stake in Kotak Mahindra Bank (a private sector bank) to 10%. This is the first time an investor has been allowed to hold more than 5% in a private sector bank since the RBI announced norms in 2005 that any stake exceeding 5% in the private sector banks would need to be vetted by them.

11. Indian Financial System

- Indian Financial System is a system in which People, Financial Institutions, Banks, Industrial Companies and the Government demand for fund and the same is supplied to them.
- There are two parts of Indian Financial System – first demand side and second supply side. The representative of demand side can be Individual investor, Industrial and Business Companies, Government etc. and the representative of supply side will be Banks, Insurance Companies, Mutual Fund and other Financial Institutions.
- The Indian financial system, which refers to the borrowing and lending of funds or to the demand for and supply of funds of all individuals, institutions, companies and of the Government consists of two parts, viz., the Indian money market and the Indian capital market.
- The Indian *money market* is the market in which short-term funds are borrowed and lent. The capital market in India, on the other hand, is the market for medium-term and long-term funds.
- The Indian financial system performs a crucial role in economic

development of India through saving-investment process, also known as capital formation.
- The financial system is, commonly, classified into: (a) Industrial finance, (b) Agricultural finance, (c) Development finance and (d) Government finance.
- *Devaluation* means lowering' the official value of the local money in terms of foreign currency or gold.
- *Balance of Payments* (BOP) is a systematic record of all the economic transactions between one country and the rest of the world in a given period.
- *Balance of Trade* (BOT) is the difference between the value of goods exported and the value of goods imported per annum. Services not included in BOT.
- BOP is divided in current account and capital account.
- EXIM Policy 2000-01 introduced Special Economic Zones Scheme (SEZ).
- 1994-95, Indian Rupee was made fully convertible on current account. Fiscal Policy is the policy relating to public revenue and public expenditure and allied matters'.
- Usually, the Indian money market is classified into organised sector and the unorganised sector.
- The unorganised sector consists of indigenous bankers including the non-banking financial companies (NBFCs). Besides, these two, there are many sub-markets in the Indian money market.
- The organised banking system in India can broadly be divided into three categories, viz., the central bank of the country known as the Reserve Bank of India, the commercial banks and the co-operative banks which includes private sector and public sector banks and also foreign banks.
- The highest financial institution in organized sector is Reserve Bank of India and in addition to this the Banks of Public Sector, Banks of Private Sector, Foreign Banks and other financial institutions are also part of organized sector.
- The Reserve Bank of India regulates and controls the money of the country.
- The RBI was established under the Reserve Bank of India Act, 1934 on 1st April, 1935 with a capital of Rs. 5 crore. It was nationalised on 1st January, 1949; on the recommendation of Parliamentary Committee in 1948. It is the Central Bank of India.
- The Reserve Bank of India is the supreme monetary and banking authority in the country and has the responsibility to control the banking system in the country. It keeps the reserves of all commerical banks and hence is known as the "Reserve Bank". Its financial year is 1st July to 30th June.

The Indian Capital Market
- The Indian capital market is the market for long-term capital; it refers to all the facilities and institutional arrangements for borrowing and lending "term funds" — medium term and long term funds.
- The Capital Market in India includes : (i) Government Securities (Gilt-edged market) (ii) Industrial Securities Market (iii) Development financial institutions like IFCI, IDBI, ICICI, SFCs, IIBI, UTI etc. (iv) Financial Intermediaries like Merchant banks.
- Individuals who invest directly on their own in securities are also supplier of fund to capital market. The trend in the capital market is basically affected by two important factors : (i) operations of the institutional investors in the market and (ii) the excellent results flowing in from the corporate sector.
- The capital market in India can be classified into :
  - Gilt-edged market or market for Government and semi-government securities;
  - Industrial securities market;
  - Development financial institutions; and
  - Non-banking financial companies.
- The gilt-edged securities market is the market for Government and semi government securities which carry fixed interest rates.
- The industrial securities market is the market for equities and debentures of companies of the corporate sector. This market is further classified into —
  (a) new issue markets for raising fresh capital in the form of shares and debentures, (commonly referred to as *primary market*) and
  (b) old issues market (or secondary market) for buying or selling shares and debentures of existing companies — this market is commonly referred to as the stock market or stock exchange.
- If shares or debentures of private corporations, primary sureties of government companies or new sureties and issue of bonds of public sector are sold or purchased in the capital market, then the market is called *Primary Capital Market*.
- *Secondary Market* includes transactions in the stock exchange and gilt-edged market.
- Merchant Bank, Mutual Fund, Leasing Companies, Risk Capital Companies etc. collect and invest public money into the capital market.
- Unit Trust of India (UTI) is the biggest Mutual Fund Institution of India.

Stock Exchange
- The stock exchange is the market for buying and selling of stocks, shares, securities, bonds and debentures etc. It increases the market ability of

existing securities by providing simple method for public and others to buy and sell securities.
- The first organised stock exchange in India was started in Bombay (now Mumbai) when the "Native Share Brokers' Association" known as the Bombay Stock Exchange (BSE) was formed by the brokers in Bombay. BSE was Asia's oldest stock exchange.
- In 1894, the Ahmedabad stock Exchange was started to facilitate dealings in the shares of textile mills there.
- The Calcutta Stock Exchange was started in 1908 to provide a market for shares of plantations and jute mills.
- The number of stock exchanges rose from 7 in 1939 to 21 in 1945.
- Under the securities contract (Regulation) Act of 1956, the Government of India has so far recognised 23 stock exchanges. Bombay is the premier exchange in the country.
- With the setting up of National Stock Exchange, all regional stock exchanges have lost relevance.
- The BSE transformed itself into a corporate entity from being a brokers association, from the middle of August, 2005.
- As a public limited company, BSE (Bombay Stock Exchange) is obliged to dilute stock brokers stake to 49%.
- To prevent excessive speculation and volatility in the stock market SEBI has introduced rolling settlements from July 2, 2001, under which settlement has to be made every day.

Important Share Price Index of India

- **BSE SENSEX :** This is the most sensitive share index of the Mumbai Stock Exchange. This is the representative index of 30 main shares. Its base year is 1978-79. BSE is the oldest stock exchange of India, founded in 1875.
- **BSE 200 :** This represents 200 shares of Mumbai Stock Exchange. Its base year is 1989-90.
- **DOLLEX :** Index of 200 BSE Dollar Value Index is called DOLLEX. Its base year is 1989-90.
- **NSE-50:** From 28th July, 1998, its name is *S and P CNX Nifty*. National Stock Exchange has launched a new share Price Index, NSE-50 in place of NSE-100 in April 1996. NSE-50 includes 50 companies shares. This stock exchange was founded on Ferwani Committee's recommendation in 1994.
- CRISIL, set up in 1988, is a credit rating agency. It undertakes the rating fixed deposit programmes, convertible and non-convertible debentures and also credit assessment of companies.
- **CRISIL 500 :** is the new share Price Index introduced by Credit Rating

Agency the "Credit Rating Information Services of India Limited" (CRISIL) on January 18,1996.

- Apart from CRISIL, there is another credit rating agency called "Investment Information and Credit Rating Agency of India Limited (ICRA)." It rates debt instruments of both financial and manufacturing companies.
- The *National Stock Exchange (NSE)* has launched a new version of its online trading software called 'National Exchange for Automatic Trading'(NEAT).

12. Indian Fiscal System

- **Fiscal System :** It refers to the management of revenue and capital expenditure finances by the state. Hence, fiscal system includes budgetary activities of the government that is revenue raising, borrowing and spending activities.
- **Fiscal Policy:** Fiscal Policy refers to the use of taxation, public expenditure and the management of public debt in order to achieve certain specified objectives.
- Indian Fiscal System includes or refers to the management of revenue sources and expenditure of the Central and State governments, Public debt, Deficit financing. Budget, Tax structure etc.
- **Sources of Revenue for Centre:** The revenue of the Central Government consists of the following elements : (i) Tax revenue and (ii) Non-tax revenue. Tax revenue comes broadly from three sources — (a) taxes on income and expenditure (b) taxes on property and capital transactions (c) taxes on commodities and services. Non-tax revenue consists of — (a) currency, coinage and mint (b) interest receipts and dividends; and other non-tax revenue.
- **Expenditure of the Centre :** The central government makes expenditures broadly under two heads : (i) Plan expenditure and (ii) Non-Plan expenditure.
- Under Plan expenditure comes outlay for agriculture, rural development, irrigation and flood control, energy, industry and minerals, transport, communications, Science and Technology, environment and economic services etc.
- The major non-plan expenditures are interest payments, defence, subsidies and general services.
- **Sources of Revenue for State:** The main sources are: (a) state tax revenue (b) share in central taxes (c) income from social, commercial and economic service and profits of state-run enterprises. State tax revenue includes among others, land revenue, stamp, registration and estate duty etc.

- **Expenditure of State:** The State Governments have two broad heads of expenditure : (a) Non-Development Expenditure; and (b) Development Expenditure.
- Public debt of the government of India is of two kinds – Internal and External.
- **Internal debt :** It comprises loans raised from the open market, compensation bonds, prize bonds etc. treasury bills issued to the RBI, commercial banks etc.
- **External debt:** It consists of loans taken from World Bank, IMF, ADB and individual countries like USA, Japan etc.
- Deficit Financing is a fiscal tool in the hands of the government to bridge the gap between revenue receipt and revenue expenditure.

Deficits
- In a budget statement, there is a mention of four types of deficits : (a) revenue, (b) budget, (c) fiscal, and (d) primary.

  (a) **Revenue Deficit** refers to the excess of revenue expenditure over revenue receipts. [In fact, it reflects one crucial fact : what is the government borrowing for ? As an individual if you are borrowing to pay the house rent, then you are in a situation of revenue deficit, i.e. while you are borrowing and spending, you are not creating any durable asset. This implies that there will be a repayment obligation (sometime in the future) and at the same time there is no asset creation via investment.]

  Revenue Deficit = Total Revenue Expenditure - Total Revenue Receipts = Non-plan Expenditure + Plan Expenditure - (net tax revenue + non tax revenue)

  (b) **Budget Deficit** refers to the excess of total expenditure over total receipts. Here, total receipts include current revenue and net internal and external capital receipts of the government.

  Budget Deficit = Total Expenditure - Total Receipts
  = (non-plan expenditure + plan expenditure) – (Revenue Receipts + Capital Receipts)

  (c) **Fiscal Deficit** refers to the difference between total expenditure (revenue, capital, and loans net of repayment) on one hand; and on the other hand, revenue receipts plus all those capital receipts which are not in the form of borrowings but which in the end accrue to the government.

  Fiscal Deficit = Revenue Receipts *(net tax revenue + non-tax revenue)* + Capital Receipts *(only recoveries of loans and other receipts)* – Total Expenditure *(plan and non-plan)*

(d) Primary Deficit refers to fiscal deficit minus interest payments. In other words, it points to how much the government is borrowing to pay for expenses other than interest payments. Also, it underscores another key fact : how much the government is adding to future burden (in terms of repayment) on the basis of past and present policy.

Primary Deficit = Revenue Deficit − Interest Payments

Monetised Deficit = Increment in Net RBI Credit to the Central Government.

Budget

▷ The Budget of the Government of India, for any year, gives a complete picture of the estimated receipts and expenditures of the Government for that year on the basis of the budget figures of the two previous years.

▷ Every budget, for instance, gives three sets of figures : (a) actual figures for preceding year, (b) budget and revised figures for the current year, and (c) budget estimates for the following year.

▷ The core of the budget is called the Annual financial statement. This is the main budget document. Under article 112 of the constitution, a statement of estimated receipts and expenditure of the Govt. of India has to be laid before the parliament in respect of every financial' year running from April 1 to March 31 while under article 202 of the constitution a statement of estimated receipts and expenditures of the state Governments has to be laid before the house of the state legislature concerned.

▷ The **Annual Budget** of the Central Government provides estimates of receipts and expenditures of the Government. The Budget consists of two parts viz; (i) Revenue Budget (ii) Capital Budget.

▷ **Revenue Budget:** All "current" 'receipts' such as taxation, surplus of Public enterprises, and 'expenditures' of the Government.

▷ **Capital Budget :** All "Capital" 'receipts' and 'expenditure' such as domestic and foreign loans, loan repayments, foreign aid etc.

▷ **Finance Bill** is ordinarily introduced every year to give effect to the financial proposals of the Government for the following financial year.

34% Jump in Job Growth in 8 Years: Sixth Economic Census 2013

According to the Sixth Economic Census 2013, the number of people employed in the country rose by 34.35% to 12.77 crore in eight years to 2013. The employment in urban areas increased by 37.46% to 6.14 crore, while in rural India the growth was 31.59% to 6.62 crore between 2005 and 2013.

The proportion of Women in total Workforce increased to 25.56% in 2013 from about 20% in 2005. In urban areas, the proportion of female workers was 19.8% compared to 30.9% in rural areas. The economic census does not include those employed in agriculture, public administration, defense and compulsory social security services activities.

Among the states, Maharashtra was on top of the list with maximum number of employees at 1.43 crore, followed by Uttar Pradesh at 1.37 crore, West Bengal at 1.15 crore, Tamil Nadu 1.08 crore and Gujarat at 90.63 lakh. Among the Union Territories, Delhi has the maximum number of employees at 29.84 lakh followed by Chandigarh at 2.38 lakh and Puducherry at 2.17 lakh.

In terms of percentage growth in total employment during the period, number of workers grew at higher rate of 83.29% in Manipur, followed by 78.84% in Assam, 77.14% in Sikkim, 75.26% in Uttar Pradesh and 68.81% in Himachal Pradesh.

New Poverty Line : ₹ 32 in Villages, ₹ 47 in Cities

Those spending over ₹ 32 a day in rural areas and ₹ 47 in towns and cities should not be considered poor, an expert panel headed by former RBI governor C. Rangarajan said in a report submitted to the BJP government last week. Based on the Suresh Tendulkar panel's recommendations in 2011-12, the poverty line had been fixed at ₹ 27 in rural areas and ₹ 33 in urban areas, levels at which getting two meals may be difficult.

The panel's recommendation, however, results in an increase in the below poverty line population, which is estimated at 363 million in 2011-12, compared to the 270 million estimate based on the Tendulkar formula–an increase of almost 35%. This means 29.5% of the Indian population lives below the poverty line as defined by the Rangarajan committee, as against 21.9% according to Tendulkar. For 2009–10, Rangarajan has estimated that the share of BPL group in total population was 38.2%, translating into a decline in poverty ratio by 8.7 percentage points over a two-year period.

The real change is in urban areas where the BPL number is projected to have nearly doubled to 102.5 million based on Rangarajan's estimates, compared to 53 million based on the Tendulkar committee's recommendations. So, based on the new measure, in 2011-12, 26.4% of the people living in urban areas were BPL, compared to 35.1% in 2009-10.

In case of rural areas, the rise is of the order of 20% to 260.5 million, compared to around 217 million based on the Tendulkar formula. Rangarajan's estimates would put the BPL share of total population in rural areas at 30.9%, compared to 39.6% in 2009-10.

Rangarajan panel has suggested to the government that those spending more than ₹ 972 a month in rural areas and ₹ 1407 a month in urban areas in 2011–12 do not fall under the definition of poverty. Thus, for a family of five, the all-India poverty line in terms of consumption expenditure, as per the Rangarajan committee, would amount to ₹ 4,760 per month in rural areas and ₹ 7,035 per month in urban areas. If calculated on a daily basis, this translates into a per capita expenditure of ₹ 32 per day in rural areas and ₹ 47 per day in urban areas in 2011–12. As per the Tendulkar methodology for 2011–12, the poverty line was ₹ 816 in rural areas and ₹ 1,000 in urban areas, which if calculated on a daily basis come out at ₹ 27 per day in rural areas and ₹ 33 in urban areas. The Tendulkar committee had pegged this at ₹ 4,080 and ₹ 5,000.

State Specific Poverty Line as Proposed by Rangarajan Expert Group		
States/UTs	Poverty Line 2011-12	
	Rural	Urban
Andhra Pradesh	1031.74	1370.84
Arunachal Pradesh	1151.01	1482.94
Assam	1006.66	1420.12
Bihar	971.28	1229.3
Chhattisgarh	911.8	1229.72
Delhi	1492.46	1538.09
Goa	1200.6	1470.07
Gujarat	1102.83	1507.06
Haryana	1127.82	1528.31
Himachal Pradesh	1066.6	1411.59
Jammu & Kashmir	1044.48	1403.25
Jharkhand	904.02	1272.06
Karnataka	975.43	1373.28
Kerala	1054.03	1353.68
Madhya Pradesh	941.7	1340.28
Maharashtra	1078.34	1560.38
Manipur	1185.19	1561.77
Meghalaya	1110.67	1524.37
Mizoram	1231.03	1703.93
Nagaland	1229.83	1615.78
Odisha	876.42	1205.37
Punjab	1127.48	1479.27
Rajasthan	1035.97	1406.15
Sikkim	1126.25	1542.67

			1081.94			1380.36	
Tamil Nadu			1081.94			1380.36	
Tripura			935.52			1376.55	
Uttar Pradesh			889.82			1329.55	
Uttarakhand			1014.95			1408.12	
West Bengal			934.1			1372.68	
Puducherry			1130.1			1382.31	
All India			972			1407	

Poverty Line

Committee	Year	Per capita Expenditure per day (₹)		Per capita Average Monthly Expenditure (₹)		All India Poverty Line (Average Monthly Expenditure per Family of 5)	
		Rural	Urban	Rural	Urban	Rural	Urban
Rangarajan	2011-12	32.4	46.9	972	1407	4760	7035
	2009-10	26.7	39.9	801	1198	4005	5990
Tendulkar	2011-12	27.2	33.3	816	1000	4080	5000
	2009-10	22.4	28.7	673	860	3365	4300

13. Banking in India

Banking in India originated in the last decades of 18th century. The first banks were: *The General Bank of India*, which started in 1786, and *Bank of Hindustan, which started in 1770*; both are now defunct. The oldest bank in existence in India is the *State Bank of India*, which originated in the *Bank of Calcutta* in June 1806, which almost immediately became the *Bank of Bengal*. This was one of the three presidency banks, the other two being the *Bank of Bombay* and the *Bank of Madras*, all three of which were established under charters from the British East India Company. For many years, the Presidency Banks acted as Quasi-central banks, as did their successors. The three banks merged in 1921 to form the *Imperial Bank of India*, which, upon India's independence, became the State Bank of India in 1955.

History of Banking

Merchants in Calcutta (Kolkata) established the Union Bank in 1839, but it failed in 1840 as a consequence of the economic crisis of 1848-49. The Allahabad Bank, established in 1865 and is still functioning today, and is the oldest Joint Stock Bank in India.*(Joint Stock Bank: A company that issues stock and requires shareholders to be held liable for the company's debt)* It was not the first though. That honour belongs to the Bank of Upper India, which was established in 1863, and which survived until 1913, when it failed, with some of its assets and liabilities being transferred to the *Alliance Bank of Simla*.

Foreign banks too started to operate, particularly in Calcutta, in the 1860s. The Comptoir d'Escompte de Paris opened a branch in Calcutta in 1860, and another in Bombay in 1862; branches in Madras and Pondicherry, then a French colony, followed. HSBC established itself in Bengal in 1869. Calcutta was the most active trading port in India, mainly due to the trade of the British Empire, and so became a banking center.

The first entirely Indian joint stock bank was the Oudh Commercial Bank, established in 1881 in Faizabad. It failed in 1958. The next was the Punjab National Bank, established in Lahore in 1895, which has survived to the present and is now one of the largest banks in India.

Around the turn of the 20th Century, the Indian economy was passing through a relative period of stability. Around five decades had elapsed since the Indian Mutiny, and the social, industrial and other infrastructure had improved. Indians had established small banks, most of which served particular ethnic and religious communities.

The presidency banks dominated banking in India but there were also some exchange banks and a number of Indian joint stock banks. All these banks operated in different segments of the economy. The exchange banks, mostly owned by Europeans, concentrated on financing foreign trade. Indian joint stock banks were generally under capitalised and lacked the experience and maturity to compete with the presidency and exchange banks. This segmentation let Lord Curzon to observe, "In respect of banking it seems we are behind the times. We are like some old fashioned sailing ship, divided by solid wooden bulkheads into separate and cumbersome compartments."

The period between 1906 and 1911, saw the establishment of banks inspired by the *Swadeshi movement*. The Swadeshi movement inspired local businessmen and political figures to found banks of and for the Indian community. A number of banks such as Bank of India, Corporation Bank, Indian Bank, Bank of Baroda, Canara Bank and Central Bank of India were established and have survived to the present. The fervour of Swadeshi movement lead to establishing of many private banks in Dakshina Kannada and Udupi district which were unified earlier and known by the name South Canara (South Kanara) district. Four nationalised banks started in this district and also a leading private sector bank. Hence undivided Dakshina Kannada district is known as "Cradle of Indian Banking".

From the First World War (1914 – 1918) to the end of the Second World War (1939 – 1945), and two years thereafter until the independence of India were challenging for Indian banking. The years of the First World War were turbulent, and it took its toll with banks simply collapsing despite the Indian economy gaining indirect boost due to war-related economic activities.

At least 94 banks in India failed between 1913 and 1918 as indicated in the following table:

Years	Number of banks that failed	Authorised capital (Rs. Lakhs)	Paid-up Capital (Rs. Lakhs)
1913	12	274	35
1914	42	710	109
1915	11	56	5
1916	13	231	4
1917	9	76	25
1918	7	209	1

Banking in the Post-Independence Era

The partition of India in 1947 adversely impacted the economies of Punjab and West Bengal, paralysing banking activities for months. India's independence marked the end of a regime of the *Laissez-faire* for the Indian Banking. The Government of India initiated measures to play an active role in the economic life of the nation, and the *Industrial Policy Resolution* adopted by the government in 1948 envisaged a mixed economy. This resulted into greater involvement of the state in different segments of the economy including banking and finance. The major steps to regulate banking included:

- The Reserve Bank of India, India's central banking authority, was established in April 1935, but was nationalised on January 1, 1949 under the terms of the Reserve Bank of India (Transfer to Public Ownership) Act, 1948 (RBI, 2005b).[1]
- In 1949, the Banking Regulation Act was enacted, which empowered the Reserve Bank of India (RBI) "to regulate, control, and inspect the banks in India".
- The Banking Regulation Act also provided that no new bank or branch of an existing bank could be opened without a license from the RBI, and no two banks could have common directors.

Nationalisation of Banks in India

Despite the provisions, control and regulations of Reserve Bank of India, banks in India except the State Bank of India, continued to be owned and operated by private persons. By the 1960s, the Indian banking industry had become an important tool to facilitate the development of the Indian economy. At the same time, it had emerged as a large employer, and a debate had ensued about the nationalization of the banking industry. Indira Gandhi, the then Prime Minister of India, expressed the intention of the Government of India in the annual conference of the All India Congress

Meeting in a paper entitled "Stray thoughts on Bank Nationalisation." The meeting received the paper with enthusiasm.

Thereafter, her move was swift and sudden. The Government of India issued an ordinance ('Banking Companies (Acquisition and Transfer of Undertakings) Ordinance, 1969')) and nationalised the 14 largest commercial banks with effect from the midnight of July 19, 1969. These banks contained 85 percent of bank deposits in the country. Jayaprakash Narayan, a national leader of India, described the step as a "masterstroke of political sagacity." Within two weeks of the issue of the ordinance, the Parliament passed the Banking Companies (Acquisition and Transfer of Undertaking) Bill, and it received the presidential approval on 9th August 1969.

The second phase of nationalisation of six more commercial banks followed in 1980. The stated reason for the nationalization was to give the government more control of credit delivery. With the second phase of nationalisation, the Government of India controlled around 91% of the banking business of India. Later on, in the year 1993, the government merged New Bank of India with Punjab National Bank. It was the only merger between nationalised banks and resulted in the reduction of the number of nationalised banks from 20 to 19. After this, until the 1990s, the nationalised banks grew at a pace of around 4%, closer to the average growth rate of the Indian economy.

Banking Reforms

- On the recommendation of Narsimhan Committee, a number of steps taken to improve functioning of banking sector. SLR and CRR were reduced.
- Banks were given freedom to open new branches. Rapid computerisation of banks was undertaken.
- Banking "Ombudsmen Scheme" started functioning to expedite inexpensive resolution of customer's complaints.

Scheduled and Non-scheduled Banks

- The scheduled banks are those which are entered in the second schedule of the RBI Act, 1934. These banks have a paid-up capital and reserves of an aggregate value of not less than Rs. 5 lakhs and satisfy the RBI that their affairs are carried out in the interest of their depositors.
- All commercial banks (Indian and foreign), regional rural banks and state co-operative banks are scheduled banks. Non scheduled banks are those which are not included in the second schedule of the RBI Act 1934. At present there is only one such bank in the country.

Regional Rural Banks

- The Regional Rural Banks (RRBs), the newest form of banks, have

come into existence since middle of 1970s (sponsored by individual nationalised commercial banks) with the objective of developing rural economy by providing credit and deposit facilities for agriculture and other productive activities of all kinds in rural areas.
- ➪ The emphasis is on providing such facilities to small and marginal farmers, agricultural labourers, rural artisans and other small entrepreneurs in rural areas.
- ➪ First Regional Rural Bank was established on 2nd October, 1975.

Co-operative Banks
- ➪ Co-operative banks are so called because they are organised under the provisions of the Co-operative Credit Societies law of the states. The major beneficiary of the Co-operative Banking is the agricultural sector in particular and the rural sector in general. The first such bank was established in 1904.
- ➪ The Co-operative credit institutions operating in the country are mainly of two kinds: agricultural (dominant) and non-agricultural.
- ➪ At the apex is the State Co-operative Bank (SCB) (co-operation being a state subject in India), at the intermediate (district) level are the Central Co-operative Banks (CCBs), and at the village level are Primary Agricultural Credit Societies (PACs); Long-term agricultural credit is provided by the Land Development Banks.
- ➪ In the year 1991, Narsimhan Committee was constituted to advice on the issue of reconstruction of banking system.

Development Banks
- ➪ *Industrial Development Bank of India* (IDBI), established in 1964.
  Main functions : Providing finance to large and medium scale industrial units.
- ➪ *Industrial Finance Corporation of India* (IFCI), established in 1948.
  Main functions: (a) Project finance (b) Promotional services.
- ➪ *Industrial Credit and Investment Corporation of India Limited* (ICICI) established in 1991.
  Main functions: Providing term loans in Indian and foreign currencies; Underwriting of issues of shares and debentures.
- ➪ *Small Industries Development Bank of India* (SIDBI), established in 1989.
  Main functions : Providing assistance to small scale industries through state finance corporations, state industrial development corporations, commercial banks etc.
- ➪ *Export-Import Bank of India* (Exim. Bank) was established in 1982.
  Main functions : Coordinating the working of institutions engaged in financing export and import trade, Financing exports and imports.
- ➪ *National Housing Bank* (NHB) started operations in 1988.

Main functions: Development of housing finance in the country.
- *National Bank for Agriculture and Rural Development* (NABARD). It was established in 1982. The paid-up capital of NABARD stood at Rs. 2000 crore as on 31st March 2010.
Main functions: to serve as an apex refinancing agency for institutions engaged in providing agricultural finance to develop credit delivery system to coordinate rural financing activities.

Insurance

- The basic concept of insurance is of spreading the loss of a few over many. The insurance industry includes two sectors — Life Insurance and General Insurance. Life Insurance in India was introduced by Britishers. A British firm in 1818 established the Oriental Life Insurance Company at Calcutta now Kolkata.
- Life Insurance Corporation (LIC) of India was established in September 1956. General Insurance Corporation (GIC) was established in November 1972.
- Indian Insurance sector has low penetration particularly in rural areas. It also has low turnover and profitability despite high premium rate. *The committee on Insurance Sector Reforms was set-up in 1993 under the chairmanship of R.N. Malhotra* which submitted its report in 1994.
- Since opening up, the number of participants in the industry has gone up from 6 insurers (including Life Insurance Corporation of India, 4 public sector general insurers and General Insurance Corporation of India as the national reinsurer) in the year 2000 to 47 insurers as on March, 2010 operating in the life, non-life and reinsurance segments (including specialised insurers viz. Export Credit Guarantee Corporation and Agriculture Insurance Company of India Ltd. AICIL)
- 36 companies in the private sector are operating in the country in collaboration with established foreign insurance companies from across the globe as on 31st March, 2010.
- The Life Insurance Corporation with its Central Office in Mumbai, 8 Zonal Offices at Mumbai, Kolkata, Delhi, Chennai, Hyderabad, Kanpur, Bhopal and Patna, 109 Divisional Offices including one Salary Savings Schemes (SSS) Division at Mumbai, 2048 Branch Offices and 1004 Satellite Offices as on 31st March, 2010, spreads the message of Insurance the length and breadth of India.
- At present LIC is operating internationally through Branch Offices in Fiji, Mauritius and U.K. and through Joint Venture Companies in Bahrain, Nepal, Sri Lanka, Kenya and Saudi Arabia. Its Representative Office in Singapore was opened on 6th Nov. 2008.

14. Adoption of Banking Technology

The IT revolution had a great impact in the Indian banking system. The use of computers had led to introduction of online banking in India. The use of the modern innovation and computerisation of the banking sector of India has increased manyfold after the economic liberalisation of 1991 as the country's banking sector has been exposed to the world's market. The Indian banks were finding it difficult to compete with the international banks in terms of the customer service without the use of the information technology and computers.

The RBI in 1984 formed Committee on mechanisation in the Banking Industry (1984) whose chairman was Dr C Rangarajan, Deputy Governor, Reserve Bank of India. The major recommendation of this committee was to introdue MICR Technology in all the banks in the metropolis in India. This provided use of standardised cheque forms and encoders.

In 1988, the RBI set up committee on Computerisation in Banks (1988) headed by Dr. C.R. Rangarajan, which emphasized that settlement operation must be computerized in the clearing houses of RBI in Bhubaneshwar, Guwahati, Jaipur, Patna and Thiruvananthapuram. It further stated that there should be National Clearing of inter-city cheques at Kolkata, Mumbai, Delhi, Chennai and MICR should be made operational. It also focused on computerisation of branches and increasing connectivity among branches through computers. It also suggested modalities for implementing on-line banking. The committee submitted its reports in 1989 and computerisation began form 1993 with the settlement between IBA and bank employees' association.

In 1994, the committee on Technology Issues relating to Payments System, Cheque Clearing and Securities Settlement in the Banking Industry (1994) was set up with the chairman Shri WS Saraf, Executive Director, Reserve Bank of India. It emphasized on Electronic Funds Transfer (EFT) system, with the BANKNET communications network as its carrier. It also said that MICR clearing should be set up in all branches of all banks with more than 100 branches. The committee for proposing legislation on Electronic Funds Transfer and other Electronic Payments (1995) emphasised on EFT system. Electronic banking refers to DOING BANKING by using technologies like computers, internet and networking, MICR, EFT so as to increase efficiency, quick service, productivity and transparency in the transaction.

Apart from the above mentioned innovations, the banks have been selling the third party products like *Mutual Funds*, insurances to its clients. The total numbers of ATMs installed in India by various banks as on end of March 2005 was 17,642. The number of ATMs is highest for the SBI and its subsidiaries and then it is followed by the New Private Banks, Nationalised Banks and Foreign Banks.

15. Tax System

- A compulsory contribution given by a citizen or organisation to the Government is called Tax, which is used for meeting expenses on welfare work.
- Tax imposing and Tax collecting is at three levels in India — Central level, State level and Local level.
- The distribution of tax between Centre and State has been clearly mentioned in the provisions of Indian Constitution. For rationalising it from time to time, Finance Commission has been constituted.
- The tax system has been divided into two parts :

    Tax Imposed by Central Government: Custom Duty, Income Tax and Corporate Tax etc.

    Tax Imposed by State Government: The state government has right to collect all the taxes in this categoriy and to spend them.
- There are two types of taxes : (i) Direct Taxes (ii) Indirect Taxes.
    - **Direct Taxes:** The taxes levied by the central government on incomes and wealth are important direct taxes. The important taxes levied on incomes are — corporation tax and income tax. Taxes levied on wealth are wealth tax, gift tax etc.
    - **Indirect Taxes :** The main forms of indirect taxes are customs and excise duties and sales tax. The central government is empowered to levy customs and excise duties (except on alcoholic liquors and narcotics) whereas sales tax is the exclusive jurisdiction of the state governments.
- However, the union excise duties form the most significant part of central taxes. The major tax revenue sources for states are their shares in union excise duties and income tax, commercial taxes, land revenue, stamp duty, registration fees, state excise duties on alcohol and narcotics etc. Sales tax forms the most important component of commercial taxes.
- **Progressive Tax :** A tax that takes away a higher proportion of one's income as the income rises is known as progressive tax. Indian Income Tax is a progressive and direct tax.
- **R. Chelliah Committee** was constituted in August 1991 for suggesting reforms in Tax Structure.
- The Chelliah committee recommended Income Tax for agricultural income of more than Rs. 25,000 p.a. The committee also recommended for lowering down the tax rates and reducing the tax slabs.

- **K.L. Rekhi** Committee was constituted in 1992 for suggesting uniform regulations for indirect taxation (Custom Duty and Excise Duty).

Finance Commission
- Finance Commission is constituted by the President under Art 280 of the constitution. Since Independence, 12 Finance Commissions have submitted their reports.
- 1st Finance Commission was constituted under the chairmanship of K. C. Neogi while 12th Finance Commission was constituted under the chairmanship of Dr. C. Rangarajan. The recommendations of 12th Finance Commission cover period from 1st April, 2005 to 31st March, 2010.
- 13th Finance Commission, for the period 2010-2015, has been constituted in November, 2007 with Dr. Vijay L. Kelkar as the Chairman.

Important Taxes imposed in India
- **Tax on Income and Wealth:** The central government imposes different types of tax on income and wealth, viz. income tax, corporate tax, wealth tax and gift tax. Out of them income tax and corporate tax are more important from the revenue point of view.
- **Personal Income Tax :** Personal income tax is generally imposed on an individual combined Hindu families and total income of people of any other communities.
- In addition to tax, separate surcharges are also imposed sometimes.
- Agricultural income in India is free from income tax.
- **Corporate Tax :** Corporate Tax is imposed on Registered Companies and Corporations.
- The rate of corporate tax on all companies is equal. However, various types of rebates and exemptions have been provided.
- **Custom Duties :** As per the Constitutional provisions, the central government imposes import duty and export duty both. Import and Export duties are not only sources of income but with the help of it the central government regulates the foreign trade.
- **Import Duties :** Generally import duties are *ad-valorem* in India. It means import duties are imposed on the taxable item on percentage basis.
- **Export Duties :** Export Duties are more important, compared to Import Duties in terms of revenue and regulation of foreign trade.
- **Excise Duties :** Excise duties are commodity tax as it is imposed on production of an item and it has no relevance with its sale. This is the largest source of revenue for the Central Government.
- Except liquor, opium and other drugs, production of all the other items is taxable under Central Excise Duties.

- On July 15, 2010 Indian rupee got the much awaited symbol, just like other leading currencies of the world viz. Dollar, Euro, Pound, Sterling and Yen.
- The new symbol is an amalgamation of *Devanagari 'Ra'* and the Roman 'R' without the stem. Till now the rupee was written in various abbreviated forms in different languages.
- On March 5, 2009 the Government announced a contest to create a symbol for the Rupee.
- Over 3000 entries received only 5 entries had been selected by the jury, headed by the Deputy Governor of R.B.I.
- The new symbol designed by D. Udaya Kumar, a post-graduate of IIT Bombay, was finally selected by the Union Cabinet on July 15, 2010.
- Though the symbol '₹' will not be printed or embossed on currency notes or coins, it would be included in the 'Unicode Standard' and major scripts of the world to ensure that it is easily displayed and printed in the electronic and print media.
- One Coin and One Rupee note belong to "Legal Tender Money" category.
- M_1 is known as Narrow Money.
- M_3 is known as Broad Money.

Types of Tax

Direct Tax	Income Tax, Property Tax, Gift Tax etc.
Indirect Tax	Sales Tax, Excise Duty, Custom Duty etc.
Taxes imposed by the Central Government	Income Tax, Corporate Tax, Property Tax, Succession Tax, Wealth Tax, Gift Tax, Custom Duty, Tax on agricultural wealth etc.
Taxes imposed by the State Government	Land revenue tax, Agricultural income tax, Agricultural Land Revenue, State Excise Duty, Entertainment Tax, Stamp duty, Road Tax, Motor Vehicle Tax etc.

Financial institutions and year of establishment

1.	Industrial Credit and Investment Corporation of India	Jan., 1955
2.	Industrial Finance Corporation of India	1948
3.	Unit Trust of India (Head Office – Mumbai)	1st Feb., 1964
4.	National Bank for Agricultural and Rural Development (NABARD)	12th July, 1982
5.	Industrial Reconstruction Bank of India	20th March, 1985

6.	Small Scale Industries Development Bank of India (SIDBI) (Head Office – Lucknow)	1990
7.	Export-Import Bank of India (EXIM Bank)	1st Jan., 1982
8.	Regional Rural Bank (RRB) (Head Office – Kolkata)	2nd October, 1975
9.	Life Insurance Corporation of India (LIC) (Head Office – Mumbai)	Sep., 1956

16. Industry

▷ India started her quest for industrial development after independence in 1947.
▷ The Industrial Policy Resolution of 1948 marked the beginning of the evolution of the Indian Industrial Policy.
▷ In the Industrial Policy of 1948, the importance of both public sector and private sector was accepted. However, the responsibility of development of basic industries was handed over to Public Sector.
▷ The Industrial Policy Resolution of 1956 gave the public sector strategic role in the economy.
▷ Earmarking the pre-eminent position of the public sector, it envisaged private sector co-existing with the state and thus attempted to give the policy framework flexibility.
▷ The main objective of the Industrial Policy of 1956 was to develop public sector, co-operative sector and control on private monopoly.
▷ There were four categories of industries in the Industrial Policy of 1948 which was reduced to three in the Industrial Policy of 1956.
▷ In 1973, Joint Sector was constituted on the recomendations of the Dutta committee.
▷ The Industrial Policy of 1980 was influenced by the concept of federalism and the policy of giving concession to agriculture based industries was implemented through it.
▷ Various liberalised steps to be taken were declared at comprehensive level, in the Industrial Policy declared on 24th July, 1991.
▷ Privatisation and liberalisation are the main thrust areas in the New Industrial Policy.

New Industrial Policy, 1991

▷ This new policy deregulates the industrial economy in a substantial manner. The major features of NIP 1991 are:
▷ **Abolition of industrial licensing :** In a major move to liberalise the economy, the new industrial policy abolished all industrial licensing, irrespective of the level of investment, except for certain industries related to security and strategic concerns, social reasons, concerns

related to safety and over-riding environmental issues, manufacture of products of hazardous nature and articles of elitist consumption.

- **Entry of foreign investment and technology made easier :** For the promotion of exports of Indian products in world markets, the government would encourage foreign trading companies to assist Indian exporters in export activities. Approval would be given for direct foreign investment up to 51% foreign equity in high priority industries.
- **Public sector's role diluted :** The new industrial policy has removed all these (the number of industries reserved for the public sector since 1956 was 17) industries from the Reserved List. Industries that continue to be reserved for the public sector are in areas where security and strategic concerns predominate. These areas are (i) arms and ammunition and allied items of defence equipment, defence aircraft and warships, (ii) atomic energy, (iii) mineral oils and minerals specified in the schedule to the atomic energy (control of production and use) order, 1953, (iv) railways.
- **MRTP Act :** Under the MRTP Act, all firms with assets above a certain size (Rs. 100 crore since 1985) were classified as MRTP firms. Such firms were permitted to enter selected industries only and this also on a case by-case approval basis. The new industrial policy scrapped the threshold limit of assets in respect of 'MRTP' and dominant undertakings.
- **Liberalisation of Industrial location policy :** The new Industrial policy provides that in locations other than cities of more than one million population, there will be no requirement of obtaining industrial approvals from the centre, except for industries subject to compulsory licensing. In cities with a population of more than one million, industries other than those of a non-polluting nature will be located outside 25 kms of the periphery.
- **Abolition of Phased Manufacturing Programmes for new projects :** To force the pace of indigenisation in manufacturing, Phased Manufacturing Programmes have been in force in a number of engineering and electronic industries.
- **Mandatory convertibility clause removed :** A large part of industrial investment in India is financed by loans from banks and financial institutions. These institutions have followed a mandatory practice of including a convertibility clause in their lending operations for new projects. This has provided them an option of converting part of their loans into equity, if felt necessary by their management. This has often been interpreted as an unwarranted threat to private firms of takeover by financial institutions. This mandatory convertibility clause put forward by the financial institutions has been abolished by the new industrial policy.

▷ In the Union Budget of 1997-98, nine public sector undertakings, which performed very well were given the name of "Navratna" and were made autonomous. These "Navratnas" included:

SAIL	Steel Authority of India Limited
IOC (Sept. 1964)	Indian Oil Corporation
BPCL (Aug. 1, 1977)	Bharat Pertroleum Corporation Limited
HPCL (Est. July 15, 1974)	Hindustan Petroleum Corporation Limited
BHEL	Bharat Heavy Electricals Limited
NTPC	National Thermal Power Corporation
BEL	Bharat Electronics Limited
HAL	Hindustan Aeronautics Limited
ONGC (Est Aug. 14, 1956)	Oil and Natural Gas Corporation
Following undertakings were also included in this list later :	
GAIL (Aug. 1984)	Gas Authority of India Limited
MTNL	Mahanagar Telephone Nigam Limited
NMDC	National Mineral Development Corporation
PFC	Power Finance Corporation
PGCIL	Power Grid Corporation of India Limited
REC	Rural Electrical Corporation Limited
NALCO	National Aluminium Company
SCI	Shipping Corporation of India
CIL	Coal India Limited

Navratna: Public sector enterprises have been given enhanced autonomy and delegation of powers to incur capital expenditure (without any monetary ceiling), to enter into technology joint ventures, to raise capital from domestic and international market, to establish financial joint ventures and to wholly own subsidiary.

Public Sector

▷ In terms of ownership, public sector enterprise (PSE) comprises all undertakings that are owned by the government, or the public, whereas private sector comprises enterprises that are owned by private persons.

▷ **The main objectives of public sector are :**
- To promote rapid economic development through creation and expansion of infrastructure;
- To generate financial resources for development;

- To promote redistribution of income and wealth;
- To create employment opportunities;
- To encourage the development of small scale and ancillary industries;
- To promote exports on the new side and import substitution on the other; and
- To promote balanced regional development.

Disinvestment and Privatisation

➪ There is a difference between privatisation and disinvestment. Privatisation implies a change in ownership resulting in a change in management. Disinvestment is a wider term extending from dilution for the stake of the government to the transfer of ownership (when govt. stake reduced beyond 51%).

➪ The Government of India constituted the Disinvestment Commission with Mr. G.V. Ramakrishna as the chairman in August 1996 to advise it on disinvestment programme of public sector enterprises. It has suggested classification of PSE into core and non core. In core sector maximum of 49% disinvestment would be allowed while in non core disinvestment would be upto 74%. PSEs shares will be given to small investors and employees to ensure wide dispersal of shares, thus introduce mass ownership and workers shareholding. It has also suggested greater autonomy to PSEs.

➪ To minimize the financial burden on the Public Sector Enterprises, the Government has started Voluntary Retirement Scheme (VRS) for the employees by giving full compensation to employees. This is called "Golden Hand Shake Scheme".

➪ Privatisation refers to a general process of involving the private sector in the ownership, or operation of a state owned enterprise. Thus, it refers to private purchase of all or part of a company.

Small Scale Industries

Small scale and cottage industries have an important role to play in a labour surplus developing economy like India. Their importance can be explained as:

(i) **Employment Generation:** Large scale industries are generally capital intensive. Small-scale industries, on the other hand, are generally labour intensive and have a substantially higher employment potential.

(ii) **Equitable Distribution:** The ownership of SSIs is more wide spread inter of both individuals as well as areas. Thus, these ensure equitable distribution of income individually and regionally.

(iii) **Mobilisation of Small Savings:** SSIs can be run with the help of small capital. Thus, they facilitate mobilisation of small savings.

(iv) **Export Contribution :** The share of small industries in the total export has increased over the years. It contributes 35% of total exports.
(v) **Environment Friendly:** As these are dispersed far away from urban centres they do not pollute urban environment.

However, Small Scale Industries are suffering from a number of problems like (i) Lack of timely, adequate and easy finance (ii) Lack of availability of raw material (iii) Lack of sound marketing system (iv) Competition with large scale sector.

Sick Industries

- A sick unit is one which is in existence for at least five years and had found at the end of accounting year that it had fully eroded its net worth. 30,000 units fall sick every year. A weak unit is one which erode 15% or more of its net worth.
- Textile industry is the largest industry in the country. The share of Textile and Clothing industry in total industrial production is about 14%. It also contributes 13.14% in total merchandise exports of the country. This industry provides employment to about 350 lakh people in the country.
- There are about 1,100 mills (900 spinning mills and 200 composite mills) in the country with 28 million spindles and 2 lakh loorns.
- There are 112 cotton mills in Gujarat. In Ahmedabad alone, there are 66 mills. It is known as Bostan of East. In Maharastra there are 104 mills out of which 54 alone are in Mumbai. Mumbai is called cottonopolis. In Kanpur there are 10 cotton mills and this city is called Manchester of North India.
- The first cycle making factory of India was established in Calcutta in 1932. India holds second place in the field of cycles production in the world. About 90 lakh cycles are produced annually in India.
- The share of small scale industries (SSI sector) in total exports of India is 32.3% in 2005-06
- Small and Cottage industries were given high priority in the Industrial Policy of 1977.
- District Industry Centres were established in 1977.
- With the aim to provide finance, *Small Industries Development* Bank of India (SIDBI) was established in 1990.
- *The Abid Husain committee* is related to reforms in small industries.
- The industries in which maximum Rs.1 crore is invested are called Small industries.
- *Industrial Finance Corporation of India* (IFCI) was established on 1st July, 1948 by a special Act of Parliament.
- The main aim of IFCI was to make available long term and mid term credit to the Industries of private and public sectors.

- Industrial Credit and Investment Corporation of India (ICICI) was established in 1955 under the Indian Companies Act.
- The function of ICICI is to support the establishment, development and modernization of industries in the private sector.
- Industrial Development Bank of India (lDBI) is an apex institution in the field of industrial finance.
- IDBI was established on 1st July, 1964.
- *Industrial Reconstruction Board of India* (IRBI) was established in 1971 with the aim to reconstruct the sick industrial units.
- Unit Trust of India was established in 1964.
- *Unit Trust of India* (UTI) collects small savings of people through sale of units and invests them into sureties.
- Life Insurance Company now Life Insurance Corporation of India or (LIC) was established in September 1956.
- The head office of Life Insurance Corporation of India is in Mumbai.
- Presently, it has 7 zonal offices and 100 regional offices.
- *General Insurance Company of India* (GIC) was established in 1972.
- Indian Industrial Investment Bank Limited was established on 17th March, 1997 by the government, under Companies Act 1956. Presently, its authorized capital is 1000 crore rupees and its head office is in Kolkata.

Industrial Growth

- The target growth of industry during the Tenth Plan (2002–07) was put at 10% consistent with an over all GDP growth 8%.
- According to the CSO's latest data, during 2006–07, (the last year of the l0th plan) the industrial growth stood at 10.0% compared to 9.6% in the corresponding period of 2005-06.
- Manufacturing production grew by 11.3% against 9.1%, electricity generation by 7.7% against 53% and mining out put by 4.5% against 3.6% between the last two consecutive years.
- Growth of industrial sector, from a low of 2.7% in 2001–02, revived to 7.1% and 7.4% in 2002–03 and 2003–04 respectively, and after accelerating to over 9.5% in the next two years, touched 10.0% in 2006–07.

Current Industrial Production

- The growth rate of Industrial Production, as per the Quick Estimates of Index of Industrial Production (IIP) with base year 1993–94, improved from an average of 5.0% per annum during 1997–2002 (9th Plan) to 10.5% in 2009–10.
- India is the second largest manufacturer of cement in the world. Cement industry is one of the most advanced industries in the country.
- At present there are 156 large cement plants with an installed capacity

of 233.94 million tonnes and more than 350 mini cement plants with an estimated capacity of 11.10 million tonnes per annum.
- The small scale, cottage and artisan sector account for over 75% of the leather production.
- More than 30% of the work force employed in this sector constitutes women.

Automobile Industry
- Automobile Industry was delicensed in July 1991with the annoucement of the New Industrial Policy.
- The passenger car was however delicensed in 1993.
- At present 100% Foreign Direct Investment (FDI) is permissible under automatic route in this sector including passenger car segment.
- The industry also offers substantial scope of employment with 4.5 lakh direct employment and about one crore indirect employment.

Textile Industry
This industry covers a wide range of activities ranging from generation of raw materials such as jute, wool, silk and cotton to greater value added goods such as ready made garments prepared from different types of man made or natural fibres. Textile industry provides job opportunity to over 35 million individuals, thus playing a major role in the nation's economy. It has 4 per cent share in GDP and shares 35% of the gross export income besides adding 14% of value addition in merchandising sector.

Food Processing Industry
In terms of global food business, India accounts less than 1.5% in spite of being one of the key food producing nations worldwide. But this on the other hand also indicates enormous possibilities for the growth of this industry. Supported by the GDP estimates, the approximate expansion of this sector is between 9–12% and during the tenth plan period the growth rate was around 6–8%.

Chemical Industry
The indian chemical industry generates around 70,000 commercial goods ranging from plastic to toiletries and pesticides to beauty products.With an approximate cost of $28 billion, it amounts to 12.5% of the entire industrial output of India and 16.2% of its entire exports. Under chemical industries, some of the other rapidly emerging sectors are petrochemical, agrochemical, and pharmaceutical industries.

Cement Industry
India has about 10 large cement plants governed by different state governments. Besides this India has 115 cement plants and around 300 small

cement plants. The big cement plants have installed competence of about 148.28 million tones per annum, whereas the mini cement plants have the total capacity of around 11.10 million tonnes per annum. Ambuja cement, J K Cement, Aditya Cement and L & T Cement are some of the major cement companies in India.

Steel Industry

The indian steel industry is a-400-years old sector which has a past record of registering 4% growth in 2005-06. The production during this period reached at 28.3 million tones. Indian steel industry is the 10th largest in the world, which is evident from its Rs 9,000 crore of capital contribution and employment opportunities to more than 0.5 million people. The key players in Steel Industry are Steel Authority of India (SAIL), Bokaro Steel Plant, Rourkela Steel Plant, Durgapur Steel Plant and Bhilai Steel Plant.

Software Industry

The Software Industry registered a massive expansion in the last 10 years. This industry signifies India's position as the knowledge based economy with a Compounded Annual Growth Rate (CAGR) of 42.3%. In the year, 2008, the industry grew by 7% as compared to 0.59% in 1994-95.

Mining Industry

The GDP contribution of the mining industry varies from 2.2% to 2.5% only but going by the GDP of the total industrial sector it contributes around 10% to 11%. Even mining done on small scale contributes 6% to the entire cost of mineral production.

Petroleum industry

It started its operations in the year 1867 and is considered as the oldest Indian industry. India is one of the most flourishing oil markets in the world and in the last few decades has witnessed the expansion of top national companies like the Oil and Natural Gas Corporation (ONGC), Hindustan Petroleum Comporation Limited (HPCL), Bharat Petroleum Corporation Ltd. (BPCL) and the Indian Oil Corporation Ltd.(IOC).

17. Foreign Trade

- Before independence, the foreign trade of India was being operated on the principles of colonialism. But after independence, there have been huge changes in its state and direction.
- After independence, inward looking foreign trade policies were accepted and the policy of import replacement was its base.
- Efforts were made for trade liberlisation during the decade of 1980 and the comprehensive policy of liberalisation and globalisation was made in the decade of 1990s (after the year 1991).

Volume of India's Foreign Trade

▷ After independence, Indian foreign trade has made cumulative progress both qualitatively and quantitatively. Though the size of foreign trade and its vlaue both have increased during post-independence era, this increase in foreign trade cannot be said satisfactory because Indian share in total foreign trade of the world has remained remarkable low.

▷ In 1950, the Indian share in the total world trade was 1.78%, which came down to 0.6% in 1995. According to the Economic Survey 2001-02 this share percentage of 0.6% continued in years 1997 and 1998. Since 1970, this share has remained around 0.6% which clearly indicates that India has failed to increase its share in the total world trade.

▷ India's total external trade (exports + imports including re-exports) in the year 2009–10 reached a level of Rs. 8,45,534 crore registering a growth of 0.57%. In US $ terms, exports reached a level of US $ 178.8 billion, registering a negative growth of –3.5% as compared to a growth of 13.6% during the previous year.

Composition of India's Foreign Trade

▷ Imports have been classified into Bulk imports and Non-bulk imports.

▷ Bulk imports are further sub-divided into petroleum, oil and lubricants (POL) and non-POL items such as consumption goods, fertilizers and iron and steel.

▷ Non-bulk items comprise capital goods (which include electrical and non-electrical machinery), pearls, precious and semiprecious stones and other items.

▷ **The structural changes in imports since 1951 show:** (a) rapid growth of industrialisation necessiating increasing imports of capital goods and raw materials; (b) growing imports of raw materials on the basis of liberalisation of imports for export promotion; and (c) declining imports of food grains and consumer goods due to the country becoming self sufficient in food grains and other consumer goods through agricultural and industrial growth.

▷ **Exports of India are broadly classified in to four categories:** (i) Agriculture and allied products which include coffee, tea, oil cakes, tobacco, cashew *kernels*, spices, sugar, raw cotton, rice, fish and fish preparations, meat and meat preparations, vegetable oils, fruits, vegetables and pulses; (ii) Ores and minerals which include manganese ore, mica and iron ore; (iii) Manufactured goods which include textiles and ready-made garments, jute manufactures, leather and footwear handicrafts including pearls and precious stones, chemicals, engineering goods and iron steel; and (iv) Mineral fuels and lubricants.

▷ Exports of India over the years show a clear decline in the importance of agriculture and allied products and a substantial increase in the importance of manufactured goods. This has been due to changing production structure of the economy and the overall growth of the economy.

Direction of Foreign Trade

- India is having maximum trade with OECD countries (mainly the USA, EU and Japan).
- The direction of Indian trade registered a change during recent past years. Indian trade has been partially shifted from West-Europe to East Asia and OECD countries.
- The high growth rate in Japan and ASEAN countries gave a high demand and favourable market to Indian exports. This has been one of the major reasons responsible for increasing Indian exports to East-Asian region of the world.

New Foreign Trade Policy (2009-2014)

- In the Foreign Trade policy for the year 2009-14 announced on 27th August, 2009, the 'Government spelt out a bold vision to double India's exports of goods and services by 2014 and to double India's percentage share of global trade by 2020 and to focus on the generation of additional employment.
- Stability of trade policy regime and need based support measures extended from time have yielded positive results since the inception of the Foreign Trade Policy (FTP) 2009-14.

India's Foreign Trade Policy 2015-20

India aims to increase India's exports of merchandise and services from US$ 465.9 billion in 2013-14 to approximately US$ 900 billion by 2019-20 and to raise India's share in world exports from 2 per cent to 3.5 per cent. Unveiling the first trade policy of the National Democratic Alliance (NDA) government, Commerce Minister Nirmala Sitharaman said the FTP (2015-20) will introduce Merchandise Exports from India Scheme (MEIS) and Services Exports from India Scheme (SEIS) to boost outward shipments. Besides, higher level of incentives will be provided for export of agriculture products under the Foreign Trade Policy (FTP), which seeks to integrate with Make in India and Digital India initiatives of the government. The FTP also seeks to establish an Export Promotion Mission to provide an institutional framework to work with State Governments to boost India's exports.

The salient features of the new Foreign Trade Policy 2015-20 are the following:

- Merchandise Export from India Scheme (MEIS) and Service Exports from India Scheme (SEIS) launched. The 'Services Exports from India Scheme' (SEIS) is for increasing exports of notified Services. These schemes (MEIS and SEIS) replace multiple schemes earlier in place, each with different conditions for eligibility and usage. Incentives (MEIS & SEIS) to be available for SEZs also. e-Commerce of handicrafts, handlooms, books etc., eligible for benefits of MEIS.

- Export obligation would be reduced by 25 per cent and incentives available under the MEIS and SEIS would be extended to the units in the SEZs to make them more attractive for investors. SEZs have lost their sheen after imposition of the minimum alternate tax (MAT) and dividend distribution tax (DDT) in 2012.
- Debits against scrips would be eligible for CENVAT credit or drawback.
- Further business services, hotel and restaurants would get rewards scrips under SEIS at the rate of 3 per cent and other specified services at the rate of 5 per cent.
- SEIS would be applied to "Service Providers located in India instead of "Indian Service Providers".
- Served from India Scheme (SFIS) replaced with SEIS.
- Under MEIS, the main sectors to be provided support includes processed, packaged agricultural and food items, agricultural and village industry goods.
- These schemes (MEIS and SEIS) replace multiple schemes earlier in place, each with different conditions for eligibility and usage. Benefits from both these schemes will be extended to units located in SEZs.
- Nomenclature of Export House, Star Export House, Trading House, Premier Trading House certificate changed to 1, 2, 3, 4, 5 Star Export House.
- Higher level of rewards under MEIS for export items with high domestic content and value addition.
- Export obligation under EPCG scheme reduced to 75% to promote domestic capital goods manufacturing.
- FTP to be aligned to "Make in India', 'Digital India' and 'Skills India' initiatives.
- Duty credit scrips made freely transferable and usable for payment of custom duty, excise duty and service tax.
- Export promotion mission to take on board state governments.
- Unlike annual reviews, FTP will be reviewed after two-and-half years. Higher level of support for export of defence, farm produce and eco-friendly products.
- Agricultural and village industry products to be supported across the globe at rates of 3% and 5% under MEIS.
- Industrial products to be supported in major markets at rates ranging from 2% to 3%.

- Branding campaigns planned to promote exports in sectors where India has traditional strength.

FTP to promote e-Commerce companies focusing on job creation :
- Under the new five-year Foreign Trade Policy (FTP), the government will provide incentives to e-Commerce companies exporting products from sectors that create jobs.
- Firms that export goods through courier or foreign post office using e-commerce of FOB (Freight on Board) value up to ₹ 25,000 per consignment will be entitled for rewards under MEIS.
- The objective of MEIS is to offset infra inefficiencies and associated costs involved in export of goods, which are manufactured in India and especially those having high export intensity, employment potential and can enhance India's export competitiveness.
- If the value of exports using ecommerce platform is more than ₹ 25,000 per consignment, then MEIS reward would be limited to FOB value of ₹ 25,000 only.
- The goods entitled for benefit under the scheme are handloom, books and periodicals, leather footwear, toys and customised fashion garments.
- Export of such goods under courier regulations shall be allowed manually on pilot basis through airports at New Delhi, Mumbai and Chennai... Department of Revenue shall fast track the implementation of EDI mode at courier terminals.

FTP proposes new institutions to boost global trade :
- The new Foreign Trade Policy proposed setting up of the following (i) Trade Council and (ii) National Committee on Trade Facilitation, to improve India's share in global trade and implement of WTO obligations.
- A National Committee on Trade Facilitation is being constituted for domestic coordination and implementation of the TFA.
- Several initiatives are under way for the simplification of procedures and digitization of various processes involved in trade transactions.
- Steps are being taken by various ministries and departments to simplify administrative procedures and reduce transaction costs based on the recommendations of two task forces constituted by the Directorate General of Foreign Trade.
- Specific measures will be taken to facilitate the entry of new entrepreneurs and manufacturers in global trade through extensive training programmes.
- "The Niryat Bandhu' scheme will be revamped to achieve these objectives and also further dovetailed with the ongoing outreach programmes.
- Capacity development efforts will focus on export promotion councils and commercial missions.

- A new institution – Centre for Research in International Trade – is being established not only to strengthen India's research capabilities in the area of international trade, but also to enable developing countries to articulate their views and concerns from a well-informed position of strength.
- Two institutional mechanisms are being put in place for regular communication with stakeholders - the Board of Trade and the Council for Trade Development (CTD) and Promotion. While the Board of Trade will have an advisory role, the CTD would have representation from State and UT governments. The CTD will be an institution between the Centre and the States with the objective of internalising the thinking and the processes and the participation of State government into central government policy making, implementation and monitoring.

Government Relaxes FDI Norms Across 15 Sectors

- The union government on the eve of Diwali went on a reforms overdrive and announced Foreign Direct Investment (FDI) and liberalisation in 15 sectors. "To further boost this entire investment environment and to bring in foreign investments in the country, the government has brought in FDI related reforms and liberalisation touching upon 15 major sectors of the economy," the government said in a press release.

The sectors included in this reforms exercise include :
   (i) Limited liability partnerships, downstream investment and approval conditions.
   (ii) Investment by companies owned and controlled by Non-Resident Indians (NRIs).
   (iii) Establishment and transfer of ownership and control of Indian companies.
   (iv) Agriculture and animal husbandry.
   (v) Plantation 100% FDI under automatic route in plantation sector — coffee, rubber, cardamom, palm oil tree and olive tree.
   (vi) Mining and mineral separation of titanium bearing minerals and ores, its value addition and integrated activities
   (vii) Defence 49% FDI through automatic route and beyond that through FIPB nod.
   (viii) Broadcasting sector 100% FDI in DTH, Cable Network, uplinking of news and current affairs TV channels, 49% from 26% for terrestrial broadcasting FM radio.
   (ix) Civil aviation 100% from 74% in non-scheduled air transport services, ground handling services and credit information companies. FDI in regional air transport services under automatic route.
   (x) Increase of sectoral cap

(xi) Construction development sector 100% FDI under automatic route in completed projects for operation and management of township, malls/shopping complexes and business sectors; minimum capitalisation norms and floor area restrictions have been removed; eased exit norms for foreign investors in this sector.

(xii) Cash and carry wholesale trading/wholesale trading (including sourcing from MSEs)

(xiii) Single brand retail trading and duty-free shops relaxed conditions for FDI in single-brand retail; 100%. FDI under automatic route in duty-free shops.

(xiv) Banking-private sector FIIs/FPIs/QFIs, following due procedure, can now invest upto sectoral limit of 74%, provided there is no change of control and management of invitee company, and

(xv) Manufacturing sector for the purpose of the FDI, Indian manufactures would be the investee company, which is the owner of the Indian brand and manufacturers in India in terms of value at least 70% of its products in house and sources at most 30% from Indian manufacturer.

For facilitating faster approvals on most of the proposals, the government also raised the threshold limit of approval by Foreign Investment Promotion Board from the earlier ₹ 3,000 crore to ₹ 5,000 crore. As per the extant policy, FIPB considers foreign investment proposals of inflow up to ₹ 3,000 crore and those above that limit are placed for consideration of the Cabinet Committee on Economic Affairs.

> **'Invest India' Constituted to Promote FDI**
>
> A joint company of public and private sectors named 'Invest India' has been constituted for promoting foreign direct investment in the country. This company will provide investment information to foreign investors. This company will work on no profit-no loss basis. In its capital of ₹ 1000 crore, the government and FICCI have the share of 49 : 51.
>
> This company will work on three principles:
> (i) to promote FDI in the country.
> (ii) to provide processing facilities to foreign investors and act as coordinator among various ministries.
> (iii) to provide feedback to government on industrial policy.

Exim Policy 2002-07

The major highlights of Exim Policy 2002-07 are :

(i) Removal of quantitative and packaging restrictions on agri exports.
(ii) Transport assistance for movement of agri goods.
(iii) Export thrust on items indentified in Medium Term Export Strategy.

(iv) Continuance of existing duty neutralisation schemes till the Value Added Tax (VAT) becomes fully operational.
(v) Extension of the period for fulfilling export obligations under Export Promotion Capital Goods (EPCG) Scheme from 8 to 12 years.
(vi) Exemption of banking units set up in SEZs from statutory requirements like SLR and CRR.
(vii) Ease of external commercial borrowing norms by permitting less than three years tenure loans.
(viii) Provision for repatriation of export earnings within 360 days instead of the earlier 180 days.
(ix) Retention of entire export earnings in Export Earners Foreign Currency Account (EEFA).
(x) Tax benefits on sales from domestic tariff areas to Special Economic Zones (SEZs).
(xi) Reduction of processing fees, fewer physical inspections, same day licensing in all offices of Director Gen. of Foreign Trade (DGFT).
(xii) Common classification for DGFT and customs department to eliminate classification related disputes.
(xiii) No licence requirement for relocation of overseas industrial plants in India.
(xiv) Industrial towns such as Tirpur, Panipat and Ludhiana to get Market Access Initiative (MAI) funds, priority for infrastructure development.
(xv) Allocation to states from Rs. 350 cr. Assistance to States for Infrastructure Development (ASIDE) fund linked to their export performance.
(xvi) Permission for captive power generation and duty free import of fuel for power generation, for exporters.
(xvii) Reduction in the eligibility for getting Export House status from Rs. 15 crores to Rs. 5 crores.

Balance of Payment : A statement of all transactions of a country with the rest of the world during a given period. Transactions may be related to trade, such as imports and exports of goods and services; movement of short term and long-term investments; gifts, currency and gold. The balance of payments may be classified into current account, capital account, unilateral transfer account and gold account.

Balance of Trade : Part of the nation's balance of payments concerning imports and exports. A favourable balance of trade means that exports exceed imports in vlaue.

Invisibles : A term used to describe those items, such as financial series, included in the current Balance of Payments accounts, as distinct from physically visible Imports and Exports of goods. Invisibles include government grants to overseas countries and subscriptions to international organizations, net payment for shiping services, travel, royalties, commissions for banking and other services, transfers to or from overseas residents, Interest, Profits and Dividends received by or from overseas residents.

Foreign Exchange Reserves in India

▷ The foreign exchange reserves of the country include three important components : (i) Foreign Exchange Assets of RBI. (ii) Gold Stock of RBI (iii) SDR holdings of the Government.

▷ After 1991, Indian foreign exchange reserves have rapidly increased due to various reasons which are as follows : (i) Devlauation of Rupee. (ii) Availability of loans from international institutions. (iii) Availability of foreign exchange from NRIs under various schemes. (iv) Increased foreign investment (both direct and indirect). (v) Full convertibility of Rupee on current account.

▷ FEMA (Foreign Exchange Management Act) came into force in July 2000. The FEMA has replaced Foreign Exchange Regulation Act., 1973 (FERA-1973).

Foreign Exchange Reserves in India, at the end of Juanuary 2013 was $ 295.60 billion.

▷ Under the FEMA provisions related to foreign exchange have been modified and liberalised so as to simplify foreign trade and payments. The FEMA will make favourable development in foreign Money Market.

India's foreign trade

Year	Exports (Rs. crore)	Imports (Rs. crore)	Total trade (Rs. crore)	Trade deficit (Rs. crore)
1997-1998	1,30,101	1,54,176	2,84,277	-24,075
1998-1999	1,39,753	1,78,332	3,18,085	-38,579
1999-2000	1,59,561	2,15,236	3,74,797	-55,675
2000-2001	2,03,571	2,30,873	4,34,444	-27,302
2001-2002	2,09,018	2,45,200	4,54,218	-36,182
2002-2003	2,55,137	2,97,206	5,52,343	-42,069
2003-2004	2,93,367	3,59,108	6,52,475	-65,741
2004-2005	3,75,340	5,01,065	8,76,405	-1,25,725
2005-2006	4,56,418	6,60,409	11,16,827	-2,03,991
2006-2007	5,71,779	8,40,506	14,12,285	-2,68,727
2007-2008	6,55,864	10,12,312	16,68,176	-3,56,448
2008-2009	8,40,755	13,74,436	22,15,191	-5,33,681
2009-2010	8,45,534	13,63,736	22,09,270	-5,18,202

(Sources: DGCI and S, Kolkata) *(Courtesy: India 2011)*

- India's total external trade (exports plus imports including re-exports) in the year 1950 – 51 stood at Rs. 1214 crore. Since then, this has witnessed continuous increase with occasional downturns.
- India's share in total world trade has gone up from 1.1% in 2004 – i.e. initial year of the Foreign Trade Policy (2004 – 09) to 1.5% in 2006.
- During 2008 – 09 the vlaue of India's external trade reached Rs. 22,15,191 crore.
- India's imports were highest from Asia and ASEAN (35.22%) followed by West Europe (21.17%) and America (7.78%), during 2005 – 06.
- During 2009 – 10 India's imports reached to Rs. 13,63,736 crore from Rs. 13,74,436 crore in 2008 – 09, registering a negative growth of 0.78% in rupee terms. In US $ terms, imports reached a level of US $ 288.37 billion in 2009 – 10, registering a negative growth of – 5.05%.
- During 2009 – 10, UAE (13.4%) has been the most important country to export destination followed by USA (10.9%), China (6.5%), Hong Kong (4.4%), Singapore (4.2%), Netherlands (3.6%), U.K. (3.5%), Germany (3%), Saudi Arabia (2.2%).
- Asia and ASEAN accounted for 60.9% of India's total imports during 2009 – 10 followed by Europe (19.2%) and America (10.2%). Among individual countries the share of China stood highest at 10.7% followed by UAE (6.8%), Saudi Arabia (5.95%), USA (5.9%).
- During 2009 – 10, the share of Asia and ASEAN region comprising South Asia, East Asia, North East Asia, WANA accounted for 53.93% of India's total exports.
- Trade deficit decreased during 2009 – 10 to Rs. –5,18,202 crore as against Rs. –5,33,681 crore during 2008 – 09. In US $ terms also, trade deficit decreased to US $ 109.6 billion from a level of US $ 118.4 billion during 2008 – 09.
- The share of Europe and America in India's exports stood at 21.56% and 15.02% respectively of which EU countries (27) comprises 20.17%.

Trade Organisations

- International Monetary Fund (IMF) was established on 27th December, 1945 on the basis of decision taken in the Bretenwood Conference and it started functioning w.e.f. 1st March, 1947.
- The total member countries of IMF in 2002 were 183.
- The function of IMF is to encourage financial and economic co-operation between member countries and to extend world trade.
- International Bank for Reconstruction and Development (IBRD) was established in 1945.
- IBRD alongwith other institutions is also called World Bank. The other institutions are International Finance Corporation, International Development Agency and Multilateral Investement Guarantee Agency.

- Presently, it is helping member countries in capital investment and encouraging long-term balanced development.
- General Agreement on Tariffs and Trade (GATT), came into being on 30th October, 1947 and started functioning from 1st January, 1948.
- The principle of GATT was equal tariffs policy, to remove quantitative ban and disposal of business dispute in a democratic way.
- On 1st January, 1995 the World Trade Organisation took over the place and position of GATT.
- The Headquarter of WTO is in Geneva and the number of its member countries in the year 2003 was 146. India is a founder member of it.
- The India-ASEAN Trade in Goods Agreement came into effect on Jan. 1, 2010, though it was signed on August 13, 2009.
- The signing of the India-ASEAN Trade in Goods Agreement paves the way for the creation of one of the world's largest free trade areas (FTA)– market of almost 1.8 billion people with a combined GDP of US $ 2.75 trillion.

www.ingramcontent.com/pod-product-compliance
Lightning Source LLC
Chambersburg PA
CBHW062218080426
42734CB00010B/1938